T0318299

Frontline Crisis Response

Frontline crisis response is challenging. Emergency responders, soldiers, and humanitarian aid workers all operate at the frontlines of threatening, uncertain crisis situations on a daily basis. Under intense pressure, they need to make a range of difficult decisions: to follow preexisting plans or improvise; to abide by top-down instructions or take discretionary actions; to get emotionally involved or keep a rational distance? These dilemmas define their work but, until now, have not been subjected to systematic investigation. This book conducts in-depth studies of eleven such dilemmas by integrating a wide array of research findings on crisis response operations. The comprehensive overview of crisis response research shows how frontline responders deal with these dilemmas amidst the chaos of crises and forms the basis for the formulation of a theory of frontline crisis response. As such, this book will undoubtedly help to understand, evaluate, and advance crisis response operations.

JORI P. KALKMAN is Associate Professor in the Faculty of Military Sciences at the Netherlands Defence Academy and was a visiting researcher at the Swedish Defence University. His work focuses on frontline crisis operations and has been published in various management journals as well as in specialized emergency response, military, and humanitarian outlets.

Frontline Crisis Response

Operational Dilemmas in Emergency Services, Armed Forces, and Humanitarian Organizations

JORI P. KALKMAN
Netherlands Defense Academy

CAMBRIDGE
UNIVERSITY PRESS

Shaftesbury Road, Cambridge CB2 8EA, United Kingdom

One Liberty Plaza, 20th Floor, New York, NY 10006, USA

477 Williamstown Road, Port Melbourne, VIC 3207, Australia

314–321, 3rd Floor, Plot 3, Splendor Forum, Jasola District Centre,
New Delhi – 110025, India

103 Penang Road, #05–06/07, Visioncrest Commercial, Singapore 238467

Cambridge University Press is part of Cambridge University Press & Assessment,
a department of the University of Cambridge.

We share the University's mission to contribute to society through the pursuit of
education, learning and research at the highest international levels of excellence.

www.cambridge.org
Information on this title: www.cambridge.org/9781009262194

DOI: 10.1017/9781009262170

First published 2024

A catalogue record for this publication is available from the British Library

A Cataloging-in-Publication data record for this book is available from the
Library of Congress

ISBN 978-1-009-26219-4 Hardback
ISBN 978-1-009-26218-7 Paperback

To Lieske

Contents

Tables

Acknowledgments

Crises are intense situations that tend to absorb all our attention. Our observations are eager but agitated, the situation is rapidly changing and uncertain, and our lives are being uprooted for some period of time. Crises may usher in progress, bring people together, and make us feel alive. But these moments are also incredibly distracting. This is why writing, to me at least, requires the absence of crises in whatever shape or size. Long timespans of dull tranquility and an undisturbed peace of mind work best for me. When other authors talk through their books and articles, I withdraw into quiet solitude to hear their stories, grasp their arguments, and contemplate their claims. Moments of seclusion helped me to write this book as well. But research is never a solitary endeavor or individual achievement. Many people have been instrumental to this book, and the depth of my gratitude is hard to bring within the confines of language. This attempt will have to suffice until I find better words or ways to express myself.

The Netherlands Defence Academy has been an excellent place to study crisis response, and several colleagues have had a formative influence on my research. Myriame Bollen has been my mentor and closest colleague for the past seven years. Her creative thinking and unmatched kindness are a source of inspiration. She demonstrates time and again that you can both be a virtuous, caring person and a good scholar. As such, she serves as an example of the researcher I aspire to be. Eric-Hans Kramer has often generously made time to share his original thoughts on crisis management and other, unrelated themes during our recurring 'existentialist talks'. I am looking forward to seeing his yet unpublished work get the recognition it deserves. Captain Huib Zijderveld and Lt. Col. Jacobine Janse are not only exceptional officers but also successful PhD candidates. I feel privileged to supervise them and benefited greatly from their in-depth knowledge about the intricacies of military life as well as their critical reflections on it. Tine Molendijk impresses me always with her great intelligence, elegant writing, and ability to reach large audiences with her nuanced messages. Working with her is always a joy. As a proud member of the Joint Research Task Force for the Dedicated Development of Defence Knowledge, I have been inspired by insightful conservations with Sofie, Lema, Naomi, Teun, Esmee, Willem, Henk, and Dave. I am also grateful to Dorine, Erik, Paul, Robert, Gwen, and Job for their various contributions to my thinking and personal development.

In the spring of 2022, I had the privilege of spending two months at the Swedish Defence University in Stockholm and Karlstad. I received a most hospitable reception and enjoyed many thought-provoking conversations during my stay. Aida Alvinius has been very supportive of this book project. Her welcoming gestures and perseverant character are equally admirable. A special note of thanks is due to Helena Hermansson and Elisa Viteri for pleasant walks, good food, and great discussions. Chiara Ruffa was kind enough to invite me to several events and shared her fascinating research projects. Sheryn Lee and Andreas Ivansson went above and beyond to make me feel welcome as well. I also wish to express my gratitude to Erik Berntson, Stefan Annell, Erik Hedlund, Monica Sjöstrand, Eva Johansson, Thomas Vrenngård, Gerry Larsson, and Lena Carlsson for their kind help and interesting talks.

Scholars from other institutions have been a source of inspiration and encouragement in very diverse ways too. I specifically wish to mention Jeroen Wolbers, Kees Boersma, Martijn Dekker, Bram Jansen, Annelies van Vark, Willem Treurniet, Marlys Christianson, and many anonymous reviewers. I also wish to thank Cambridge University Press for their trust and support. Writing for this press is a dream come true. I am especially grateful to Valerie Appleby who kindly and skillfully guided me through the book proposal process.

I am also very much indebted to the many frontline crisis responders who have shared their stories, experiences, and expertise with me. Over two hundred of them participated over the past few years in interviews and controlled experiments. In formal and informal settings, they took ample time to tell me about their work in general or particular response operations. Invariably, they shared their captivating stories with passion. Their information has been instrumental to my understanding of the research themes in this book. Their generosity and support is deeply appreciated. I have gained the greatest respect for their professionalism and their altruistic dedication to the job. My hope is that this book makes them feel heard and will be of use to them.

Finally, I owe everything to the people who are closest to me. I wish to thank my family, both the one I gained by birth and the one gained by marriage, for their continuous affection and support. I am grateful as well to Max, Dani, Laura, Ramon, Eva, Stratton, and Britt for their friendship. My gratitude also extends to Fyodor and Kyra who have been among my closest companions during the writing of this book. Most importantly, I am immensely grateful to Lieske who has carefully reviewed most of the book and offered many useful suggestions. Her love and approval are all that matters. Ultimately, she makes all of this worthwhile.

1 | *Operational Dilemmas in Frontline Crisis Response*

A crisis is a shocking and dramatic moment that radically disrupts our ordinary lives. It wreaks havoc suddenly and unexpectedly, leaving destruction and suffering in its wake. As a result, a crisis site produces a disturbing scene: buildings and other material objects are damaged, wounded victims are hurt and in pain, and the tragedy of death causes profound grief. Inevitably, aid will come from all sides, but for many survivors, crises have a lasting impact on their lives nevertheless. Societies try to reduce and minimize crises, but despite their efforts, crises of all sorts and sizes continue to have major effects across the globe. Even more concerning, crises appear to grow increasingly destructive and unpredictable with tragic consequences for communities and individuals alike. This means that crisis response activities are becoming more important.

Crisis response operations are carried out by frontline personnel of crisis organizations. These crisis professionals intervene to resolve the situation on the ground. Emergency responders (or first responders) rush to the scene of the incident to rescue victims, extinguish fires, control riots, and resuscitate patients. Soldiers engage enemy troops in combat or attempt to bring and maintain stability in volatile settings. And humanitarian aid workers provide live-saving relief and alleviate human suffering during catastrophic disasters. These frontline responders have very different backgrounds and tasks, but all need to urgently react to threatening, uncertain situations. Similarly, all of them face hardships in their work and take considerable risks to help others in desperate need. Their operational activities and experiences are therefore comparable.

One of the most defining aspects of their work is the recurrence of complicated dilemmas: Do I follow preexisting plans or do I improvise? Do I wait for instructions of a superior or take urgent decisions myself? Do I coordinate my activities with other crisis organizations or am I more efficient working independently? Emergency responders, military personnel, and humanitarians face these dilemmas again and again, but there are no simple solutions. In fact, we know surprisingly little about how frontline responders deal with these crisis response dilemmas. This book aims to address this knowledge gap and offers a comprehensive overview of how frontline crisis responders organize and implement their activities amidst the chaos of crises.

1.1 What Is a Crisis?

Crises have become ubiquitous in recent years, or so it seems. News media report on new crises every day, and the apparent continuous series of crisis situations is by some described as "the new normal." Yet, this perspective risks an inflation of the word. Crises, by definition, are not ordinary or normal, but disorderly, undesirable, infrequent, disruptive, and confusing. The term is often misused to dramatize circumstances: saying "crisis" is a sure way to attract attention. When societal problems vie over the spotlight, depicting a problem as a crisis suggests that it is more deserving of publicity. A crisis situation may also be invoked or declared to legitimize (otherwise) contentious decisions or even power grabs (cf. Buzan et al., 1998). Politicians and managers can speak of crises to justify autocratic or unpopular measures, and those who contradict them, make themselves suspect of harboring ill will to their country or organization. Such (ab)use of the term may be attractive to opportunistic leaders (Spector, 2019) but also diffuses the concept. This is concerning, because crisis response can only be improved if we have a clear understanding about what the word "crisis" means. Unfortunately, even scholars do not see eye to eye. Part of the problem is that there are many terms that have similar meanings, such as emergency, incident, accident, and disaster. These terms emerged from different research disciplines but have overlapping connotations. While some researchers consider it important to clearly separate these terms, others use the concepts as synonyms. Here, crisis is used as an umbrella term.

A crisis is viewed as any situation that is characterized by a physical threat, uncertainty, and time pressure (see Boin et al., 2016). A physical threat endangers the life or safety of either responders or victims. Uncertainty features in the fact that these situations are often hard to grasp, so that the causes, evolution, and consequences of a crisis are typically unknown and ambiguous. Time pressure, finally, refers to the need for a rapid response, because a postponed intervention will likely lead to an escalating impact or cause irreversible harm. A situation must have all three characteristics to qualify as a crisis.

Inevitably, these characteristics raise new questions. People are often not in agreement over whether there is a threat. There have been contentious societal debates over COVID-19, terrorism, and climate change. While some view these phenomena as threats, others remain skeptical or believe there is little need to address these issues. Time pressures and uncertainty, likewise, are perceived and cannot always be easily measured or determined. Nurses in an emergency trauma center are used to urgent work and developed expertise with operating in ambiguous situations, so they will be resilient against stress, but less experienced persons might be rapidly overwhelmed by the time pressure and uncertainty of emergencies. In practice, it is therefore difficult to definitively or objectively label a situation as a crisis. This should not be taken to mean that there is nothing beyond our perceptions or that any crisis declaration is equally valid. From a critical realist point of view, there is a real world, independent from us as observers, even if it can only be accessed through our own fallible observations that are influenced by our social positions in the world. This perspective implies that various constructions of reality can be judged on credibility and legitimacy. Thus, even though crisis understandings rely on our individual perceptions, some situations can be more reasonably and convincingly defined as crises than others.

The definition of a crisis as a threatening, uncertain, and urgent situation enables the inclusion of a variety of empirical cases without becoming overly broad and thereby meaningless. A crisis can range from common medical emergencies and building fires to unique disastrous events, such as the Indian Ocean tsunami, the European refugee crisis, or the global COVID-19 pandemic. Next, crises might primarily pose a risk to ordinary citizens (e.g., a traffic accident) or members of crisis organizations (e.g., an isolated wildfire). A common denominator, however, is that a crisis is an extreme context for those who experience it from nearby (Hällgren et al., 2018).

The selected crisis definition also helps to exclude situations from the study that lack one of the three characteristics of a crisis (i.e., threat, uncertainty, or urgency). First, for a situation to qualify as a crisis, it must pose a direct, physical threat to those affected or the frontline personnel aiming to resolve the situation. Since danger to individuals' lives and safety is crucial, this book excludes reputational and organizational crises, which only threaten the performance of organizations or the positions of managers (cf. Bundy et al., 2017; Pearson & Clair, 1998). Likewise, in financial and political crises, people's lives are not directly at stake, so these cases are excluded from the analysis as well. Second, uncertainty is also a necessary condition for a situation to be defined as a crisis, so the selected crisis definition excludes situations that are threatening and urgent, but not uncertain. Some routine emergencies fall within this category. Single-vehicle incidents and scheduled medical procedures are risky moments, which require time-pressured actions, but these situations are also fairly contained and usually quite predictable. Similarly, heatwaves and periods of extreme cold necessitate an urgent response, but the nature of the threat and the type of interventions needed can be anticipated. A complicating factor is that these situations might escalate into crises, particularly when responders have misinterpreted and oversimplified these situations. Still, in most cases, such situations can be addressed by regular, procedural interventions and do not constitute crises. Third, the definition excludes situations in which there is no pressing urgency to act. Limited urgency means that the situation does not require immediate intervention, while high time pressure suggests that a situation will rapidly escalate if actions are not taken instantly. Threatening and uncertain developments, such as the buildup of enemy troops or changes in the natural environment, are worrying trends, but do not demand a reaction in a matter of minutes or hours, so lack the need for a time-pressured response that characterizes crises. Of course, if no actions are taken, these situations will likely produce crises, which demand urgent reactions after all.

At this point, it is also useful to make a distinction between hazards and crises. Hazards are potential sources of damage or harm. A hazard can be contained through pre-crisis measures and policies that keep it from escalating. Hazard management activities can reduce the chances and impact of a crisis in various ways. Flood hazards, for example, can be managed by building dykes, creating floodplains, and prohibiting construction in flood-prone areas. Crisis organizations can also set up warning systems, give timely evacuation orders, and instruct populations on how to act in case of rising water levels. These efforts can avoid a crisis, even when water levels reach unprecedented heights and areas are flooded, because the harmful effects of the extremely hazardous situation are minimized by pre-impact interventions. Vice versa, floods become problematic if fragile houses have been built in low-lying areas near rivers or seas, if people do not earn enough to have savings for evacuating or storing supplies, and if victims have no access to health care or good sanitation, so that they are susceptible to homelessness, starvation, and epidemics. Crises, therefore, can be viewed as mismanaged hazards. The view on crises as mismanaged hazards also explains why some scholars no longer use the term "natural disaster." They argue that this mistakenly puts responsibility for disasters on nature. But it is not the natural hazard that causes the disaster. The problem is that poor public policies leave people vulnerable, thereby creating the social conditions that allow a hazard to develop into a crisis (Chmutina & Von Meding, 2019; O'Keefe et al., 1976; Tierney, 2007, 2019). This view also challenges the traditional approach to crises as exceptional, temporary events, which have clear origins, are restricted in time, and can be characterized as disturbing interruptions of normality. Instead, crises are deeply rooted in a society and reflect preexisting societal vulnerabilities that have become normalized in society over time (Roux-Dufort, 2007; Williams et al., 2017). For instance, governmental neglect of hazard management measures in combination with policies that lead to rising socioeconomic inequality create ideal conditions for a disastrous crisis. Regardless of the hazard, the resulting disaster can only be understood in the context of failing public policy in the affected society. Such social roots of crises are important to acknowledge in order to better grasp the nature of crises. A better understanding of crises, in turn, may improve crisis response and reduce dramatic suffering and loss.

1.2 What Is Frontline Crisis Response?

The focus of this book is on frontline crisis response. This means that there are two main boundaries to the book that need to be discussed. First, the analyses in this book are restricted to frontline (or operational) issues, questions, and processes. Most literature on crisis management, instead, is about high-level leaders and decision-makers. In particular, there is ample research on crisis management in political science and public administration literature, focusing on public leaders and the political implications of their decisions (see Allison, 1971; Boin & Hart, 2003; Boin et al., 2016). In addition, many studies address decision-making by CEOs and other senior managers during organizational crises (see James et al., 2011; Pearson & Clair, 1998; Williams et al., 2017). This strategic focus can be explained by the fact that our attention is usually grasped by the decisions and statements of top-level leaders in times of crisis. As a result, there has been much less attention for frontline responses to crises. Yet, frontline personnel ultimately resolve crisis situations and often run great risks during these operations (Groenendaal et al., 2013; Kalkman, 2020b). Thus, this book focuses on the organization and implementation of crisis operations. It is about the "boots on the ground," the women and men who get their hands dirty, and the professionals who make decisions on life and death in a matter of minutes or seconds. This frontline focus includes organizational members who coordinate frontline crisis activities. These organizational members are often physically and psychologically close to the frontlines of the crisis and make a real impact, but desk-bound policy-makers and senior decision-makers work at a greater distance from crisis operations and fall outside the scope of this book.

Second, this book is about responses to crises. Crisis response is one of the stages of crisis management. Management of crises begins with crisis prevention or mitigation, which consists of reducing vulnerability to hazards and avoiding accidents or dramatic organizational failures. Next, organizations need to prepare for potential crises by training, exercises, and planning. When a crisis unfolds or has just happened, the response phase aims to minimize its effects through delivering critical, lifesaving assistance, reducing suffering and damage, and resolving the situation. Afterwards, communities or societies go through a period of recovery from trauma and loss as well as infrastructure reconstruction (e.g., Tierney, 2019). While the separation between these stages is clear on paper, they are not always as distinct in practice. For instance, when exactly do organizations shift from crisis preparation to response during an emerging pandemic or a river flood and when exactly does a planned combat mission turn into a crisis to resolve? It can be hard to detail transitions between different crisis phases, but it is usually possible to give an indication of what constituted the response phase. As a general direction, this book specifically focuses on operational dynamics from the moment that a crisis manifests itself and the situation can be characterized as threatening, uncertain, and urgent.

In practice, crisis response is conducted by a variety of crisis organizations, primarily emergency services, armed forces, and humanitarian organizations. Frontline responders of emergency services include firefighters, emergency medical teams, police officers, search and rescue teams, coast guard personnel, border patrol officers, and dispatchers. Soldiers operate in crisis situations as they are deployed to engage in combat and stabilization operations or provide aid in the aftermath of emergencies. And humanitarian aid workers deliver basic goods and services after destructive conflicts or disasters. For these organizations, crisis response is a primary responsibility, but members of other organizations may also periodically encounter crises, such as operators of advanced technological systems (e.g., aircraft, nuclear power plants) and expedition members in extreme environments (e.g., mountain climbing, space exploration). An interesting aspect about the work of all these frontline responders is that it consists of very hands-on, practical activities, but that many of their occupations are also increasingly professionalizing, so that members need extensive education and training, have much control over their own work, and enjoy considerable prestige (e.g., McCann & Granter, 2019). This professionalization is necessary, because crises are growing more complex, so responders need advanced knowledge and skills to handle them. A core assumption of this book is that all frontline crisis responders, in spite of the differences in organizational and crisis contexts, operate under similarly challenging circumstances (i.e., threat, uncertainty, and urgency), which means that their professional challenges and operational activities can be usefully compared and contrasted.

1.3 Why Study Crisis Response?

There are multiple reasons to study frontline responses to crises. One prominent reason is that there appear to be more and more crises in modern-day societies, even if we correct for the prevalent misuse of the word. To some extent, this is simply the result of growing population numbers, which lead to a rising number of emergencies and also means that more people are affected by large-scale disasters. However, there have also been significant changes in the natural environment (e.g., global warming and biodiversity loss) over the past decades, which increase the likelihood of natural hazards. At the same time, many communities still face poverty, extreme inequality, and failing public services, leaving people vulnerable to these hazards. The intersection of these processes results in an increasing number and impact of crises.

Worryingly, attempts to prevent crises continue to fail and might even increasingly do so. Ideally, governments and organizations intervene before a hazard gets a chance to develop into a crisis and cause harm. Avoiding crises does not only reduce suffering but is often also cheaper than crisis response and reconstruction. Still, crisis prevention and preparation fail in practice, because both activities are very difficult. Charles Perrow (1984) has perhaps most convincingly demonstrated the (growing) difficulties of crisis prevention and preparation in his research on accidents in complex, socio-technical systems. He noticed that there are often incomprehensible interactions between elements in complex systems, which can produce accidents that were not anticipated and are hard to contain once they emerge. Since these systems are also defined by tight couplings, failures reverberate throughout the system, causing new problems elsewhere and resulting in escalating crises beyond the understanding of the humans that are supposed to control the system. Generalizing these insights to society at large, it is very hard (and increasingly harder) for crisis organizations to foresee future crises and preemptively intervene due to the complexity of modern-day societies, so that many crisis plans are symbolic documents at best (Clarke, 1999). Even when prevention and preparation are possible, pre-crisis investments are politically unattractive, because decision-makers prefer to spend scarce resources on other public services that sort more immediate or visible effects. It is not necessarily in the interest of crisis response actors either, since they gain their legitimacy from responding to crises, so fewer crises means less visibility (McConnell & Drennan, 2006). In fact, effective crisis prevention and early neutralization of emerging threats may even facilitate cutbacks on crisis organizations. Paradoxically, public leaders and crisis organizations have therefore little interest in avoiding crises altogether, increasing the need for crisis response operations.

There is another reason for studying frontline crisis response: The activity is growing increasingly complicated. Over time, crisis situations have changed in nature and gained new dimensions. Given that our societies are highly interconnected (cf. Perrow, 1984), an incident is likely to have broad repercussions, interact with other dormant threats, and escalate into larger, complex crises (Ansell et al., 2010; Robert & Lajtha, 2002). Political, functional, and temporal boundaries are easily crossed in the process, which complicates response efforts. Take the European refugee crisis. For years, Western European states had intervened militarily in Syria, Afghanistan, and Iraq, participating in the conflicts from which people fled away toward these same European countries, which then responded by reinforcing border checks at the EU external border and brokering an EU–Turkey deal to reduce migration numbers but also by expanding reception facilities and policing against violent, anti-immigration protests at home. In other words, crisis response unfolded over a long period of time, across multiple countries, on various political levels, and required interventions by a range of actors to handle its various manifestations. Transboundary crises clearly make responding to crises more complex.

Clearly, crises will continue to affect our societies. With the growing number and impact of increasingly complex crises that are not preemptively addressed, there is an urgent societal need for studying how frontline personnel resolve crises. Studying crisis response practices may help us to better understand frontline response processes and contribute to improving their success. To do so, crisis response success needs to be defined, but the crisis literature is surprisingly silent on the topic of crisis response performance. Certainly, researchers speak about effectiveness when introducing new crisis management approaches (e.g., Ansell et al., 2010; Robert & Lajtha, 2002) or study clear response failures in post hoc analyses (Snook, 2002; Weick, 1993), but they generally refrain from describing how success can be measured in the context of emergency, military, and humanitarian operations. Typically, assumptions about response effectiveness remain implicit. For instance, there is a lot of research on interorganizational collaboration in crises, which builds on the assumption that better coordination and cooperation between crisis organizations will benefit crisis operations (e.g., Comfort & Kapucu, 2006; Moynihan, 2009). Even though this assumption makes sense, there is usually little evidence provided. Evidently, it is difficult to define what exactly successful crisis response entails (Hilhorst, 2002; McConnell, 2020). Some of the confusion results from the fact that evaluators have different conceptions of crisis response goals (see Chapter 12). At the frontline, however, responders do not only struggle with ambiguous goals but also grapple with a range of other challenges in their response efforts. An in-depth, comprehensive study of these crisis response challenges can serve as a starting point for exploring opportunities for crisis response improvements.

1.4 Dilemmas in Crisis Response

A comprehensive analysis of frontline crisis response begins with bringing together a broad range of crisis studies. The result of this endeavor is surprising: Crisis researchers often reach diametrically opposed conclusions on how to organize and implement crisis response operations. For instance, a top-down hierarchy has proven popular among some scholars (Bigley & Roberts, 2001; Van Wart & Kapucu, 2011), while others have propagated decentralization instead (Drabek & McEntire, 2002; Quarantelli, 1988). In another example, some analysts emphasize cohesion as extremely important to frontline crisis teams (Godé, 2015; Wong et al., 2003), whereas others advocate for heterogeneity and internal debate (Rosenthal et al., 1991; Weick & Sutcliffe, 2001). Scholars, likewise, disagree over numerous other questions related to organizing and operating in crises. Yet, due to the fragmented nature of the literature on crisis response, these contradictions have received little attention. Findings that are published in specialized journals (e.g., emergency services, military, or humanitarian journals) are not always taken up by crisis researchers that focus on other contexts. As a result, the complexity of crisis response is not always acknowledged and there has been little attention for the contradictory suggestions that researchers have put forward over time in different outlets. These contradictory suggestions indicate that frontline members of crisis organizations face persistent dilemmas during their crisis response operations.

Crisis response dilemmas are difficult and contentious choices that frontline responders face when they are reacting to a crisis. Examples include the choices between abiding by organizational norms or following individual convictions, getting emotionally involved or keeping a rational distance, and involving or excluding spontaneous volunteers during the response efforts. These dilemmas do not have straightforward solutions and inconsistent findings can be found in different studies, testimony to the complexity of crisis response work. The fact that crisis response is complex should not be taken as an end-point of the discussion though. It would be a rather disappointing conclusion that rightfully criticizes simplistic answers but also paralyzes the

Table 1.1 *Frontline crisis response dilemmas*

Chapter	Themes	Crisis response dilemmas
2	Leadership	Command and control versus decentralization
3	Sensemaking	Creating clarity versus embracing ambiguity
4	Acting	Planned routines versus spontaneous improvisation
5	Ethics	Organizational norms versus individual convictions
6	Emotions	Involvement versus detachment
7	Ties	Cohesion versus contestation
8	Structures	Organizing versus disorganizing
9	Coordination	Integration versus fragmentation
10	Civilians	Inclusion versus exclusion
11	Technology	Early adoption versus skepticism
12	Goals	Restoring order versus social transformation

scholar and the professional responder into a pessimistic stance as to what further research can achieve. Clearly, the complicated nature of managing crises should not close it for further inquiry. This would be unacceptable to the victims of these crises and to frontline personnel who spend a lifetime responding to them. A focus on crisis response dilemmas does not have to mean passively accepting that these dilemmas are unmanageable either. Instead, by systematically comparing and contrasting research findings, it is possible to find recurring patterns and explain divergent outcomes. This gives us a deeper understanding about the nature of crisis response dilemmas, which can serve as a basis for reflective thinking about alternative ways to dealing with these difficult and contentious choices.

Eleven crisis response dilemmas form the backbone of this book. The selection of these eleven dilemmas followed an inductive process. I read the academic literature on frontline responses to crises and grouped publications in research themes. Over time, it became possible to identify eleven research themes that have received considerable attention by crisis scholars over the past decades (see Table 1.1). Some of these research themes play out primarily on the individual level of analysis (e.g., sensemaking), others on the level of crisis teams (e.g., ties), and others again on the organizational level (e.g., goals). All research themes, however, are directly related to frontline crisis response, because they bear directly on the operational activities of crisis organizations. Further review of the existing scholarship enabled the identification of a core dilemma for each research theme, in which scholars defend alternative perspectives. In each chapter, a frontline crisis response dilemma is clarified by elaborating the arguments for each side in the debate.

While the research themes are discussed separately, these themes are connected in practice. Crisis responders who are trying to make sense of a threatening situation will be influenced by their superiors' instructions, their own emotions, and the organizational structure in which they operate (Colville et al., 2013; Weick, 1995). Indeed, no research theme can be understood in a social (or analytical) vacuum. Yet, on a more abstract level, these themes are clearly distinct and are worthwhile studying separately to better understand and address the specific crisis response dilemmas at stake. Throughout the book, there is therefore a fine line between the practical connections and the analytical distinctions of the selected research themes.

1.5 Sources and Contributions

This book is strongly rooted in the academic literature and synthesizes findings from a variety of studies. Publications in journals are a main source of information for this book. Relevant articles are published in various crisis journals, including those dedicated to research on emergency services, military operations, and humanitarian aid. In addition, there are prominent outlets in organization and management studies as well as in public administration that published relevant work on crisis response operations. Another source of inspiration are renowned books that contributed to our understanding of crises and crisis response (e.g., Perrow, 1984; Snook, 2002; Weick & Sutcliffe, 2001). The analysis also draws from book chapters and dissertations focusing on crisis response operations. To a lesser extent, information is retrieved from agency reports, manuals, and practice-oriented (hand)books. Although these are helpful sources for explaining specific crises and for the training of (future) members of crisis organizations (Bullock et al., 2017; Canton, 2019; Fagel, 2011; United States Congress, 2006), they mainly offer insights in how specific crisis management systems are organized and contain useful empirical illustrations.

My own research also serves as a source of information for this book. Throughout the book, elaborate examples are provided, which are derived from my own empirical studies on frontline crisis response efforts. Specifically, I draw insights from a disaster relief operation by a military task force that was deployed after Hurricane Dorian struck the Bahamas in 2019. Next, there are examples from a series of emergency response exercises, during which crisis teams had to resolve difficult scenarios. Moreover, I studied Dutch border guards who were deployed to the external border of the European Union during the European refugee crisis. I also researched the implementation of humanitarian operations in risky conflict areas. Finally, I systematically analyzed veterans' war novels to understand how frontline personnel in crises struggle with operational dilemmas. Examples from my own empirical research are primarily presented to clarify the theoretical arguments in this book.

Building on these sources, this book aims to make multiple contributions to the literature. First, it integrates a wide range of research findings on frontline crisis response. As such, this book gives a broad overview of the main research topics and theories in literature on crisis response operations. Next, the in-depth analysis of eleven frontline response dilemmas brings competing research results to the fore, problematizes simple solutions to crisis response dilemmas, and provides a basis for reflective thinking about possible crisis response improvements. Finally, based on an analysis of the eleven crisis response dilemmas, the concluding chapter adds to the current literature by presenting a theory of frontline crisis response. In general, this book therefore helps to understand, evaluate, and advance crisis response operations.

2 | *Leadership*
Command and Control
versus Decentralization

Ask people what is most important during crises and you will often get leadership as an answer. It is widely believed that crisis situations require strong authority figures, who can take command and lead people out of chaos. But hierarchical authority structures face some recurring challenges in crises. Take the example of a paramedic who is called to the site of a traffic accident and finds a man with serious neck pain. The paramedic thinks he has a broken neck and wants to send him to the trauma center. This takes only a short car drive, but he knows the road is bumpy since there are trolley tracks along the way, so he decides to call in a helicopter instead. His superior must give permission though, and refuses. The paramedic now faces a tough and urgent dilemma: ignore the top-down decision or risk the patient's health (see Henderson & Pandey, 2013). In another example, a military commander plans for battle and his subordinates look to him for orders. He knows the battle is bound to be unpredictable and cause many casualties. Should the commander be directive, assertive, and resolute or be restraint, ask for soldiers' input, and allow for discretionary behaviors? Perhaps even more crucially, the commander wonders whether it is even possible to exercise control over hundreds of soldiers that are confronted with unforeseeable combat scenarios and are struggling to survive (Tolstoy, 2001).

These are very different examples but both show that operational leadership in a crisis is not self-evident, nor easy. In the first case, the paramedic willfully ignores his superior's order, the helicopter flies the victim to the trauma center, and the man fully recovers. In the second example, the commander accepts that he has limited influence when the fighting breaks out and gives some general guidance, but refrains from intervening in operations. Clearly, these examples challenge the traditional view on leadership in crises, because top-down hierarchies are relaxed and superiors' instructions are contested. The issue of leadership in crisis response is therefore not a settled matter. Instead, crisis responders face a recurring organizing dilemma, because crises seem to demand both centralization and decentralization of decision-making power.

2.1 Command and Control as Leading Principles

We have high expectations of operational leaders in crises. Leaders are supposed to have a superior grasp of the crisis situation and have to choose a clear course of action in complex, chaotic situations. When they make their choice, they also need to be decisive and inspiring, so their subordinates will closely follow their instructions, no matter if they understand their leader's intentions or whether they agree. The decisions of these great leaders, moreover, should quickly and efficiently resolve crises to general satisfaction. Sometimes, it may even seem like these "exceptional individuals" single-handedly relieve us from disaster (see Clarke, 2013; Uhr, 2017). This perception of leaders has not only been popular in fictional accounts of crisis response but has also been the basis for authority structures in many professional crisis organizations.

It is based on the assumption that responders might freeze or panic when they are suddenly confronted with danger. The anxiety resulting from an external threat causes people to look at their leaders and makes them rely on their decisions as a way of coping with their anxiety (cf. Staw et al., 1981). Early research has indeed suggested that a crisis results in centralization of decision-making power: Fewer individuals are involved in the decision-making process and more decisions are made at higher organizational levels (Hamblin, 1958; Hermann, 1963). In general, if leaders are uniquely capable of saving us from disaster, it makes sense to shift responsibilities to them and trust that they will make decisions that will be in our common interest.

The authority structures that have been created in crisis response organizations mimic traditional military ways of organizing (Clarke, 2013; Drabek & McEntire, 2002; Dynes, 1994; Suparamaniam & Dekker, 2003). The idea is that armed forces are extremely successful in operating under conditions of danger and uncertainty, so other crisis organizations should adopt a similar, para-military approach. This approach is defined by the terms "command and control" (or C2). It refers to a top-down hierarchy, in which a designated leader gives orders to their subordinates through which the organization regains its grip of a chaotic situation. Every subordinate only receives instructions from one superior along clearly defined command lines and is expected to implement these faithfully. Subordinates may not even be informed of the broader context, but receive only limited information by their superiors, because there is no need for them to know the rationale or justification of the instructions. They have to follow orders without questions and leave forecasting, analysis, and contemplation to commanders. At the same time, they are accountable to their superiors and are supposed to report the outcomes of their actions, so their leaders can use this information for future decision-making. This approach can be found in crisis response organizations around the world, for instance in Incident Command Systems (Bigley & Roberts, 2001), ambulance services (Harrison, 2019), coast guards (Jin & Song, 2017), and humanitarian agencies (Clarke, 2013).

It has not only influenced the design of authority structures in crisis organizations but also affected our views on (failing) crisis leadership. For instance, Van Wart and Kapucu (2011) found that emergency management officials considered strong leadership of crucial importance in crises: Officials emphasized that leaders should be decisive, take responsibility, have analytical skills to make unilateral decisions, and display self-confidence. These characteristics fit the command and control approach closely. Likewise, when the United States Congress (2006) investigated the disastrous governmental response to Hurricane Katrina, which left 1,800 people dead and most of New Orleans flooded, it blamed the failing management of this crisis on a lack of command and control. Claiming that effective crisis response requires unity of command and a clear hierarchy, the report recommended that command and control structures are better protected, further clarified, and more closely followed in future crises.

In the aftermath of the COVID-19 pandemic, researchers have again argued for strong leadership, because critical situations "need a commander to coerce her or his followers into line to avoid a catastrophe" (Grint, 2020, p. 315). The militarization of this crisis, in which politicians declared war on the virus and spoke about fighting the disease (Bernhard, 2020), has invoked calls for military-style, strong leadership (Jetly et al., 2020; Pearce et al., 2021). Command and control remain, therefore, the preferred organizing principles for authority structures in crises.

2.2 The Impossibility of Centralized Control

It may be very appealing to centralize power in the hands of one great leader. Yet, it is also bound to fail. In crises, leaders do not have as much power as most people, including leaders themselves, may like to believe. This was a key finding from early research on large-scale crises. Members of the Disaster Research Center in the United States studied community-wide disasters with natural or technological causes and noticed something unexpected (Dynes, 1983; Quarantelli, 1997b; Quarantelli & Dynes, 1977). There was no centralization of decision-making power during these situations. And there were good reasons to explain this. For instance, these disasters can last days or weeks, so senior decision-makers get quickly overworked and need to rest or be replaced. These crises also create new tasks (e.g., mass burials and removing waste), which are often unforeseen or different from expected, so there is no leader clearly in charge and many of these tasks will be spontaneously taken up by responders on the ground. Even for common tasks, it might be unclear who is responsible in a particular situation. For instance, security provision after a hurricane can be taken up by the local police, national police, or the armed forces. In many cases, a new crisis-driven hierarchy simply emerges ad hoc in the aftermath of crises (Neal & Phillips, 1995). This convinced the researchers that authority conflicts are more common than a centralization of authority in post-disaster situations.

While the preferred top-down leadership approach is borrowed from the armed forces, it is ironically not even used (or even possible) in most military operations. To illustrate this, it is useful to refer to Tolstoy, a veteran himself, who writes in his masterpiece *War and Peace* that the French emperor Napoleon did not (and could not) exercise his authority during the Battle of Borodino. He was simply so far from the battlefield that "he could not know the course of the battle and not one of his orders during the fight could be executed" (Tolstoy, 2001, p. 621). Instead, officers on the spot took the lead and they "did not fear getting into trouble for not fulfilling orders or for acting on their own initiative, for in battle what is at stake is what is dearest to man – his own life – [...] and these men who were right in the heat of the battle acted according to the mood of the moment" (Tolstoy, 2001, p. 634).

Still, it is not just large-scale disasters and military operations that render leadership challenging. Scholars found that centralized control has proven equally impossible in a range of other crisis situations. Crises, in fact, trigger several processes that undermine a centralization of decision-making power (Hart et al., 1993). These processes can be illustrated by analyzing one of the most momentous crises of the past decades: the attacks on the World Trade Centre in New York on 9/11. Dearstyne (2007) paints a picture of chaos and disbelief among responders. Reliable information was hard to come by in the early phase of the crisis, so commanders did not understand what was happening, could not conceive the collapse of the towers, or even knew which units were present at the incident site. Vague and contradictory information made it challenging to lead the response operations, but it became truly impossible for them to interact with subordinates when radio communication broke down. In the immediate aftermath of the attack, commanders could not find their command posts and ambulance personnel failed to locate their superiors. Even when there were opportunities for giving orders, senior officers had no advice or their instructions proved unworkable. Frontline responders of all emergency services made their own decisions.

The 9/11 response offers clear indications of how centralized control can break down in crises. Leaders might be paralyzed by the overwhelming ambiguity or profound uncertainties surrounding the situation, failing to give instructions even when subordinates ask for them. Other leaders may send out orders, but often these simply cannot be implemented, are very vague, or are outdated as soon as frontline responders receive them. It seems that the higher leaders are in the hierarchy, the less they can oversee and guide what happens on the ground and the less likely their instructions are implemented. While the command and control approach implies that responders become passive in the absence of clear crisis command, this is outright wrong. Responders take initiative, ignore ill-informed orders, and, more generally, do what they think needs to be done (see Comfort & Kapucu, 2006; Hart et al., 1993).

Suparamaniam and Dekker (2003) confirm this in their study on international disaster relief work, where they noticed a gap between those in charge and those with the relevant knowledge. It is hard, they report, to get the relevant knowledge to authority figures, because it is often challenging to find out who has formal authority in the first place. In practice, therefore, it is common for frontline personnel with the relevant local knowledge and the required resources to step up and take the lead. They feel compelled to act, take charge, and initiate crisis response efforts, either with the consent of official leadership or without. Another confirmation of this theory comes from an innovative study on leadership during small emergency incidents (Groenendaal & Helsloot, 2016). Frontline commanders of Dutch fire services were equipped with helmet-mounted cameras during incidents, so the researchers could follow how they made and communicated their decisions. While commanders may inadvertently overstate their role and influence in crises during post hoc interviews and in evaluations reports, this methodological approach enabled the researchers to study how commanders actually lead during crises. Interestingly, during half of the incidents, not a single order was issued. Even when there were instructions, many proved to be ambiguous and allowed for a broad array of discretionary behaviors. Monitoring took place less than half of the time, and over a third of the orders were not properly carried out. This empirical study demonstrates that, even in minor crises, leaders often play a modest role. Those in authority positions may have to go to great lengths to elicit compliance among those who are supposed to follow their instructions, as is confirmed in a study on communications between dispatchers and police officers (Karunakaran, 2021). Dispatchers have formal authority during emergencies, but police officers have a higher status and may not always comply with dispatchers' directions or simply fail to respond to them. By putting pressure on them through sharing information about their noncompliance with other officers in the police unit, the dispatcher can exercise influence and induce the police officer in question to comply with their instructions after all. Authority is clearly not equal to power and functional superiors need to work to ensure obedience of their subordinates.

Researchers have formulated several explanations for the limited dependence of frontline responders on their commanders. Based on Naturalistic Decision-Making theory, they argue that responders are primed by their previous experiences when responding to a critical situation. Lower-level Army commanders, firefighters, and paramedics do not analyze and compare multiple approaches in a deliberate way, but assess a situation, recognize it as a typical case, and (re)act. Ultimately, their experiences are a stronger guide for these actions than top-down instructions (Klein, 1993). As such, it makes sense that commanders often have little to do during response operations (Groenendaal et al., 2013; Rake & Njå, 2009). In addition, literature on street-level bureaucracy shows that frontline responders, like other street-level bureaucrats, enjoy considerable discretion in translating policies and guidelines into concrete actions (Lipsky, 1983). Implementation of orders typically deviates from the leaders' intent, because frontline responders enact top-down instructions as they deem fit. Since their superiors are often remotely located and their instructions will be necessarily general due to their reduced situational awareness, the discretionary power of responders is significant in crisis operations (Henderson & Pandey, 2013; Kalkman & Groenewegen, 2019). Both explanations boil down to the argument that operational leadership in crises will often be symbolic. Decisions are not deliberately taken through centralized control, but simply "happen" on the ground as frontline personnel respond to crises.

2.3 The Undesirability of Centralized Control

Even if centralized control in crisis response was possible, there are reasons to question whether it would be desirable. There are strong indications that a strict hierarchy impedes rapid and effective crisis response. It may foster a passive attitude in frontline personnel and lead to rigidity rather than flexibility in operations, thereby undermining adaptation to changing circumstances. This became painfully clear during the 2014 Sewol ferry disaster when the South Korean Coast Guard failed to rescue around 300 passengers after the ferry capsized (Jin & Song, 2017). The authority structure was based on command and control, so senior officers gave instructions that were faithfully obeyed by frontline personnel. The hierarchy was so strong that even when the orders failed to match the situation at hand, rescuers did not take discretionary actions themselves, but passively awaited new instructions, resulting in a failed and heavily criticized response effort. Similarly, in the Heysel stadium disaster, a stampede before the 1985 European Cup final between Juventus and Liverpool, tensions between supporters had continued to rise and were witnessed by police on the ground, who failed to intervene and prevent the escalation of the situation. They had received no orders to be proactive, nor were they allowed to approach their superiors and ask for instructions. As a result, they awaited the disaster rather than taking actions to avoid it (Hart et al., 1993).

Clearly, flexibility is often critically important, because frontline responders will be much more likely than their superiors to sense that something is off, a crisis is about to occur, or an incident might blow up into a full-scale disaster. The rescuers at the Sewol ferry accident and the police during the Heysel stadium disaster felt and knew that a tragedy was unfolding, but the hierarchical structure left them little power to act on this knowledge. A similar dynamic has unfolded in other disasters. Kayes (2004), for instance, studied the 1996 Mount Everest climbing disaster, during which several climbing teams tried to reach the top but failed to safely return. Things went terribly wrong when a snowstorm struck the mountain, and multiple mountaineers did not return in time, dying near the mountaintop. Kayes explains that a strong reliance on directive leadership rendered individual team members unable to cope with the deteriorating situation themselves. They failed to adapt, even though discretionary adaptation was crucial to saving lives and limbs. Likewise, when Weick (1990) explained the causes for the Tenerife air crash, during which a KLM aircraft collided with a Pan Am airplane on a foggy runway, he found fault as well with the strict hierarchy in the cockpit. The first officer and the flight engineer both indicated they had doubts about whether it was safe to take off, but to no avail. The crash left 583 people dead.

Apart from thwarting flexible responses, a leadership approach based on centralized control also burdens communication channels with the wrong type of information (Dynes, 1994). In the early phase of a crisis, there is considerable uncertainty as to what is happening and responders urgently desire to gain a better understanding of the situation (see Dearstyne, 2007). Yet, rather than gathering this information and sharing this throughout the response network, communication channels are used for issuing orders. This may add to the confusion, particularly when orders are based on outdated or contradictory information. It also risks creating an information overload. Responders' limited cognitive capacities are distracted from grasping the crisis at hand to interpreting top-down instructions. Moreover, in transboundary crises, during which multiple organizations have to collaborate in the response, a directive leader is likely to antagonize others. Crisis partners may easily estrange from an unfamiliar leader, who is assertive, dominant, and imposing. Instead, leaders should recognize that their expertise may be limited, that others have a better or complementary situational awareness, that they necessarily share power with a range of other actors, and that they need to reach compromises when opinions differ or risk producing conflict and rivalry (Rosenthal et al., 1991; Uhr, 2017).

These examples show why crisis researchers have grown skeptical of a hierarchical authority structure. Commanders that allow their frontline responders little leeway may make the response rigid and ineffective. Leaders that are higher up the chain of command are generally not well positioned to lead the crisis response in an adaptive, successful manner. This made Quarantelli (1988, p. 381) argue for loosening or decentralizing the command structure.

2.4 Decentralizing Decision-Making Power

If centralized control is both impossible and undesirable, crisis organizations have to involve frontline responders in the decision-making process. There are different ways of realizing this. Some crisis researchers argue that operational leaders should engage responders to voice their concerns when they notice anomalies and share their divergent perspectives on the situation (Barton & Sutcliffe, 2009; Barton et al., 2015). Similar findings are reported in a study on operating room teams learning to use a novel cardiac surgery technology (Edmondson, 2003). It shows that team leaders could reduce power imbalance and encourage subordinates to speak up for the benefit of organizational learning and performance. Likewise, Hannah et al., (2009) argue that some extreme contexts may benefit from a more adaptive, shared leadership style, in which there is a smaller distance between subordinates and commanders to incorporate frontline input in leaders' decision-making. In these studies, the leader remains the essential authority figure in crisis response operations and should mainly change their posture or approach.

Other researchers, instead, have advocated for a decentralization of decision-making power in crisis, building on the idea that effective crisis response requires autonomous, adaptive behaviors at the frontline. If crises confront responders with rapidly changing conditions, discretionary initiatives by frontline personnel are crucial to an effective response, so decision-making should be deferred to lower organizational levels (Drabek & McEntire, 2002; Dynes, 1994). This means that frontline responders adopt their own crisis approach as they seem fit, take actions they consider necessary, and deploy resources over which they might not even formally have control. It requires a delegation of decision-making responsibilities to those with relevant knowledge or closer familiarity with the crisis, despite the fact that this person is lower in rank.

Such a decentralized decision-making structure is already used by some highly reliable organizations, including aircraft carriers and nuclear power plants (Weick & Sutcliffe, 2001). In these organizations, decisions are pushed down toward the frontline, because someone who can see, smell, and feel the (emerging) crisis is more likely to make the right choices than an off-site commander. In practice, frontline personnel often dynamically solve unanticipated problems in creative ways and should be granted the discretionary power to do so (Meshkati & Khashe, 2015). Even armed forces have increasingly adopted "mission command," an approach that prescribes the devolution of responsibilities to lower-level military personnel, who have the most recent information and are best positioned to make decisions in uncertain, and threatening situations. Although a decentralized way of operating in crisis has gained traction in theory, it still faces problems in practice (LaPorte & Consolini, 1991; Vogelaar & Kramer, 2004).

2.5 Fragmented Decision-Making in Crises

The report by the United States Congress (2006, p. 195) on the dramatic response to Hurricane Katrina concludes that the failing command and control structure resulted in "an agonizingly disjointed and slow response to the disaster." This conclusion highlights that the lack of integration is a concerning weakness of a decentralized crisis approach. Integration of different response actions is important for various reasons. Bigley and Roberts (2001) describe the Incident Command Systems, the standard approach for emergency response in the US, as hierarchical and argue that operational leaders play an important role in embedding or "nesting" operations of various responders on the scene into the wider response effort. While the lowest operational responders may only have to focus on their task, operational commanders also need to avoid a dissolution of the response. A commander, ideally, has a general overview and can shift resources or priorities to match the changing situation without sacrificing cohesion in the process. In a similar vein, the "very rigid hierarchy" of emergency trauma centers, and particularly the attending surgeon's undisputed leadership, enables coordination in uncertain, urgent situations (Klein et al., 2006, p. 602). In other words, hierarchy is necessary to ensure that actions are synchronized and to prevent inefficient or counter-productive actions by disparate team members. Groenendaal and Helsloot (2016) write about a fire services' scuba team that tried and failed to open a car in a lake, even though another team had tried and failed to do the same just before. In this example, there were no adverse consequences, but such minor inefficiencies are a waste of resources that are often scarce in crises, while it also unnecessarily exposes responders to risks.

Apart from resulting in a disjointed approach, decentralization of decision-making power may render crisis response also problematically slow when coordinated action is required. In the face of a need for collective action, synchronizing activities without clear, hierarchical directions means delays. This is problematic since crises are characterized by a high degree of urgency. When fast decisions are needed, there may not be time to wait for consensus among responders to emerge. At those moments, there is a premium on rapid choices. Thus, collective action under time pressure produces an imperative for hierarchical command (Moynihan, 2008, 2009). When there are multiple organizations involved, such as in domestic emergencies or international humanitarian operations, conflicts are common, because responders have differing views and interests. In such situations, as well, it might be more attractive to grant commanders the authority to resolve disputes, make decisions, and direct the integrated response effort without stalling the process and losing the initiative (Bigley & Roberts, 2001; Clarke, 2013).

A final challenge to a decentralized crisis response revolves around questions of accountability. Crisis responders will be guided by their professional understandings and experiences when taking discretionary actions, but they still make errors. Take the example of the Stockwell shooting, during which Jean Charles de Menezes, a man who was mistaken for a suicide bomber by the London Metropolitan Police, was killed. A police officer shot him dead, believing that his actions were within the operational mandate, but still going far beyond his superior's ambiguous instructions to stop the suspect (Colville et al., 2013). Clearly, discretionary actions can have disastrous results. When people have power over life and death, as crisis responders typically do, there is merit in respecting the authority structure to ensure that operational decisions are legitimate and accountable. In turn, a clear line of command may protect responders against having to make tough moral decisions without leadership support. For instance, medical staff had to decide on what to do with dying patients after days of enormous hardships in the aftermath of Hurricane Katrina that brought their hospital to a standstill. As they evacuated the hospital, they should not have had to make the choice between euthanizing patients or leaving them behind to slowly die alone (Boin & Nieuwenburg, 2013). In crises, there are often situations in which it is not easy to distinguish right from wrong, so it makes sense to defer these decisions to leaders who have been appointed to make such decisions and can be held responsible afterward.

Empirical Example

In early September 2019, the category 5 Hurricane Dorian hit the Bahamas and caused massive destruction on several islands. Seventy-five percent of the houses on the Abaco islands, for instance, were damaged and over two hundred people were reported missing. A task force, consisting of two Navy ships and 650 military personnel from the Dutch, German, and French armed forces, was deployed to provide disaster relief and humanitarian aid after a request for support. The task force was led by a Command Center, which was created on board of one of the ships and consisted of a commander, deputy commander, and eighty-seven other officers. They were supposed to analyze all available information, decide on the priority of tasks, and control the response efforts. Almost immediately, however, this authority structure failed. An Army sergeant noticed that their instructions became "quickly often too simplistic, not up to date, not realistic," while a general admitted that "things developed so rapidly that [control] proved impossible." Alternative centers of power emerged on the island instead. A lower-level commander from the Marines was in charge of the Command Post that was created upon arrival as a central hub for land-based operations and he decided to take charge to speed up decision-making processes. At the Emergency Operations Center, military liaisons began to take initiative as well by relaying only some requests for military support and rejecting others, while at the main airport, helicopter personnel decided to take control over air operations. With top-down command clearly failing, land-based units increasingly began to take discretionary actions and military leadership felt a need to shift to "mission command", thereby giving frontline soldiers much more discretion. A Navy colonel explained that "you can design [the command and control structure] like you want, but if it doesn't work in practice, you need to change." Marines and Engineers, particularly, went their own way and operated almost autonomously. One major of the Engineers confided: "I don't let them control me that much." Personnel from these units also felt little or no obligation to document their activities and report back to the Command Center, so their senior officers could improve their situational awareness or hold the units accountable for their decisions, because they prioritized rapid actions on the ground. Even when the Command Center was informed, the reports did not meet the requirements, which a Navy lieutenant justified by mentioning that "everyone is working at maximum capacity and is not thinking about reporting things correctly [...]. We have better things to do." Although the response was flexible, the frontline unit began to disintegrate after a few days with soldiers operating in small teams or alone. At the same time, their actions became disjointed and were guided by immediate requests rather than attempts to use scarce resources efficiently. Perhaps most disturbing, infighting between different units was looming and inter-unit frustrations were increasingly voiced. None of these consequences spiraled out of control before the mission ended after ten days. Once all were back on board, the preexisting leadership structure was rapidly restored (Kalkman, 2023a).

2.6 Co-constructing Authority

The outline of the dilemma of leadership for crisis response is now clearer (Table 2.1). Proponents of a hierarchical approach argue that a top-down authority structure enables a rapid, coordinated crisis response effort in which responsibilities are clearly allocated, while supporters of a decentralized approach claim that delegating power to the frontline is needed for an adaptive, effective response to the chaotic situation. In short, frontline crisis responders face an operational dilemma, because there is a simultaneous need for centralization and decentralization.

Table 2.1 *The leadership dilemma*

	Command and control	Decentralization
Characteristics	Strict hierarchy	Delegating decision-making power
	Clear lines of command	
	Bottom-up obedience	Discretionary initiatives
Advantages	Rapid decision-making	Adaptive frontline behaviors
	Coordinated actions	Well-informed decisions
Shortcomings	Implementation problems	Inefficiency
	Passive attitude of responders	Slow consensus-building
	Rigid operational response	Undermines accountability

It is important to begin with noting that crisis organizations have to design an authority structure that can shift between centralized command when rapid, integrative decisions are needed and decentralized decision-making when there is a need for adaptive, flexible responses. Traditionally, most researchers have either argued for a strong hierarchy with limited room for frontline discretion (see Bigley & Roberts, 2001; Klein et al., 2006; Moynihan, 2008) or for a decentralized approach in which frontline responders are the main decision-makers (Drabek & McEntire, 2002; Dynes, 1994; Meshkati & Khashe, 2015). Yet, different crises demand different leadership approaches and even one single crisis response may benefit from changes in the authority structure over time. The implication of this proposition is that preexisting authority structures need to be continuously tested and potentially revised to ensure that crisis response efforts remain effective.

Although it is clear that crises differ and crisis situations evolve, there is a tendency to design leadership structures for use in all response operations. The Incident Command System, for instance, offers a "highly formalized" structure that is "supposedly suitable for almost any type of emergency (such as massive disasters, riots, and terrorist attacks) and for emergencies of nearly any size, ranging from a minor incident involving a single small team, such as a fire engine company, to a major event involving numerous agencies" (Bigley & Roberts, 2001, p. 1282). But some incidents, such as recurring house fires or a car crash, may demand a different leadership approach than more complex, large-scale, uncertain crises (see also Hannah et al., 2009). Faraj and Xiao (2006) show that emergency treatments in trauma centers may range from habitual and predictable trajectories to problematic ones. These different trajectories require different organizational responses. For instance, attending surgeons are more likely to devolve some responsibilities when tasks are familiar and less time-pressured (Klein et al., 2006). In other words, an authority structure needs to be adapted to the crisis it aims to resolve.

Leaders' roles in relatively familiar and straightforward crises can be planned and anticipated: They delegate tasks or merely supervise, create the boundary conditions for frontline responders to do their work, and take charge sparingly to intervene in operations when responders engage in unsafe behavior or the response effort disintegrates (see e.g., Groenendaal & Helsloot, 2016; Wolbers et al., 2018). The operational leaders' role becomes more difficult when a crisis turns problematic or more complex.

Typically, response organizations cannot know up front if a crisis is a manageable situation in which the planned authority structure will suffice, or if it is (or will evolve into) a difficult crisis situation for which the authority structure needs to be adapted. Critically, this requires an observation of cues, which may signify the need for changes to the authority structure. Sometimes, these cues may be very clear, such as a patient who is not responding to treatment, a coordinated terrorist attack, or a hurricane crippling a state. However, these cues are usually subtle and equivocal in other cases. It can, for instance, be a small change in the weather conditions that causes increased risks to mountaineering teams and wildland firefighters (see Kayes, 2004; Weick, 1993). What is important here is that frontline personnel will be the first to sense that something is off. Their key role in noticing the problematic development of a crisis means that frontline responders should trigger the reconsideration of the existing authority structure. When they express concerns or uneasiness, operational leaders have to take these signs seriously. A leader's attitude and behavior toward team members are therefore very important. They should encourage and enable frontline subordinates to use their voice and develop a trusting relationship so that these warning signals are heeded (Barton & Sutcliffe, 2009; Cherry, 2014). In those cases, a novel authority structure is needed and must be co-constructed through interactions between frontline responders and leaders.

As soon as a crisis grows more complex, frontline personnel will typically take more autonomy and improvise to flexibly adapt. Top-down directions are likely to be ignored, because these may be based on outdated information, are not received, or will be perceived as misguided. Interestingly, and perhaps paradoxically, the role of leaders increases at the same time. When responders believe that the crisis requires them to go beyond their formal responsibilities, they simultaneously undermine the authority structure and trigger a need for leaders to rethink the distribution of power in the response effort. Leaders may have to grant more autonomy to subordinates, but they also have to set the external boundaries of frontline discretionary behavior. They need to define which choices are of such functional or moral importance that these have to be taken by them, possibly in a directive manner, because as leaders, they still have to guarantee a coherent effort and remain responsible for (ethical) response outcomes. In this way, a new distribution of power emerges ad hoc. In the past, researchers have been more interested in finding the appropriate allocation of power than in how influence is exercised and circulates in crisis response, but leadership structures cannot be static in the complex and dynamic contexts of crisis response. It needs dialogue and negotiation between responders and operational leaders, who co-construct a new, evolving authority structure throughout the response effort.

2.7 Conclusion

During crises, it is important to continuously test whether the existing authority structure is still appropriate, challenge leadership when it is overly directive, and implement top-down interventions when the response grows too disjointed or stalls. To deal with the dilemma of a simultaneous need for centralization and decentralization in crisis response, authority structures need to be co-constructed by frontline responders and their operational leaders.

It will be particularly useful to learn more about how influence and decision-making power shift between responders during crises. In particular, future studies may identify different processes through which authority structures are co-constructed and offer new insights on how to design crisis organizations that enable such co-construction. Frontline experiences on changing authority structures during crises need more attention as well. Finally, a flexible approach to authority also requires operational leaders who can both delegate and take control depending on the situation. Further research may focus on how to best prepare leaders for adopting such different styles and when to switch between them.

Resources for Educators and Professionals

PRACTICAL LESSONS

- Top-down command and frontline discretion might both be needed in crises
- Different crisis situations require different ways of organizing leadership, so authority structures should be adaptable rather than fixed
- Frontline personnel are best positioned to indicate when the authority structure needs change in a particular situation
- More complex crises will inevitably lead to increased frontline autonomy, but operational leaders have to guarantee a coherent effort and remain responsible for response outcomes
- Frontline responders and their leaders construct new authority structures together during a crisis by discussing and negotiating how crisis response decisions are made

QUESTIONS FOR REFLECTION AND DISCUSSION

- During which recent crisis situations did a hierarchical approach work well? What were its advantages?
- What images of leadership are dominant in your crisis organization? How do people talk about leadership and what do they find important?
- Frontline discretion may be inevitable, but it is not always encouraged: When are autonomous actions lauded as proactive and when are they criticized as irresponsible?

3 | *Sensemaking*
Creating Clarity versus
Embracing Uncertainty

Crises are chaotic to the people that have to respond to them. When a crisis is first encountered, frontline personnel face a potentially dangerous situation about which they know very little. This is exemplified in the story of a team of smokejumpers, deployed to put out a wildfire at the Mann Gulch area, in Montana. The fifteen smokejumpers were dropped with their tools near the fire and met up with a ranger who was already involved in fighting the fire. They had some information about the fire, such as the fact that it was between ten and ninety-nine acres and the spotters' estimation that it would be contained by 10:00 am the following morning. Yet, they sensed the fire was more serious than that. When the team started approaching the fire, they collected bits of information (e.g., from the smoke, vegetation, wind, and exploding trees) that gave them a better grasp of it, but they could not fully oversee the situation, nor how it would develop. This became dramatically clear when, nearing the fire on the safe side of the gulch, they suddenly saw that it had crossed the gulch and it was moving toward them at a very high speed. They turned around, trying to flee. Their operational commander lighted an escape fire, but the others did not understand what he was doing and continued to run. Most of them failed and died in the attempt. Their overly optimistic view on the fire and their inability to revise their view of the situation along the way ultimately led them toward tragedy (Weick, 1993).

The firefighters in this example failed to properly make sense of the changing situation. Failed sensemaking led them to take disastrous actions. Most crisis researchers believe that responders need to continuously (re)make sense of their environment to gain an adequate understanding, which enables them to respond to the crisis in an effective manner. The implicit assumption is that responders should always pursue more clarity about their environment and abstain from committing to a certain understanding until more is known. Yet, the smokejumpers could not have waited and passively observed until they had a full picture of the situation either. The resulting sensemaking dilemma for responders is that they need to balance gaining a better understanding with embracing uncertainty.

3.1 Gaining an Understanding of a Crisis Situation

Research on sensemaking is heavily indebted to the American scholar Karl Weick, whose analyses of the Mann Gulch disaster and other crises continue to exercise a major influence on crisis sensemaking studies. Weick (1988, 1993) has demonstrated that crises confront responders with unexpected situations, which disrupt previous ways of working and challenge the existing understanding of the situation (see also Maitlis & Christianson, 2014; Maitlis & Sonenshein, 2010). When responders think they know what they are facing (e.g., a small fire) and are suddenly proven wrong, they urgently need to gain a renewed sense of what is happening in their environment to avoid their response from collapsing into failure (Weick, 1993). The sensemaking process orders the chaotic situation into a comprehensible understanding: It gives responders the confidence that they are aware of the situation again and it offers them a framework for their future activities (Brown et al., 2015; Weick, 1995, 2010; Weick et al., 2005).

At the same time, sensemaking is extremely challenging in practice. In an early stage of the crisis, frontline responders know close to nothing, while the cues, the bits of information, that they do receive or register, will often be confusing. Cues can be confusing due to their ambiguity and their equivocality (Weick, 1995). When cues are ambiguous, it is hard to make out what they signify. Charles Perrow (1984) famously analyzed the partial meltdown of the Three Mile Island nuclear power plant, where complex interactions and tight couplings between elements of the plant left the operators in utter oblivion about what was happening. The operators were confused and misled by the indicators, dials, and lights on their control panel that did not make sense and seemed contradictory. The signals were doing little more than puzzling the operators and it was ultimately an act of desperation (rather than a solid understanding of the situation) that averted disaster. Similar accounts of pervasive confusion due to ambiguity are recurring. Frontline personnel after the 9/11 attack reported being overwhelmed, unable to figure out what occurred, and simply unable to grapple with the fact that the towers had collapsed (Dearstyne, 2007). Still, other cues tend to be equivocal, which means that they can mean multiple things, rendering sensemaking equally difficult. In the run-up to the Stockwell shooting, the London Metropolitan Police team following Jean Charles de Menezes faced a lot of equivocal cues. As they were preparing for the operation, frontline officers received specialist ammunition and were informed about the possible need for "unusual tactics," suggesting that they were facing a suicide bomber, although this was never officially stated. Later, during the attempt to identify the target, one surveillance officer states that the target is "possibly identical" to the terrorist suspect that the team members think they are chasing, which is again a very dubious piece of information. Later, the operational commander orders the firearms officers to stop the suspect, but the word choice is vague as well: The operational commander intended them to detain him, but fire arms officers interpreted it to mean that they had to stop the suspect at all costs and shot him dead at close range (Colville et al., 2013; Cornelissen et al., 2014). In short, crises present situations in which information is limited and unclear, as cues can often not be made sensible or are open to multiple interpretations.

It will come as no surprises that responders spend considerable effort on gathering as much reliable information as possible when they face a crisis. All senses are strained to their maximum capacity to collect, check, and interpret any incoming data. Svensson and Hällgren (2018) listened in on emergency calls and interviewed emergency operators, discovering that they do not just listen to the (factual) information of callers but the whole range of audible cues. Wheezing sounds may indicate breathing difficulties, screaming and running noises mean that a reported fire is real and significant, traffic sounds hint at a car accident, and panic suggests the need for urgency. On route to a crisis, the responders want as much information as well. Using ethnographic observations and video recordings inside a fire truck, Landgren (2005) finds that firefighting teams try to get insights into the nature, exact location, and size of the incident. In the early stage of a crisis, responders will therefore often ask question after question (Kalkman, 2019b).

Frontline responders do not make sense of crises in social isolation but will rely on others for information and analysis. People also influence each other's sensemaking through the ways they are acting in and talking about a situation (Sandberg & Tsoukas, 2015; Weick, 1995). The social element of sensemaking is useful for understanding how teams and organizations react in crises. Indeed, crisis response typically requires coordination between multiple individuals, so involved personnel need to arrive at similar or overlapping understandings to enable collective efforts (see Wachtendorf & Kendra, 2006). Clearly, when organizational members have wildly different ideas on the nature or trajectory of the crisis, their actions might be inconsistent or even conflicting. For instance, after a blast in a building, firefighters may be primed to think of gas leaks and fragile structures, while police might identify a potential terrorist attack. This can lead to police officers trying to cordon off the area to take out the perpetrator and allow for crime scene investigation, while firefighters will want to enter the building to evacuate people inside (Kalkman, 2019b). In these situations, it is helpful if involved crisis responders co-create a picture of the situation by exchanging information and negotiating the implications of the scarce data initially available (Merkus et al., 2017; Wolbers & Boersma, 2013). Such collective sensemaking efforts offer a basis for coordinated crisis response activities.

3.2 Sensemaking Processes

Sensemaking has often been confused with interpretation, but it is considerably more complex than that. The original sensemaking model consists of three recurring processes: enactment, selection, and retention (Weick, 1979; Weick et al., 2005). When an environment is chaotic, such as in crises, it is virtually impossible to simply observe and define the nature of the situation. Frontline personnel are not inclined to wait and see either. They will begin with taking actions that they have been trained to implement or that come intuitively (i.e., enactment). Vietnam War veteran Tim O'Brien (2015) tells of the time that he saw an enemy combatant who

carried his weapon in one hand, muzzle down, moving without any hurry up the center of the trail. [...] I had already pulled the pin on a grenade. I had come up to a crouch. It was entirely automatic. I did not hate the young man; I did not see him as the enemy; I did not ponder issues of morality or politics or military duty. [...] There were no thoughts about killing. The grenade was to make him go away – just evaporate – and I leaned back and felt my mind go empty and then felt it fill up again. I had already thrown the grenade before telling myself to throw it.

In fast-evolving, uncertain crises, such enactment typically precedes a full understanding of the situation.

These actions also focus information gathering efforts. Ambiguous and equivocal cues initially puzzle and overwhelm responders, but once actions are taken, the responder can focus on the effects of these actions. For instance, members of O'Brien's unit will likely focus attention on signs that enemy combatants are either returning fire or retreating. This information will be used in the so-called selection process, during which organizational members use their previous experiences and earlier training to find the right frame for the situation or may come to the conclusion that an entirely new understanding is required when familiar definitions of the situation do not apply. The soldiers may, for example, conclude that this soldier was operating alone and likely a scout, engage in a firefight with a possibly experienced enemy unit, or face new recruits that flee at the first sign of danger. Such an understanding is always preliminary, as definite crisis understandings are unlikely, but nevertheless help responders to slightly improve their grasp of the environment. Moreover, their initial actions have affected the environment, because these evoked a reaction from enemy soldiers or showed that this soldier was operating alone in which case the initial action neutralized the threat. Either way, the environment has changed. The environment is clearly not a static given to be interpreted but a dynamic situation, which is to a large extent influenced (or enacted) by the responders themselves that subsequently select relevant cues for sensemaking (Weick, 1979, 1988; Weick et al., 2005).

Products of successful sensemaking of the crisis are retained and serve multiple goals. Retained understandings provide a basis for decision-making during the crisis and offer a frame for interpreting new cues that emerge out of further actions. Ideally, understandings will therefore grow increasingly specific and adequate. But retention has implications for sensemaking beyond the specific crisis incident. It inspires new training and drills, guides future enactment, and steers information gathering and analysis in later, similar episodes (see Colville et al., 2013). This may explain why experienced professionals are typically better at sensemaking in the aftermath of incidents and disasters than less-experienced colleagues (Gacasan & Wiggins, 2017; Whiteman & Cooper, 2011). Indeed, a soldier who has been in multiple combat situations is more likely to rapidly assess the nature of the situation and anticipate the possible effects of different actions. Retained understandings, in summary, serve as a reference for crisis situations in times to come (Weick, 1979; Weick et al., 2005).

Over time, crisis researchers have proposed alternative sensemaking processes, for instance, by referring to action–interpretation cycles (Maitlis & Christianson, 2014) or suggesting alternative sensemaking pathways (Kalkman, 2020c). In spite of these adaptations to the original model, sensemaking scholars share the belief that a crisis situation cannot be grasped by exhaustive intelligence work prior to the operations. Decision-making models that suggest observations precede actions, such as the Observe–Orient–Decide–Act loop in military doctrines, are believed to be useless in crises, because the complex environment cannot be understood by external observers and crucial information will be released only through action-induced cues. Sensemaking theory states that actions and situational interpretations, particularly in crises, coincide and understandings are slowly produced as the response is already underway. You can only know what you are dealing with, once you are already deeply involved in the situation.

3.3 Sensemaking Failures

A recurring finding in research on crisis sensemaking is that frontline personnel often commit to a certain understanding of the situation, until they are proven wrong in a disastrous manner. The example of the Mann Gulch smokejumpers provides an example. In spite of contradicting cues, the smokejumpers committed to the understanding that the wildfire was small and would be quickly contained. New information that they collected along the way, such as observations of the smoke or the sound of exploding trees, was either fitted in this frame or filtered out as unimportant. New cues were used only to support the existing understanding rather than to test or challenge it. As a result, they recognized too late that their sensemaking was wrong, because the fire was actually exploding and much larger than originally anticipated. Many similar sensemaking failures have been studied by crisis scholars, such as the failure to realize that the Mt. Everest expedition was gradually becoming more dangerous (Kayes, 2004), the misguided belief that helicopters were those of the enemy rather than friendly aircraft until after they were shot down (Snook, 2002), or even the mislabeling of a fire as taking place in an electrical power house rather than in someone's stove (Landgren, 2005). The adverse consequences may vary, but the common denominator in these examples is that frontline personnel were (overly) committed to a mistaken understanding and unable to revise it. This raises the question of why professional, skilled responders suffer from sensemaking failures.

In practice, it is often the first cues that people receive about a situation that trigger a particular understanding, which seem to match these cues. Responders will take new actions on the basis of this situational assessment to confirm, in the selection process, that new cues match the chosen understanding. Yet, when understandings guide actions and perceptions, people may create blind spots for themselves so they do not see deviant cues, as they are seeking for confirmation. Take the example of NASA's Columbia shuttle disaster. When the shuttle was launched, foam broke off and struck the orbiter, rendering it vulnerable. Mission Management, however, viewed it from the onset as a familiar, acceptable risk, acting toward the incident in that manner. They spent little effort on seeking alternative explanation and failed to heed to those with concerns, creating constraints for alternative sensemaking that simply could not be overcome, until the concerns tragically turned out to be justified when the shuttle crashed (Dunbar & Garud, 2009).

Particularly in stressful situations, it may be very hard to remain open-minded toward alternative explanations, so that responders engage in familiar behaviors even when these are futile (Ben-Shalom et al., 2012; Colville et al., 2013; Staw et al., 1981). Much of this has to do with expectations. Expectations about uncertain situations are risky, because they lull people into believing that they know what is going on, even when they should be most alert. When a highly toxic gas leaked from a pesticide plant in Bhopal, India, the plant operating team could not conceive it initially. They were committed to the idea that the plant was safe. One of the operators smelling methyl isocyanate was told he was only smelling mosquito spray, and the concerns of another who reported unusually high-pressure measurements were likewise discarded. The frontline operators held onto their belief that the plant was safe until they discovered too late that large quantities of gas were escaping into the atmosphere, killing thousands of nearby inhabitants and injuring many more (Weick, 1988). In a study on Israeli soldiers, Ben-Shalom et al. (2012) show that extensive drills and clear battle plans can likewise blind military personnel to the fact that their analysis of the situation is mistaken and needs revising. Even when they are under fire and their own lives are in danger, they may repeatedly engage in futile actions, such as storming a target with no success, which demonstrates the tenacity of frames in crises.

Sometimes, commitment to a specific crisis understanding is built into the crisis organization. Responders' roles and responsibilities focus their actions and perceptions, and simultaneously narrow their sensemaking. This became painfully clear when military personnel were deployed to New Orleans after Hurricane Katrina and the commanding officer told the *Army Times* that hundreds of troops would engage in combat operations to bring the city back under control, representing a far-reaching militarization of the response. People needed food, water, and medicine, but a soldier is primarily trained to bring security and might focus on security threats, even in a humanitarian crisis. Similarly, a police unit tasked with a surveillance operation of a notorious criminal was nearby when he was murdered, but failed to pursue and arrest the perpetrators, as the team was unable to shift to a different situational understanding and operating frame, being unprepared and not equipped for revising their sensemaking (Schakel et al., 2016). If frontline personnel have very specific tasks and capacities, they are likely to only have one or a few frames to fall back upon, which turns problematic when they suffer from good memory and are unable to engage in mindful reflection or creative, unprepared actions as a basis for new sensemaking (see Weick, 2010).

In the context of teams and organizations, members may also suffer from groupthink and conformity-seeking behaviors, failing to share crucial information that could induce reconsideration, thereby reinforcing a shared (but mistaken) understanding of the situation. In the example of the Mann Gulch disaster, for instance, smokejumpers had reasons to doubt that the fire was small, but no one voiced these doubts. Since no one suggested an alternative understanding or focused attention on deviant cues, every smokejumper had reason to believe that all others agreed that the fire was small and that their own doubts were likely misplaced. No one spoke up, and they distrusted their own senses and intuition rather than raising questions about the group frame (Weick, 1993).

When responders finally realize that their frame of reference is misguided, but do not have an alternative understanding of the crisis ready, their sensemaking and the response effort may collapse and needs to be rebuilt. This is often impossible in the stress and urgency of crisis situations. Responders who fail to remake sense will face a "cosmology episode," a situation in which not only the existing understanding collapses but also any means to rebuild it, as responders' worldview is profoundly shaken and its members succumb to fear (Orton & O'Grady, 2016). Usually, this is preceded or coincides with organizational disintegration. Indeed, as long as the organizational structures remain intact, team members may not fall victim to fear, but continue to do their work without fully understanding the situation. The combination of not grasping the environment and not being able to fall back on others, however, heralds a certain onset of organizational collapse, as displayed by the smokejumpers overrun by the exploding fire or by soldiers whose lives are in immediate danger by a surprise enemy attack (Kalkman, 2020c; Weick, 1993). Such sensemaking failures precede crisis response failures.

3.4 Adaptive Sensemaking

Sensemaking needs to keep up with the changing crisis situation. Indeed, crises are dynamic, evolving events. A patient may deteriorate or not respond to treatment, refugees may take new routes when existing ones are closed off, and a wildfire that cannot be controlled will expand and threaten villages or towns. Crises may also change in nature over time. A small fire in a building can suddenly turn into a different type of crisis when this building is a chemical plant, a fireworks warehouse, or a critical infrastructure. Likewise, natural hazards, such as volcano eruptions or hurricanes, often have a disastrous direct impact, but can in the long run also cause crop failure, water shortage, and epidemics, so that a community moves from one crisis to the next. Frontline responders who fail to keep up or have a mistaken understanding, to begin with, will likely engage in failing response efforts.

There is therefore a need for ongoing adjustments to one's understanding of the crisis through a process called adaptive sensemaking. This term is actually a pleonasm. Sensemaking is by definition continuous and adjusting, even if it only increasingly reinforces an existing (mistaken) understanding. If not, we might be speaking of situational awareness or intelligence products, but it would not be sensemaking. Still, scholars use the term to indicate that sensemaking can be renewed in light of changing environmental circumstances and may become a better fit with the situation over time. The term has a strong normative undertone. The faster and better responders adjust their understanding to the evolving crisis situation, the more adaptive is their sensemaking. Adaptive sensemaking, thus, refers to the ability to adopt a new understanding that better matches recently acquired information and enables a flexible response (Maitlis & Sonenshein, 2010).

A starting point for adaptive sensemaking is openness to the idea that the current understanding of the crisis may be mistaken. Ideally, responders seek out anomalies, which are critical signals that one's frame of reference is flawed. They should be encouraged to share differing opinions in order to seek out cues that may suggest that their operating frame is outdated or simply wrong (Barton et al., 2015). Sometimes, they can literally look at the crisis situation from different sides or they might contemplate various scenarios to make sure that they do not develop tunnel vision. Subsequently, responders will need to adjust their understanding once they discover their previous frame of reference is no longer applicable. This process of revising one's understanding has been dubbed updating (Maitlis & Sonenshein, 2010). It implies that a perfect understanding of the crisis situation is possible as long as responders continue to adjust and refine their sensemaking. One manifestation of updating is that frontline personnel shift from an old understanding to another frame of reference that is readily available in the organization. Police units, for instance, could switch from a surveillance situation to a chase and arrest scenario (Schakel et al., 2016). In other cases, responders need to build a new understanding from scratch.

Practice shows that updating is important but not easy, because it is difficult to fully discard previous understandings and rapidly reinterpret a situation as radically different from previously thought. Updating is also challenging when there is no clear alternative understanding readily available, but a new frame has to be constructed in situ. Combatants, for instance, have to actively search for information and engage in free thinking to come up with creative solutions when battle plans no longer apply (Ben-Shalom et al., 2012). Likewise, emergency department teams, treating a patient, need to simultaneously develop an understanding of a patient's condition and take immediate care of that same patient (e.g., giving medication and fluids, and performing CPR). When treatments are not sorting effects as anticipated, medical personnel have to continue multi-tasking, providing emergency care while trying to get a grasp of the origins of the health problems through collecting information, formulating explanations, and testing hypotheses (Christianson, 2019). When a new understanding is emerging that adequately explains the patient's condition and guides action that helps him improve, the team has successfully updated their understanding after all. Adaptive sensemaking is therefore manifested in frontline response teams who manage to rapidly update their frame of reference to one that best matches the crisis, improving their response efforts.

3.5 Embracing Uncertainty

Sensemaking theory has often been used to explain dramatic response failures (Orton & O'Grady, 2016). When firefighters or mountaineers die because their environment has turned much more dangerous than they anticipated or when police units misinterpreted a situation and their operation fails, something clearly went wrong and a better understanding should have been pursued. But there are pitfalls to selecting these dramatic cases for studying sensemaking. If cases are about misread situations that lead to accidental shootings or the deaths of organizational members, it does not come as a surprise that researchers find that responders need to continuously seek for updated or more exact explanations until they find the right one. These studies do typically not mention that there are reasons to be cautious with promoting continuous updating and pursuing increasingly exact understandings as well.

One of the main reasons to be cautious is that a perfect crisis understanding is not only impossible but also counterproductive. The implicit aim of adaptive sensemaking appears to be a full and accurate understanding of the crisis, since this is supposed to enable the best possible crisis response effort. But crises are by definition uncertain and unpredictable. An understanding is always based on incomplete information and will be quickly outdated, as the situation continues to evolve. A perfect understanding is therefore an unrealistic goal during a crisis. It is also counterproductive, because it costs a lot of time and energy. When frontline personnel are focusing efforts on gathering and analyzing more information, there is less time for taking actions. As a result, a detailed understanding of the situation can come at the cost of actual operational interventions.

Moreover, understandings are abstractions, driven by frames, and results of conceptual processing. This has the great advantage of facilitating coordination, because responders can use these concepts to quickly describe the world and their (collective) actions to each other. At the same time, conceptualization comes with a loss of attention for details, narrows your view, and risks oversimplifying reality. You can only observe what your concepts allow you to observe, thereby confirming your earlier conceptualization. This easily turns problematic because crises are unique events, in which blind spots may be disastrous. Thus, it may be sensible to temporarily forego sensemaking rather than to continuously update it. Likewise, there is merit in complicating understandings rather than specifying them, as this allows responders to collect a broader range of cues and develop richer awareness of their context (Weick, 2004, 2011).

One way of achieving this is by actively employing sense-discrediting methods, which refers to questioning and undermining one's existing understanding. There are various ways in which crisis organizations can discredit earlier understandings to ensure frontline teams are open to challenging their operating frame. Of primary importance, here, is creating space for meaningful argumentation and voicing contradictions in teams, so that past sense is not taken for granted but actively doubted (Kramer, 2007). In general, these strategies mean that frontline responders have to accept and embrace uncertainty. Many sensemaking studies do not allow for such uncertainty. Even when scholars encourage responders to seek out anomalies or challenge existing frames, the implicit goal is to renew sensemaking in pursuit of an optimal understanding. But uncertainty is unavoidable and to some extent even useful in crisis sensemaking.

Interestingly, and paradoxically, it may also be advisable to occasionally commit to preliminary, uncertain understandings. Researchers have typically viewed commitment as problematic in crisis sensemaking, since commitment in their case studies often preluded failure. This finding points at selection bias though, because commitment might be a recurring phenomenon in successful responses as well. Weick (1995) recounts a story by the Czech poet Holub, which tells of a military reconnaissance unit that gets lost in the snowy Alps, thinking that they are doomed, when one of them finds a map in his pockets. This calmed the soldiers, who were about to give up, and they used it to find their way back. As they returned, they present the map to their lieutenant who discovers that it is a map of the Pyrenees and not the Alps. Yet, by committing to a (mistaken) understanding, they gained the confidence to act and ultimately survived. This shows that acting in an uncertain world is sometimes more important than collecting

Table 3.1 *The sensemaking dilemma*

	Creating clarity	Embracing uncertainty
Characteristics	Adaptive sensemaking Ongoing updating to achieve perfect crisis understanding	Incomplete understandings Sense-discrediting and temporary commitments Action over information
Advantages	Optimal response effort Flexible operations Facilitates coordination	Rich awareness of context Avoids blind spots and paralysis
Shortcomings	Difficulty of discarding earlier understandings Limited information Time- and energy-intensive	Counterintuitive Demanding for responders

more and better information. A temporary commitment to even the wrong understandings can provide a foundation for action that is vital to keep people moving forward under seemingly hopeless conditions, constructing new meanings along the way, and ultimately averting a dangerous crisis or outright failure.

Thus, these crisis studies show that responders may have to commit to an unproven frame, which they doubt, when they are compelled to respond due to time pressures or simply to evade paralysis. In addition, they would benefit from avoiding increasingly detailed sensemaking as well in order to keep an open mind and gain rich experiences before adopting a frame of reference. Accepting uncertainty in the response is bound to be counterintuitive to responders who want to grasp what is happening and are likely to develop explanations and understandings unconsciously. Moreover, responders who face enormous uncertainty and stress tend to resort to trained behaviors and frames, which are familiar and trusted (Staw et al., 1981). Regardless, they will only succeed when they tolerate anxiety, uncertainty, and chaos, focusing on new cues despite their tough operating conditions, which is a skill that renders US Navy Seals, for instance, highly attentive in volatile situations (Fraher et al., 2017; Stein, 2004). While accepting uncertainty in crises is extremely demanding for responders, it facilitates their sensemaking. In general, these findings challenge the predominant idea of sensemaking as a means to reducing ambiguity by propagating embracing uncertainty (Table 3.1).

Empirical Example

Soldiers in combat situations do not only face the very real danger of impending annihilation but are also confronted with profound uncertainty. Without fail, veterans write in their autobiographical, fictional novels about the so-called fog of war. In this context, soldiers desperately try to make sense of what is happening, but this turns out to be extremely challenging. They lack crucial information about the enemy and are unable to develop an overview of the battlefield. Even when there are a lot of noises, scents, and movement, these sensory impressions make things only more confusing and puzzling, because they seem to make no sense or appear contradictory. Still, soldiers develop an increased awareness to gain as good an understanding as possible, for any information might be lifesaving. O'Brien, who fought in the Vietnam War, writes: "It's a hard thing to explain to somebody who hasn't felt it, but the presence of death and danger has a way of bringing you fully awake. When you're afraid, really afraid, you see things you never saw before, you pay attention to the world." In addition, soldiers look at others for information by exchanging perceptions and impressions, hoping that this will give them a clearer image of the situation. When feeling lost, they typically ask a lot of questions, as illustrated by Tolstoy's depiction of a young officer hearing shots and asking: "What does it mean? What is it? Whom are they firing at? Who is firing?" When individual sensemaking fails, such interpersonal interactions give guidance on how to comprehend the situation. Clearly, uncertainty remains pervasive, but soldiers cannot sit and wait. They will have to spring into action. Such actions are often intuitive, following instincts or resulting from endless drills. Remarque's protagonist, fighting in WWI, is told about an impending gas attack: "I grab for my gas-mask. Some distance from me there lies someone. I think of nothing but this: That fellow there must know." In another episode, he suddenly faces an enemy soldier: "I do not think at all, I make no decision – I strike madly home, and feel only how the body suddenly convulses, then becomes limp, and collapses." He only makes sense of these situations in hindsight. Interestingly, even in the absence of individual sense, soldiers may continue to do their work, simply because they believe that others still understand the situation, judging by their behavior. If they talk and act as if they comprehend the situation, the soldier will likely fall in line, induce others to play along, and thus commit and contribute to the shared fiction that the situation is still sensible and that continued fighting is appropriate. They forego sensemaking until they can act their way toward a new understanding. As such, committing to the shared fiction serves as a pragmatic alternative to an adequate individual understanding. Panic and paralysis can be overcome by (temporarily) accepting failed personal sensemaking without overt reflection. Or as Remarque formulates it: "[T]error can be endured so long as a man simply ducks; but it kills, if a man thinks about it." In other words, responders sometimes have to accept that crises are uncertain and that sensemaking can be slow in producing a clearer understanding of the situation (Kalkman, 2020c).

3.6 Plausible Sensemaking

Interestingly, Weick's own thinking about sensemaking in crises seems therefore in contrast with much of the research based on his work. While crisis researchers generally argue that frontline crisis responders need to pursue updated, exact understandings, Weick argues for foregoing sensemaking and occasionally committing to understandings even when these are uncertain. Clearly, this introduces a sensemaking dilemma for responders: They have to gain an adequate and up-to-date understanding of the crisis to which they are responding, but they are also encouraged to embrace uncertainty during the response effort.

To find out how responders can manage this challenge, it is worthwhile reminding that the goal of sensemaking is the construction of a plausible understanding. Although it often does not receive the attention it deserves, plausibility was originally a key word in sensemaking research. It means that the understanding that responders develop fits the available cues but does not necessarily have to be perfect or complete (Weick et al., 2005). Sensemaking, ultimately, is not about veracity, but about instrumentality. It must give frontline responders a workable understanding of the crisis, an understanding that gives them the confidence to operate and one that can guide their actions. Weick (1995, pp. 56–60) has written that "perceptions, by definition, can never be accurate" in a world that is constantly and rapidly changing, so that ultimately, "an obsession with accuracy seems fruitless, and not of much practical help." Sensemaking, instead, is a pragmatic process.

This is often missed in existing case studies of sensemaking failures that sometimes rely on unrealistic assumptions of linear shifts to increasingly better and more detailed understandings. Since sensemaking studies are predominantly based on post-hoc interviews and reports, and written with the benefit of hindsight, it is indeed much easier to say where and how things went wrong and what the best understanding would have been at particular moments in time. Yet, this does no justice to the uncertain operational realities in which responders try to gain a plausible understanding for guiding their efforts. In reality, crisis sensemaking can be a messy process. During the 9/11 attack, for instance, members of the Northeast Air Defense Sector, tasked with defending the airspace, simultaneously held incongruent frames of reference: first, that it was a training and a hijacking, and later that the crisis was an anticipated hijacking and a coordinated attack. Operating frames emerged and solidified with new cues, while fading out with increasing deviant information (Waller & Uitdewilligen, 2008). Likewise, during the European refugee crisis, border guards were deployed under a security mandate but faced humanitarian tragedies, and as a result mixed and moved between both sensemaking accounts in their work (Kalkman, 2019a). These examples serve to show that multiple understandings may be plausible to responders at one and the same time, while there is no way of telling or proving which one is correct at that moment (see also Dunbar & Garud, 2009).

If any crisis understanding is plausible and preliminary at best, responders should often act as if their operating frame is correct, while actively trying to seek indications for the opposite. It requires an awareness that updating may lead to more plausible understanding and more appropriate response activities, but also to the risk of poorer situational experiences and increased chances of ultimate failure, particularly when updating toward a more exact frame causes blind spots. Responders need an ambivalent attitude in which they treat what they doubt as certain, and doubt what appears certain to them (Weick, 1979). This demands considerable imagination on the part of crisis responders. They have to imagine the opposite of what they believe to be true, imagining that they are wrong when they feel confident and imagining their hunches are right when they feel uncertain. In this way, they remain open to cues without paralyzing. It also demonstrates how plausibility as an essential characteristic of crisis works in practice. It helps responders to take bold action on the basis of a preliminary sensemaking account if pressing urgency is pushing them, while it pushes them to doubt their understandings when there is time for reflection. They may even take actions that appear contradictory or misaligned when multiple, alternative operating frames seem plausible at the same time, and the cues that return from these actions will help them with further sensemaking.

Such an attitude is particularly important in the early phases of crises, when teams are tempted to commit to one particular understanding of the situation, even though situational uncertainty is still at its highest. When all information seems uncertain, it is attractive to adopt a clear understanding as a means of navigating the chaotic environment. Problematically, early understandings are most likely to be misguided or in need of change, as crises evolve and are unpredictable. Over time, when the situation is stabilizing and one understanding is confirmed time and again, plausibility increases and sensemaking can become more specific, but responders always need to be aware of the fact that plausibility does not equal certainty.

This requires an attitude of modesty, a recognition that previous sensemaking may be wrong, so that an open-minded stance to alternative views is adopted. To ensure that responders keep an open mind, it is equally important that they are not socialized into strict roles, which constrict their focus prematurely. This means that responders preferably have broader responsibilities, which is a challenge to coordination, but protects them against missing important cues and reduces the odds of sensemaking failures. In crisis teams, moreover, there is value in the promotion of competing viewpoints and organizing imagination (e.g., the construction of various crisis scenarios befitting different situational understandings). The goal of such measures is that responders continue to challenge and renew their sensemaking, even when (or maybe, particularly when) they think this is not necessary. Even though there has been a growing, almost uncontested emphasis in the literature on the importance of updating and specifying crisis sensemaking to avoid commitment to a flawed frame, original work on sensemaking shows the added value of accepting some uncertainty in the process, which contributes to plausible sensemaking in crises.

3.7 Conclusion

By reintroducing plausibility as a key element in crisis sensemaking, it becomes clear that foregoing, updating, specifying, and doubting sensemaking need to happen continuously and even simultaneously in crisis response teams. Frontline responders may deal with the sensemaking dilemma by valuing clarity and uncertainty in crisis understandings equally.

This is bound to be taxing and difficult to responders and they may even feel overwhelmed if they are discouraged from adopting clear understandings during their response efforts. It is therefore important to study responders' experiences of these contradictory attitudes to their operating frames, particularly to find out why some succeed while others do not. Different ways of organizing for this approach to sensemaking also need to be studied to find out which practices allow for the simultaneous pursuit of clarity and acceptance of uncertainty in crisis sensemaking in practice. Finally, future research must move beyond explaining sensemaking outcomes in specific cases and study the varied, complicated results of particular sensemaking attitudes and processes.

Resources for Educators and Professionals

PRACTICAL LESSONS

- A perfect situational understanding is impossible during a crisis, so responders should avoid it becoming an obsession.
- Crisis responders should pursue a plausible, workable understanding of a crisis.
- A detailed informational picture is likely to create blind spots and renders responders overly confident in their grasp of a situation that is uncertain and evolving.
- Particularly in the early phase of a crisis, responders have to take bold action on limited information and force themselves to doubt what seems certain.
- Crisis organizations can take measures to ensure that response teams keep an open mind.

QUESTIONS FOR REFLECTION AND DISCUSSION

- When did a crisis response go wrong due to a mistaken or incomplete informational picture? What was the reason that sensemaking failed?
- How long into an operation does it usually take you to have a good understanding of the situation? How long do you wait until you start taking actions when faced with a crisis?
- What safeguards does your organization have to avoid sensemaking failures and are they working sufficiently well?

4 | Acting
Planned Routines versus
Spontaneous Improvisation

Shoreham Nuclear Power Plant was built on Long Island, New York, but opposition against its construction rose in the late 1970s. Proponents and critics debated if people in a ten-mile radius could be evacuated in case of an emergency. The plant owner, Long Island Lighting Company, made an evacuation plan which it tested through several exercises. In one exercise, personnel that was instrumental to the evacuation had to be given information during the exercise on their basic responsibilities, while others, despite being officially notified, did not show up or were extremely delayed. Bus drivers, responsible for evacuating children and other vulnerable groups, were drilled before the exercises, but many of them forgot to read their dosimeters, were unaware of the limits of the evacuation zone, and failed to follow their assigned routes. People who were playing the residents asked for information and instructions, but received none or only after a long time. And finally, traffic guides were only dispatched hours after the emergency started. Given all the failures in this carefully planned exercise, the evacuation in a real meltdown would almost definitely have been a disaster. The evacuation plan was nothing more than a "fantasy document," a plan of almost no instrumental use, which described how people would ideally behave in a given situation without leaving space for uncertainty or unexpected surprises (Clarke, 1999). In practice, the plan would have been of little use to the crisis responders, who would have had to improvise on the spot to save as many lives as possible.

Preparedness plans offer guidance to crisis responders. In this example, the plan was supposed to support the actions of frontline personnel in a situation of enormous stress and pressure. But these same prescribed actions turned out to be hard, if not impossible, to implement during the simulation. Specific situations were not anticipated and protocols did not produce the desired results, producing a decisive planning failure and forcing responders to improvise. As in other crises, standard procedures create predictability and stability, while spontaneous actions ensure flexibility of the response. The resulting dilemma for responders is to choose the right action in light of these conflicting action patterns in crises.

4.1 Planned Actions

In many crisis situations, frontline responders will initially engage in planned activities. Planned actions are laid down in (operational) planning documents, but also in routines, scripts, drills, protocols, and standard operating procedures. Soldiers that are about to engage in combat will implement actions that have been drafted by military planners, abiding by predetermined Rules of Engagement. Paramedics arriving at the incident scene will start with triaging casualties in line with a predefined approach and scoring system (e.g., Major Incident Medical Management and Support). And airline crews are expected to resort to standard operating procedures when confronted with unexpected events during a flight. Frontline personnel that frequently operate in crisis situations need to be aware of these prescribed actions and participate in trainings to make sure that they will do the right thing if a crisis occurs. They are typically extensively drilled to ensure that they are familiar with the preplanned actions that they have to carry out during critical incidents, because people tend to fall back on familiar action patterns when confronted with crises (Staw et al., 1981).

Emergency plans are not new, but are increasingly important with the rising number of crises and growing non-acceptance toward crisis response failures. A plan serves various purposes. It renders crisis response more efficient, creating predictability and ensuring that responders are clear about the activities they are supposed to implement. It also benefits effectiveness, because planners can make sure in advance that all needs will be covered, while it boosts coordination between involved responders through creating a common language and shared goals. It may even make the operations safer, because risks to frontline responders can be identified and managed beforehand (Alexander, 2017). The fact that plans remain popular among crisis researchers can be derived from the fact that analyses of failed responses are often concluded with the recommendation to introduce or revise plans. For instance, studying the New Orleans Police Department's response to Hurricane Katrina, two police researchers state that "it is most imperative that police organizations have a clearly thought out plan to anticipate all necessary organizational and functional adaptations to adequately deal with an emergency situation" (Deflem & Sutphin, 2009, p. 47). Likewise, studying Thailand's management of the 2004 tsunami, Moe and Pathranarakul (2006, p. 403) identified that the "main cause of the problems was obviously [...] that the country lacked a master plan," before suggesting a detailed, comprehensive planning approach covering all phases and aspects of disaster management.

However, crisis plans have gained somewhat of a negative connotation over the last few decades. In practice, these plans often proved unworkable or even counterproductive for guiding the actions of frontline responders. This is partly due to the fact that the number and variety of crises were unfathomable and no plan could prepare for every possible event, as demonstrated by the many unforeseen contingencies in the failed evacuation exercise by Long Island Lighting Company. Thus, crisis scholars began to emphasize planning (instead of plans) to signify the processual and adaptive nature of crisis plans, arguing that plans need to be continuously tested against the evolving crisis situation and frequently revised to ensure that they remain up to date (Perry & Lindell, 2003). Shifting the focus toward planning also allows for giving frontline responders a little more discretionary space, for instance by formulating broader principles and moving away from detailed instructions for particular cases. As such, this flexible planning approach may still aim to discourage "impulsive reactions and to encourage the adoption of appropriate actions necessary to meet the challenges of the immediate situation" (Quarantelli, 1985, p. 24). Clearly, preplanned solutions for anticipated crisis situations continue to enjoy considerable support among crisis scholars (Bigley & Roberts, 2001; Perry & Lindell, 2003, p. 343).

Even if not laid down in plans, the activities of frontline responders are often predetermined by protocols and scripts. Schneider (1992) even goes so far as to claim that standard operating procedures are the best means to resolving crises, while deviations from bureaucratic guidelines are only counterproductive. From this view, response failures should not be blamed on the procedures, but on responders' incomplete abidance with these preplanned scripts for action, as they apparently lacked training, resources, or experience. And when responders face large, complex crises that render routines unworkable, there is simply a need for putting additional procedures in place on higher administrative levels. Ultimately, there always need to be protocols and scripts to guide actions of organizational members in crisis situations. Sometimes, such preplanned actions are straightforward and a specific set of behaviors are prescribed in a given situation. One example of this is soldiers seeking cover when there is incoming artillery or rocket fire, in which case there is a drill that is extensively trained so that it becomes instinctive when sirens go off. In many crises, however, there is an opportunity to choose between alternative scripted action patterns. When attacking an enemy position, for instance, a frontline unit can choose from several familiar tactics to achieve its goal, including a frontal assault, a flank attack, or an ambush (Friesendorf, 2018). Similarly, police units may need to choose between surveillance and interception routines, both of which come with specific action patterns, tools, and identities (Colville et al., 2013). Even when it may be challenging to find the right script in a given situation, these studies show that actions of frontline responders are often preplanned to a considerable degree in the end.

4.2 Planning Failures

A large group of crisis researchers has pointed out that contingencies, such as those experienced by Long Island Lighting Company in its failed exercise, will never be fully prevented by new plans or planning approaches. Following Prussian field marshal Von Moltke, soldiers will often even claim that "no plan survives first contact with the enemy." Carl von Clausewitz, another Prussian general, had written that "all action must, to a certain extent, be planned in a mere twilight, which in addition not unfrequently – like the effect of a fog or moonshine – gives to things exaggerated dimensions and an unnatural appearance" (Von Clausewitz, 1997, p. 90). As in other crises, be they emergencies, challenging mountain expeditions, or humanitarian operations, contingencies in combat situations are often not anticipated. This is not (necessarily) a failure on the part of members of crisis organizations. The issue is that many crisis scenarios are simply impossible to predict.

Even though risks are known (e.g., hurricanes, terrorism, and floods), it remains unpredictable when and how these situations will play out in practice (e.g., the collapse of the Twin Towers or the flooding of New Orleans). This means that response organizations often develop detailed plans that are very unlikely to be used and that responders cannot be expected to remember. Alternatively, they can create generic plans, which do not give ready answers to specific circumstances (Lu & Xue, 2016; McConnell & Drennan, 2006). Perfect crisis protocols cannot exist in an unpredictable world. Robert and Lajtha (2002, p. 184) are perhaps most outspoken in their critique of crisis response plans, claiming that most are quickly outdated and rarely updated, are unknown to responders for whom they are written, and contain a lot of useless information, leading them to conclude that they are often "worse than having no plan at all [as] such emergencies may well develop into larger scale crises for the organizations concerned because of inept/bungled emergency response actions/inactions."

Ideally, misguided plans are revealed during crisis exercises (Perry & Lindell, 2003). Crisis exercises are a great way for frontline responders to get familiar with their routines and see how to best implement these in a number of situations. For this reason, exercises are often encouraged and praised by scholars. Research results about the actual effects are mixed. Some participants self-report considerable benefits in terms of learning about others' crisis management systems and confidence in the ability to work as a team (Perry, 2004). Others, instead, find that exercise outcomes are only moderate (Berlin & Carlström, 2015; Magnussen et al., 2017). Indeed, training exercises do not always necessarily improve response practices in the end (McConnell & Drennan, 2006). One problematic feature of many crisis trainings is that responders are not really tested, but go through similar, predictable scenarios without experiencing stress or making any mistakes (Hart, 1997). For this reason, Clarke (1999) compares crisis exercises to scripts for plays: Frontline responders are the actors who play their part, but the real benefit for actual crisis responses is negligible. Kim (2013) even reports on a series of three simulation exercises in Korea, which were observed by notable dignitaries. As a result, all exercises had been rehearsed several times down to the point where the involved crisis actors memorized lines and movements in the detailed script, so no mistakes would be made during the performance. Clearly, such organizational activities are closer to theatre that may serve the palliative purpose of soothing an audience or the symbolic function of showing that a threat is being taken seriously, but it does little in the way of testing plans for relevance in crises.

Problematically, when frontline responders simply implement routines, there is a chance they do so in a mindless manner, without heeding potential signals that deviations from plans or protocols are needed. This has an adverse effect on organizational performance, particularly if a crisis situation is rapidly evolving and the scripted response has become outdated (Weick & Sutcliffe, 2001). One example can be drawn from a police unit that was surveilling a notorious criminal (Schakel et al., 2016). He was shot and killed, only meters away from members of the police unit. Despite multiple teams, including a helicopter, being nearby, the perpetrators escaped. An analysis of the surprising failure to move away from one preplanned approach to another shows that team members were engaged in their own predetermined practices and were unable to adapt after facing the unexpected event. Similarly, information-sharing procedures and coordination practices were very efficient for the surveillance task, but once disrupted could not be restored to implement another routine. With other impediments introduced by complex communication technologies, inadequate team composition, and problematic field conditions, the team failed to shift away from the preexisting plan. Case studies like this suggest a risk of producing mindless engagement among frontline responders as a result of preplanning activities.

4.3 Improvisation

If planned actions are often insufficient or even counterproductive to crisis response, it is of the utmost importance that frontline responders are able to improvise crisis response actions as well. Several researchers have argued just how important improvisation is during crises by arguing that crisis situations require creative solutions by definition. Indeed, crises are defined as uncertain situations that require urgent reactions, and protocols and routines are necessarily of limited value under these circumstances. Even stronger, the operators at nuclear power plants would under normal circumstances follow standard operating procedures (Meshkati & Khashe, 2015; Perrow, 1984), but when things go wrong, this is in itself unforeseen and unanticipated, so no procedures are available to the responders, because the situation is never supposed to present itself in the first place. Clearly, if plans do suffice in practice, one may wonder whether the situation should have been defined as a crisis at all. An outcome of this reasoning is that a society's resilience in crises can be measured by the improvisational skills of its crisis response organizations and their frontline members. They need to prepare for improvisation and be encouraged to use their creative abilities in their activities (Tierney, 2003; Webb & Chevreau, 2006). This does not only apply to members of emergency services, but also to soldiers, humanitarians, and operators of complex infrastructural systems, such as aircrafts and nuclear power plants. When planned actions fail during incidents, these frontline members are often the only ones that can prevent a full-blown, deadly escalation (see Meshkati & Khashe, 2015).

Crisis improvisation can take various forms. Personnel of crisis organizations may adapt how a plan is implemented by changing how they enact procedures, use tools, or employ resources, but they may also neglect the plan altogether and seek novel and creative solutions for urgent problems (Kendra & Wachtendorf, 2003b; Webb, 2004). Of course, this is extremely challenging when there is considerable uncertainty about the consequences of improvised actions, because such actions are by their very nature invented and tested on the spot. What makes improvisation in crises even harder is the speed with which these have to be carried out. A deteriorating patient or exploding forest fire does not allow for lengthy exchange of ideas between responders. Research on airline crews even suggests that the rapidity of adaptation to non-routine events was the primary explanatory factor that distinguished high-performance teams from other crews (Waller, 1999).

Given that fast improvisation by frontline responders is key to successfully resolving crisis situations, improvisers need to be enabled to do their work. Primarily, they require considerable autonomy and discretionary power to act on their own initiative (Kalkman, 2020b; McConnell & Drennan, 2006), regardless of whether they are emergency services personnel, operators of critical infrastructures, or soldiers. To draw an example from the latter context, Brady (2011) has argued that the Soviet Union beat the German forces at the Battle of Stalingrad, because General Chuikov allowed for improvised actions by his subordinates in contrast to his more rigid adversary, Field Marshall Friedrich Paulus. Even if they are not granted autonomy though, frontline personnel (including soldiers) might take it anyway. The improvised truce by soldiers on both sides of the First World War, who stopped the fighting and met peacefully during Christmas, 1914, was an act of resistance against their superiors (Wiedemann et al., 2021). Clearly, autonomy for improvisation may be granted, but it can also be taken by frontline personnel.

It is worthwhile noting that improvisation is not an undirected testing of impulsive ideas, but is grounded in existing knowledge and skills. Improvisation has even been compared to a craft. When foreman Dodge and his team were about to be hit by the Mann Gulch fire, he lighted an escape fire, a sudden invention that saved his life. His creativity probably stemmed from his intimate familiarity with wood and fire, enabling him to come up with this solution, despite the intense time pressure and direct threat to his life (Weick, 1993). The combination of training, experience, and involvement in the environment is a recurring set of preconditions for effective improvisation in crises. It enables frontline responders to come up with unanticipated alternative actions to achieve goals after plans have failed (Kendra & Wachtendorf, 2003b).

To gain a better insight into the practice of improvisation in crisis situations, it is useful to look at the heroic attempt of six mountain climbers to reach the summit of the Mount Everest via the Kangshung face, the most remote and one of the hardest routes. The study shows that, in these extreme circumstances, routine responses frequently broke down, and the team had to resort to improvised actions by deviating from routines by adopting novel temporary scripts (heuristics) or inventing completely new solutions to unexpected problems (improvisation). The route of the climbers included a 4,000 feet wall, from which rocks and ice were constantly falling and where avalanches were frequent. The wall was first ascended based on a routine where the climbing route was established in advance, but the expedition required more flexibility and shifted to a heuristic in which the first climber chose the route. Likewise, potentially lifesaving ropes were often damaged due to the harsh conditions. The routine way of working was that specific members would inspect and replace fixed ropes that were permanently in place at difficult sections, but when one member saw a damaged rope, he decided it would be better to instantly fix it. The team adopted a new heuristic prescribing that anyone seeing a damaged rope fixed it immediately, increasing trust in the ropes and thus allowing for a quicker and safer ascent. The team adopted more improvised actions, such as the heuristic that support members (i.e., members who were supporting the summit team members that would go on to try and reach the mountain peak) would always return to lower camps for sleep to save scarce resources. Later, the team even deviated from this temporary script when, due to exhaustion, four members stayed a night at the highest camp regardless of the fact there were insufficient supplies (e.g., oxygen, food, and sleeping bags). During the final push, finally, ropes were not even used at all, another improvised reaction to deal with the heavy load of carrying ropes at such a height (Suarez & Montes, 2019). The authors show that, in the face of crisis, improvised responses at the frontline are inevitable, often of a temporary nature, and grounded in expertise. Improvised actions serve as preliminary solutions to sudden contingencies, which can easily be replaced by returning to plans or inventing new solutions depending on the situation. Such ongoing improvisation often works out well, even under the riskiest of circumstances.

4.4 The Limits of Improvising

Improvisation is not a guarantee of success though. Scholars have at times been very skeptical of relying on improvised actions by frontline responders during crises. One of the reasons is that it is very hard to realize in practice, so improvisation may not always materialize. When individuals are facing a threatening situation, and experience anxiety or stress, they face psychological impediments on processing information and are very likely to rigidly resort to familiar, drilled responses, preventing adaptive, improvised responses to novel circumstances (Staw et al., 1981). A study of frontline Israeli commanders in combat situations demonstrates as well that soldiers, under fire, may implement futile drills or freeze rather than come up with creative solutions (Ben-Shalom et al., 2012). It is a sobering realization, but improvising is most important when it is most difficult and most likely to fail.

Even if improvisation does occur under these extreme conditions, it is not necessarily beneficial either. In fact, it can be very inefficient. Alexander (2017) argues that improvisation ultimately represents a failure of anticipation and preparation. The problem with improvisation is that there is no time to design efficient operating procedures during emergencies on the spot, so improvisation will always fall short and should therefore be avoided as much as possible, while any failure to do so is a sign of negligence. Other researchers are usually not as outspoken against improvisation, but do point out that people might unnecessarily circumvent efficient, functioning systems as they start improvising. For instance, some members of the Swedish crisis response team after the 2004 tsunami went to find supplies (e.g., coffins) by themselves rather than referring to the established organization with logistical expertise (Lundberg & Rankin, 2014). Improvisation may also lead to a situation in which multiple responders recognize different needs and engage in contradictory activities. During the EU refugee crisis, for example, some team members were treating migrants as potential security threats, while others viewed them as refugees. When both acted on their own initiative, they effectively counteracted each other's efforts (Kalkman, 2019a). These examples show that improvisation may undermine coordination between frontline responders at the cost of an efficient response effort.

Reliance on the improvisational skills can also increase risks for frontline workers operating in potentially dangerous environments. Humanitarian aid workers and soldiers, for instance, are often deployed to volatile settings and may incur harm if there are no solid operational plans in place that ensure that they can do their work safely or that they can be evacuated if the need arises. Another example comes from the UK fire services. One of its crews found a man close to drowning in a park pond. The standard procedure would be to request support for a boat rescue, since firefighting outfits make swimming risky. Two crewmembers worried the man would not hold out much longer and waded as far into the water as they could. Next, they improvised: They tied ropes to the waists, swam to the man, and rescued him. They falsified the official report afterward out of fear for repercussions for violating safety precautions with their improvised actions. Something similar happened to members of a Rapid Response Unit, which was a small firefighting unit set up to quickly deploy to minor fires. These crewmembers had limited possibilities to equip themselves for larger fires. Responding to an alarm call from a care home, the crew commander violated multiple protocols that should have prevented him from entering a smoke-filled flat, while being alone and without breathing apparatus, for a snatch rescue. The attempt was successful, but posed a considerable risk to the improvising crew commander (Macpherson et al., 2021). Such improvisations during crisis response have also been described in a derogatory way as freelancing and are deemed to be unacceptable

Table 4.1 *The dilemma over how to act*

	Planned routines	Spontaneous improvisation

Characteristics	Predesigned activities
	Protocols and exercises
		Creative solutions to
		  unforeseen situations
		Relying on training and
		  experience

Advantages	Supports action under pressure Predictability	Flexible responses Avoids inapplicable actions
Shortcomings	Impossibility of having a plan for every event Often unrealistic in practice Produces mindlessness	Practically challenging Inefficient operations Safety risks

for putting people at risk (Bigley & Roberts, 2001). Improvisation can indeed have disastrous results, as evidenced by the sinking of the cruise ship Costa Concordia, when captain Schettino improvised a sail-by salute to Giglio island and hit a rock as the ship came too close to shore (Giustiniano et al., 2016). These illustrations make clear that improvisation has its limits (Table 4.1).

Empirical Example

A team of crisis professionals of the relevant emergency organizations convenes when confronted with a possible terrorist attack at a concert venue, which has caused many victims and massive damage to the building. They rapidly need to define their approach and activities. This is the scenario of a controlled experiment with multiple teams. The experiment demonstrates notable differences in response trajectories, which indicates that preexisting plans do not produce uniform outcomes. This should not be taken to mean that preparation has no relevance. Rather, planned actions feature in the crisis response on multiple occasions. In the early phase of the response, the team risks being overwhelmed by the ambiguity of the scarce information available and resorts to preexisting protocols and standard operating procedures. Almost instantly, a range of activities are triggered related to victim tracing, activation of public crisis information channels, and provision of psychological care to witnesses. These services are needed in almost any significant emergency and these actions are therefore well prepared. The resulting actions are scripted routines and require little improvisation. The direction of the operational response, however, is less straightforward. Here, the team needs to agree on which strategy best applies to the situation at hand. Is this first and foremost a terrorist incident or a collapsed building? In the first case, the crisis location is a crime site. In the second case, priority will be given to organizing search and rescue activities. There are plans for either of the cases separately, but not for a situation in which both coincide, so the responders have to improvise. They still use elements of the preexisting plans in their new decision-making, as they contemplate how available plans might apply under the current circumstances. At one point, they discuss whether to enter the damaged building and accept a risk to firefighters, who will be carrying out the rescue activities, as one professional refers back to these plans: "If you'd ask me, we haven't made these protocols for nothing." While these protocols prescribe that frontline responders should not take unnecessary risks, it proves hard to judge how high the risks are in this situation and whether they qualify as unnecessary or not. Similarly, the team hears rumors that possible terrorists have fled the incident site by train. One professional, who prefers to improvise a response to this news, asks: "Well, do we leave the other train stations open?" Another immediately intervenes: "That depends on what the [counter-terrorism plans] state. We have made agreements on that." But even if the plan prescribes closing other train stations, the team needs to decide which ones exactly, what to do with the stranded trains, and how to deal with the large group of passengers that relied on this mode of transport to get home and have no alternative. These contingencies are not antici-pated by planners, so choices require considerable improvisation on the part of the team. Clearly, implementing planned actions is complex, because it is not immediately clear which plan applies or how exactly to implement it. Flexibility and creative solutions are therefore inevitable. Still, responders refer back to plans repeatedly in the exercises, because scripted routines, protocols, and procedures offer much-appreciated guidance in chaotic situations that might quickly become overwhelming or lead to incoherent decision-making (Kalkman, 2019b).

4.5 Reflective Acting

Frontline personnel of crisis organizations have to figure out how to act in specific situations. Plans guide the work of responders, who familiarize themselves with operating procedures and train for implementing scripted routines. The aim of this planned response is an efficient and predictable intervention. Yet, crises present unanticipated situations, undermining the relevance of plans, while planned actions may result in mindless response efforts as well. Improvisation, instead, resolves some of these issues by introducing creativity and flexibility into the response, and leading to more adaptive efforts, but it is also hard to achieve in practice and potentially increases risks to responders. The dilemma for frontline responders is that they have to abide by planned actions (e.g., protocols, drills, and routines) to ensure that they implement an efficient and coordinated response effort, but they are also encouraged to improvise for a more adaptive approach to an unpredictable situation.

The antagonism between scholars in both camps has been quite explicit and impeded a reconciliation between both approaches, even though most scholars will likely agree that plans and improvisation will both be needed to some extent in crisis response. Excessive reliance on planning is ultimately unhelpful to crisis responders in unforeseen crisis situations, but overly relying on improvisation will undermine coordinated, decisive organizational efforts. The contradiction between both action patterns is not so clear-cut, nor necessarily polemical though.

In fact, plans are not as fixed as they are sometimes presented. Given a crisis situation, frontline responders typically have multiple protocols and routines to choose from to achieve a set objective (Bechky & Okhuysen, 2011; Friesendorf, 2018). Once they have made a choice, responders have to adjust preplanned actions on the spot to move from an abstract, general script into operational activities that fit the evolving situation (see Canton, 2011). Firefighters may have been deployed to dozens of house fires before and been drilled on how to respond to such incidents, but they will still need to come up with a very basic plan on how to approach this specific fire in this specific house. Organizational scholars studying routines make a distinction between the ideal-typical (ostensive) and practical, implemented (performative) routine. The latter is based on the former, but will always be affected by contextual factors and vary per situation. Danner-Schröder and Geiger (2016) studied the training and simulated response by a German search and rescue unit in the aftermath of an earthquake, and demonstrate how routines (e.g., setting up camp, triage, and searching) are both flexible and changing with performance varying every time the routine is implemented. In addition, scripted actions patterns, although seemingly stable, may disappear and be replaced. Members of the UK fire services unlearned and forgot previous routines over time, such as the manual prescribing the use of powdered asbestos when dealing with metals on fire (Brooks et al., 2021). Planned actions, in other words, are not fixed, but subject to change and every implementation of a protocol or routine is a variation of the plan that entails some improvisation.

Plans also enable improvisation in various ways. Batista et al. (2016) studied the actions of doctors in an emergency unit and noticed something interesting. The medical professionals seemed to comply with protocols, but engaged in "under the radar" improvisations when they did not believe the rules fit the situation. Abidance with clinical guidelines and protocols was sometimes ceremonial, shielding doctors and the hospital against liabilities in case of negative outcomes, while doctors were actually improvising their treatment of a patient. Plans may therefore direct actions, but also still leave or create space for frontline responders to creatively come up with alternative approaches. As such, protocols can justify compliant and deviant behavior at the same time. In addition, plans may facilitate improvisation by creating a (misguided) sense of controllability over the crisis. Even if protocols and drills serve as a palliative (Clarke, 1999), they might reduce the stress and anxiety of frontline responders in an environment that can easily overwhelm them (Ben-Shalom et al., 2012), and give them the peace of mind to improvise. When the crisis still seems unfathomably ambiguous, enacting plans is a sure way to start and is almost always preferable to paralysis. Finally, if improvisation builds on preexisting knowledge and skills (Weick, 1993), training exercises and guidelines may serve as a basis for implementing actions that are only loosely based on preexisting scripts. For good reasons, scholars have recommended professionals to plan and train for improvisation (Trnka et al., 2016; Webb & Chevreau, 2006). Research on the emergency medical response to the 2011 Norway terrorist attacks confirms that individual protocols (or "actions cards") and regular training facilitated creative improvisation by health-care workers that were responding to the unprecedented situation (Brandrud et al., 2017).

Vice versa, improvisations can also have an influence on plans. Improvised actions contribute to organizational learning, which might result in the formulation of new standard operating procedures.

Sometimes, frontline improvisation creates new informal norms that become a standard for frontline operations, regardless of formal plans. Firefighters in the UK were familiar with the protocols for attacking a fire in high domestic buildings, which stated that frontline personnel should be fully equipped on the floor below the fire before moving forward. Experienced commanders, however, would go to the door of the flat on fire and directly contain the fire when this would be possible. Inexperienced commanders following the procedures were criticized for not using common sense. The emerging norm became prominent, was reviewed, and new procedures were put in place. Similarly, in a more formal way, commanders were confronted with fast-moving riots in the region that posed risks to firefighters and demanded a reconsideration of the standardized approach to firefighting. They relaxed rules and procedures that slowed the rapid evacuation of units (e.g., no longer fixing hoses to static fire hydrants but emptying tanks instead) as an improvised, but institutionalized, operating procedure in response to the changed situation (Macpherson et al., 2021). The mountain climbing team, attempting to summit the Mount Everest via the Kangshung side, also came up with improvised, temporary scripts or heuristics, when the old plans did not work properly and needed to be replaced (Suarez & Montes, 2019).

In many ways, plans and improvisation are not bipolar opposites, but two alternative ways of achieving one purpose (Villar & Miralles, 2021). Indeed, action patterns can be scaled from fully prepared to completely experimental, with intermediate forms frequently emerging in crisis response efforts. In practice, crisis teams often make preliminary operational plans. Airline crews, for example, conduct in-process or contingency planning activities during flights so they can rapidly adapt to incidents. Both a lack of planning and excessive planning negatively affect team adaptation and performance (Lei et al., 2016). In a similar vein, McEntire et al., (2013) analyzed the response to a pipeline explosion in San Bruno, California. First responders engaged in "spontaneous planning," which refers to the creation of new operational plans to respond to the specific crisis, in which improvisation and preexisting plans both serve as input (see also Harrald, 2006).

Some crises demand a lot of ad hoc improvisation, while others can be tackled with a planned approach. A higher degree of uncertainty is a main explanatory factor in this regard, as early research on hospital emergency units shows that uncertainty moves response efforts toward non-programmed approaches to maintain effectiveness (Argote, 1982). Ultimately, however, every crisis will require some mixture of planned and improvised action. It is therefore important to train both drills and how to act when these fail. Finding the right balance between both action patterns will be challenging in practice. It requires a reflective attitude by frontline responders during the response. Research on medical teams facing emergency scenarios shows that in-action reflection is indeed possible during crises and happens particularly during unfamiliar emergencies. These reflections include contemplation of future action trajectories through dialogue about possible next actions, but also contingency plans for when these actions do not produce the intended effects. Such in-action reflection contributes significantly to team performance (Schmutz et al., 2018). On a practical level, reflective action requires humility and creative capabilities as well (e.g., Jordan, 2010; Weick, 1993). Crisis organizations can try to promote these qualities among personnel, so their members will be able to implement reflective actions that are key in producing an adequate crisis response effort.

4.6 Conclusion

Both planning and improvisation are important to frontline responders in crises. These seemingly opposing action patterns influence each other and are complementary approaches to resolving crisis situations. Responders require a reflective attitude to find the right combination of these action patterns, because they will need to decide when and how to rely on scripted routines or protocols and when creative experimentation is needed.

Since crisis scholars have primarily focused on the implementation and effects of crisis response actions, there has been limited attention for the actors that need to balance plans and improvisation, so there is a need for further research on why and how responders come to certain actions. We also know insufficient about how they experience working around plans under extreme pressure and uncertainty. Finally, with reflection being a key process in choosing crisis response actions, it is useful to learn more about the reflective practices that are currently used in crisis teams and how these can be trained in future exercises.

Resources for Educators and Professionals

PRACTICAL LESSONS

- Operational efforts during a specific crisis incident combine planned and improvised actions.
- A strict compliance with pre-crisis protocols or drills is unlikely to work well in more complex and uncertain crises, but pure improvisation is both difficult and risky.
- Plans require some degree of improvisation to implement and enable improvised actions, while improvised actions set new norms and standards in turn.
- Frontline responders need to train for implementing plans and what to do when these fail.
- A reflective attitude is needed to strike a right balance between both action patterns and requires contemplation of future actions, contingency plans, creativity, and humility.

QUESTIONS FOR REFLECTION AND DISCUSSION

- During the last operation in which you were involved, to what extent did the frontline response follow preexisting plans, and when did frontline responders start to improvise?
- How is improvisation perceived in your organization? How common is it to train for improvisation?
- To what extent do people in your organization have a reflective attitude during response operations? How could this be improved?

5 | Ethics
Organizational Norms versus
Individual Convictions

The COVID-19 pandemic led to an unprecedented number of patients in need of intensive care. Across the globe, physicians had to make tough decisions on whom to prioritize when intensive care units (ICUs) reached capacity. Should they select on chances of survival or the potential of a long life after recovery? Should they prioritize those who might later participate in tackling the pandemic or simply help patients in their order of arrival? Can an intensivist expedite patient discharge from the ICU to make space for new arrivals? There are no simple answers to the tough questions with which medical personnel were confronted during the pandemic and different moral theories would offer competing answers. Guidelines were developed to support them with their decision-making, but the choice and responsibility of patient admission and discharge rested with intensivists in the end. They could choose to deviate from guidelines, for instance, by refusing to withdraw ICU support from critically ill patients, either on principle or because COVID-19 patients often became worse before improving. Regardless, any choice would be profoundly moral and could only ever be suboptimal. Ultimately, these moral decisions did not only affect the outcomes for patients with COVID-19 but also influenced the psychological well-being of involved caregivers themselves (Baker & Fink, 2020; Emanuel et al., 2020; Robert et al., 2020).

As the example of ICU admission during the COVID-19 pandemic shows, frontline crisis response creates challenging moral dilemmas, in which none of the available options produces a satisfactory outcome. Frontline responders, like the intensivists during the COVID-19 pandemic, ultimately need to make decisions during crises and can either abide by organizational norms and guidelines or feel compelled to follow their own normative beliefs, even if these do not align with those of their organization. In other words, when facing a moral dilemma, they have to ask themselves the question: Will I do what

I am expected to do by my employer or do I follow my own moral inclinations instead?

5.1 Ethics and Crisis Response

Research on crisis response often takes a functionalist approach by focusing on how the performance of responders can be improved. The ethics of crisis response has received much less attention. Research on the ethics of crisis response is limited to studies on emergency medical ethics, the ethics of international humanitarian aid, and military ethics. These studies are often fairly context-specific and do not easily allow for generalization to an ethics of crisis response in a broader sense. Moreover, ethical reflections on crisis response in other situations (e.g., emergency response and expeditions in extreme contexts) remain very rare (e.g., Etkin & Timmerman, 2013). The disjointed state of research on the ethics of crisis response is surprising, because the reason for societies to have crisis organizations in the first place is the normative belief that those who suffer from crises should receive help.

Perhaps, this gap can be explained by the fact that crisis response is often viewed as an inherently moral activity. After all, responders are trying to save lives, reduce human suffering, or pursue another lofty societal goal that is broadly supported by the general public. As a consequence, doctors, humanitarians, firefighters, police officers, and soldiers are not infrequently depicted as heroes and saints. In addition, all dominant ethical approaches offer support for the work of crisis response agencies. Crisis response can be viewed as the practical realization of our moral duty to help those in need, it produces the greatest good in a society by significantly reducing suffering and pain, and compassion and humanity are generally viewed as moral virtues. If crises are undesirable and deplorable events, it makes sense that the organizations that resolve such situations enjoy a high level of moral legitimacy.

Even though there is a strong moral basis for crisis response, the actions of crisis organizations are often contested in practice nevertheless. Criticism focuses not only on whether crisis response actions are functionally effective but are also directed at the morality of certain crisis response efforts. For instance, there have been debates over how extensive emergency and humanitarian aid need to be and to whom it should be delivered. Notably, the EU refugee crisis triggered a conflict over the (geographical) limits to moral responsibility and compassion, with those favoring a liberal immigration policy fiercely criticizing the work of border agencies. In a different context, protests against police brutality in the United States showed that police departments lost their moral legitimacy in the eyes of the communities they were supposed to serve after several black victims were killed by the police's excessive use of force. Citizens wanted to defund particular police departments with histories of violence and racism in response. Crisis organizations can therefore not expect unequivocal support but may find the morality of their work questioned.

Even when organizations are generally perceived to do what is right, this does not legitimize all their actions. Since crises produce significantly harmful consequences (e.g., death, injury, and trauma), a range of moral questions about humanity, responsibility, fairness, and justice will emerge in specific crisis situations (Bundy et al., 2017; Geale, 2012), creating ethical dilemmas and moral conflicts. Some interesting examples can be found in the humanitarian sector. Humanitarian aid, although broadly viewed as morally right, has not always had the intended effects and might occasionally even have exacerbated crises. In conflict settings, concerns have risen over aid being used by belligerents to prolong or fuel the fighting, worsening the living conditions for local populations. The allocation of humanitarian support in many disasters has also been subject to scrutiny, as resources were concentrated in places that aid organizations were easily able to access or which ensured media exposure rather than following a needs-based strategy for resource allocation. Humanitarian aid delivery, moreover, relies on a significant power asymmetry between beneficiaries and providers, and may also upset the local relations through the way scarce resources are allocated (Hunt, 2011; Leader, 1998; Stoddard et al., 2017). Clearly, it is not easy to translate good intentions into good crisis responses. While few people would be opposed to crisis response on principle, crisis response practices clearly invoke ethical discussions and may lead to opposition against specific organizations or their frontline response efforts on moral grounds.

In practice, crisis response is not as straightforward as it may seem and difficult moral choices have to be made. Frontline responders are inevitably confronted with such moral choices and the complexity of these choices may well be experienced as traumatic (Lentz et al., 2021). Over time, crisis scholars have come up with different principles to support the decision-making processes of frontline responders. They emphasize values such as respect, professional competence, fairness, openness, and integrity (Dean & Payne, 2013; Schneider, 2006). A shared assumption in these moral principles is that people are not objects that need to be managed or merely kept alive, but dignified human beings to be served, empowered, and supported (see Etkin & Timmerman, 2013). Still, these ideas have to be translated into practical behavioral standards for use in specific crisis contexts or operations. This is why organizational norms are useful.

5.2 Organizational Norms

The work of crisis responders is guided by certain organizational norms. Norms reflect the values to which a crisis organization adheres. Among the most famous of such values are the humanitarian principles, which guide humanitarian activities in crisis settings: Humanity (i.e., preventing and alleviating suffering), Impartiality (i.e., no discrimination in the delivery of aid), Neutrality (i.e., not choosing sides in conflicts), and Independence (i.e., autonomy from non-humanitarian objectives) (ICRC, 2015). Norms translate such values into practice and offer behavioral standards for use in complex operational contexts. They are meant to help responders when they are confronted with morally complicated situations. Norms tell them how to implement crisis response activities and ensure that their efforts meet organizational benchmarks. These norms can be laid down by the organization or a professional association in codes of conduct, rules, frameworks, professional standards, or guidelines (Dean & Payne, 2013; Hunt, 2011). Take, for example, triage in emergency medicine. This facilitates the sorting of victims into categories based on their medical condition to prioritize treatment of some over others. The practice of triage has military roots, as military doctors faced massive numbers of casualties on the battlefield. Initially, doctors selected based on rank. Higher-ranking officers received medical care before common soldiers, regardless of their injuries. Nowadays, triage is based on utilitarian thinking and fits the norm that emergency medical care serves to save as many lives as possible (see Geale, 2012).

Organizational norms are very useful for various reasons. Crisis responders are often confronted with moral dilemmas. A scarcity of resources and significant human suffering are characteristic of crises, and will regularly lead to difficult choices regarding whom to help first or how to distribute much-needed aid when there are more people that need it than can be served. In these situations, norms give answers to emerging questions in situations where organizational members do not have the luxury to contemplate and discuss alternative responses (Hunt, 2011). Medical professionals cannot and should not have to discuss which patients to prioritize during each specific incident. This would be very stressful, cost valuable time, and probably lead to interpersonal conflicts. Norms prevent this and offer clear instructions on how to prioritize.

To victims, organizational norms also offer transparency about responders' way of operating and ensures that response organizations can be held accountable for the outcomes of specific response efforts (Dean & Payne, 2013; Hunt, 2008). This is particularly important in contexts where emergency or humanitarian aid is not viewed as mere altruism, but victims are entitled to such help. Transparency and accountability also increase trust in the process, because it makes clear that other, morally questionable motivations have not unduly influenced decisions during the response effort.

Give these advantages of organizational norms, one might expect compliance. Even more so because organizational norms exercise considerable influence over employees. As norms are reflections of an organizational (moral) culture, norms steer crisis responders' identities, views, and behaviors (Granot, 1997; Resseguier, 2018). Because of their disciplinary power, norms are not easily violated either. Norm violations may lead to criticism from colleagues and self-blame, both of which frontline responders will try to avoid (Thornborrow & Brown, 2009). Thus, they will comply with norms to a disturbing extent, as exemplified by the My Lay massacre. Norms on obedience to superiors' orders and aggression toward the enemy contributed to this sanctioned mass violence, during which US Army soldiers killed hundreds of innocent civilians. It provides a most shocking example of how a strong sense of duty to authority may overrule all personal moral inhibitions and shows how frontline personnel absolve themselves from moral responsibility of heinous acts by reference to organizational norms (Kelman & Hamilton, 1989). The armed forces, more than any other crisis organization, have been criticized for undermining members' abilities to think and act as moral agents. Soldiers have indeed been willing to violate the most basic moral principles, after being told that their actions are necessary to achieve some higher moral goal (Neitzel & Welzer, 2012). Military organizations also leave little to no room for competing professional norms (e.g., medical ethical standards) or opposing individual convictions (Sidel & Levy, 2003). While armed forces provide an extreme example in this regard, similar dynamics are present in other crisis organizations. Generally, leaders of these organizations can therefore expect their subordinates to comply with organizational norms and may assume that responders do what they are expected to do.

5.3 Moral Distress in Crisis Response

Practical experience, however, shows that if crisis responders have to closely abide by organizational norms, they will frequently face moral conflicts. These moral conflicts may be dormant until a crisis situation forces the responder to either comply or deviate from the norm. Utilitarian principles in emergency health care provide an illustration. Unplugging COVID-19 patients to make space for others will not be supported by all doctors, even if this makes sense from a utilitarian point of view (Baker & Fink, 2020; Robert et al., 2020). In fact, "withdrawing ventilators or ICU support from patients who arrived earlier to save those with better prognosis will be extremely psychologically traumatic for clinicians" (Emanuel et al., 2020, p. 2052). Generally, an emphasis on organizational interests and performance metrics rather than patients and people is distressing to health-care workers and other crisis professionals (Gotowiec & Cantor-Graae, 2017; Wolf et al., 2016). Likewise, in a humanitarian context, the norm to consider the political implications of humanitarian actions is deplored by frontline aid workers responding to disasters. And existing rules concerning procurement, working hours, and safety, which make sense under normal circumstances, hinder the rapid implementation of humanitarian activities, which humanitarian aid professionals obviously prefer to see prioritized during crises (Nilsson et al., 2011). Similar moral conflicts will emerge in every new crisis situation.

In other cases, frontline responders face conflicts, because they do not think that organizational norms apply to a particular (unprecedented) crisis situation. For instance, border guards are working in a rules-based profession (Olsthoorn & Schut, 2018), but many of them struggled during the EU refugee crisis with following rules that prescribed using security-based practices toward people who were clearly in need of help (Kalkman, 2019a). Some contexts may also make it nearly impossible for responders to do what they believe to be right or meaningful, because there is so much senseless and futile suffering around them that their practical experiences defy preexisting norms and beliefs for handling the situation (De Rond & Lok, 2016). Support for organizational norms may also dwindle over time, as the effects of doing so become clearer to frontline responders. For example, initial enthusiasm for the First World War was replaced by growing moral opposition, when the brute violations of humanity and dignity became increasingly visible (Wiedemann et al., 2021). Veterans also increasingly dissociated from organizational norms, as they became more and more aware of the immense suffering and hopelessness of war (Kalkman, 2023b). These examples show that organizational norms may cause moral distress when frontline personnel are troubled or tormented due to their inability to discard organizational norms and act in line with their own moral standards (Gustavsson et al., 2020).

Responders who follow organizational norms reluctantly are engaged in "dirty work," which are morally ambiguous occupational activities that many people shun or disdain but are inevitable to their jobs. Examples include subjecting patients to painful procedures, arresting and imprisoning suspects, letting wildfires burn, or attacking enemy troops. Frontline responders feel a need to defend themselves and shift responsibilities for these actions to their organization, the law, or regulations, so they can uphold their own moral identity and legitimize their actions (Dick, 2005). They engage in "necessary evils," while realizing that these cause human suffering, because the unfortunate actions are claimed and believed to serve a greater good (Margolis & Molinsky, 2008). In practice, crisis responders' duties and professional responsibilities nevertheless clash with their compassion and their wish to help people (Lentz et al., 2021). Indeed, frontline workers admit that they frequently struggle with the normative demands of their work (Maynard-Moody & Musheno, 2003). Moral distress is therefore not uncommon among frontline responders.

5.4 Individual Convictions

Faced with such moral conflicts, many responders are willing to follow their own moral convictions and assume moral responsibility. This requires that they are able to make a free choice between multiple options and that their choices have real-world effects (Schneider, 2006). If so, they can choose to act in defiance of organizational norms. This is never an easy choice and, during a crisis, one that needs to be made under immense time pressure and uncertainty. Traditionally, research in this domain often tries to find general explanations for frontline members' deviation from organizational norms and points to social pressures (e.g., community values) that undermine obedience to rules and guidelines. Yet, it may be more insightful to listen to the stories of responders themselves in an attempt to discover their personal reflections, considerations, and meaning-making efforts that lead them to act in accordance with their own values. This does more justice to the situational complexity amidst which ethical thinking and acting takes place during crises (Kalkman, 2020b).

To understand why responders, follow their own moral inclinations rather than preset norms, it is important to note that members of crisis organizations often have very personal reasons for their career choices. For many of them, frontline response is a vocation and they feel very strongly about their occupation (Mastracci et al., 2014). Humanitarian aid workers, for instance, strive to be useful and most are motivated by a normative desire to help people in need (Resseguier, 2018). An interesting example comes from Friesen (2021), who analyzed the memoir of James Orbinski, the Canadian physician who became president of Médecins Sans Frontières and accepted the 1999 Nobel Peace Price on the organization's behalf. Through several face-to-face encounters with human suffering in his early life, Orbinski came to recognize his moral responsibility toward others, motivating him to dedicate his life to humanitarian work. Such a moral conviction makes it impossible to distinguish between personal and organizational life, and defines "humanitarians' ethics". In other crisis professions, responders report similar motives. Firefighters, for example, are primarily committed to the job, more so than to the organization or their superiors. They are most strongly motivated by their belief that their work is important to the community and are therefore willing to make great sacrifices in carrying out their responsibilities (Lee & Olshfski, 2002). In practice, these responders are committed to the moral worth of their actions rather than to organizational norms. When facing complex crisis situations, in particular, the self-identity as a crisis professional is central to responders' beliefs and judgments, guiding their actions often more than official standards (Mastracci et al., 2014).

In addition, organizational norms, similar to crisis plans, leave space for interpretation in specific situations. Frontline responders are willing to make full use of this discretionary space to act on their own moral convictions (Maynard-Moody & Musheno, 2003). To many frontline members, their work is about fairness rather than strict rule abidance. Police officers, for instance, may feel that some people deserve punishment while others do not, despite both participating in the exact same behavior (Vinzant & Crothers, 1998). The moral worthiness of the suspect or victim affects the reactions of frontline personnel: police officers will sometimes consider the suspect unworthy and treat them harshly, while in other cases giving offenders a break, because they work through something, try to cope with a situation, or are "basically good" persons (Maynard-Moody & Musheno, 2003). Since responders work in situations that are hard to oversee and monitor, discretionary actions might deviate strongly from the spirit and letter of organizational norms. In a study on paramedics, Borry and Henderson (2020) explored prosocial rule breaking among emergency medical service professionals. Prosocial rule-breaking behaviors are inconsistent with protocols, but in the interest of the patient, and include administering or withholding medication and making important decisions on the hospital of destination or mode of transport. They report indications that professional standards induce deviant behaviors, since paramedics will attach more value to professional than to organizational norms. Moreover, complex patients and those with poor prognoses are particularly likely to induce paramedics to bend or break rules, suggesting that frontline responders are more likely to deviate from organizational norms when it really matters.

Other empirical studies confirm that responders violate norms if they believe this to be in the best interest of the people they are serving. Relations and empathy take center stage in this approach. A tragic example comes from the Memorial Medical Center in New Orleans, where medical personnel were left with some 200 patients to shelter in place during Hurricane Katrina. When the city flooded in the aftermath of the hurricane, the choice was made to evacuate the hospital over the next few days. As the days passed by, the conditions in the hospital deteriorated dramatically due to a power outage, stifling heat, and poor hygienic circumstances. In a last-ditch attempt to complete the evacuation, exhausted staff believed that several patients would not be evacuated and considered some patients too weak for the rescue operation. They decided to relieve these patients of their suffering by injecting them with a deadly mixture of pain medication and sedatives rather than letting them die alone after their departure (Boin & Nieuwenburg, 2013). Against professional and organizational norms, they considered it in the better interest of their patients to die a peaceful death instead of suffering through an abandoned, slow demise.

It is interesting to look more closely at the justification of such norm deviations. Responders will often tell that they make a difference between their organizational role and their individual responsibility. They insist that, sometimes, they do what they need to do "as a human" without heeding organizational norms. They embrace their subjective experiences and try to comfort victims and deliver personalized support. Being sensitive to their needs, organizational members customize their treatment in spite of official guidelines and standards (Margolis & Molinsky, 2008). Although a violation of organizational norms, their actions build on ethical considerations nevertheless. Even soldiers during war may refuse to shoot and resist all organizational norms against insubordination due to their strongly felt moral convictions (Kelman & Hamilton, 1989; Wiedemann et al., 2021). In short, in times of crisis, frontline responders might ignore norms and do what they feel they need to do.

5.5 Moral Dilemmas

Frontline responders' attempts to deliver personalized care and their resistance against perceived unethical organizational norms can be laudable, but comes with new risks and problems as well. When frontline responders interpret the moral worthiness of victims to determine how to act in a particular situation, the result might well be arbitrary. Crisis responders are not necessarily free of discriminatory prejudices, so inequitable allocation of support based on their assessments of victims could be the undesirable outcome. Moreover, it is difficult to hold individual responders responsible for broader response effects, so unfair outcomes might be hard to contest or resolve. In turn, clear organizational norms can help to protect victims against arbitrary decisions and unconscious biases from responders.

Apart from protecting victims, norms protect crisis professionals as well. Frontline responders are active in complex moral environments, in which hard moral choices need to be made under difficult circumstances. Without the guidance and direction of organizational norms, the crisis situation may easily be experienced as overwhelming and troubling. It is telling that humanitarians report feeling frustrated and nervous, when they are left to choose for themselves whether they will take responsibility for someone in need (Resseguier, 2018). One group of humanitarians, expatriate health-care workers, struggle with various recurring moral questions and doubts in their work. They may, for instance, be confronted with tensions between following their own moral beliefs and respecting local customs that deviate from these beliefs. In other situations, they "bear the burden of choice" in choosing between several patients that are in equal need of help or have to weigh public health concerns against the interests of individual patients (Gotowiec & Cantor-Graae, 2017; Hunt, 2008). The Ebola outbreak offers some specific examples. During the response, a choice had to be made on whether to continue operations in under-resourced facilities, creating deadly risks for health workers. Next, over time, gates were shut at night and patients were practically imprisoned, so they would not leave the medical care facilities and spread the disease. Finally, at some point during the epidemic, frontline personnel felt the need to send away infected patients and contemplated the use of untested drugs, which provided further moral dilemmas (Walsh & Johnson, 2018). In these crisis settings, as Slim (1997) argues, the moral integrity of responders is threatened as they have to make impossible choices and are being forced to accept moral compromises.

Clearly, responders are likely to be confronted with impossible moral dilemmas. These situations may cast long shadows, as any such choice has potentially traumatic consequences. Humanitarians, soldiers, firefighters, police officers, and emergency medical personnel might develop moral injury, as they witness, fail to prevent, or even engage in activities that violate their core moral values, leaving them with feelings of guilt, anger, distrust, shame, and despair (Gustavsson et al., 2020; Lentz et al., 2021; Molendijk, 2021; Wolf et al., 2016). While clear organizational standards will not necessarily prevent the development of moral injury, codes or guidelines at least enable responders to dissociate from the responsibility of adverse outcomes of a crisis response effort and might sometimes reduce psychological suffering. It is beyond doubt that there are often hard choices to make during crises and that it is unfair to leave these choices to responders who would have to make these decisions without guidelines or standards under immense uncertainty and stress (Table 5.1).

Table 5.1 *The ethical dilemma*

	Organizational norms	Individual convictions
Characteristics	Behavioral standards	Moral beliefs
	Reflecting values of the organization	Sense of personal responsibility
		Empathy and relations are key
Advantages	Helps to make difficult choices	Moral worthiness and fairness of actions are decisive
	Protecting victims from unfair treatment	Customized treatment of victims
	Transparency and accountability	
Shortcomings	Moral distress	Impossible choices deferred to responders
	Potential lack of support	
	Risk of unreflective obedience	Potential biases
		Risk of moral injury

Empirical Example

During the European refugee crisis, over a million people fled from war and conflict toward the European Union in search of a better life. Many of those refugees came from Syria, Afghanistan, and Iraq, taking the Eastern Mediterranean route through Turkey and crossing the Aegean Sea to the Greek islands. One of the islands receiving the highest number of refugees was Chios. In response to a Greek request, the Dutch government decided to send several, consecutive teams of border guards toward Chios with the task to support the local Greek authorities. Border guards were given considerable leeway, but organizational norms prescribed border security activities. Border security efforts consisted of intercepting and apprehending illegal migrants before interviewing and registering them. After border guards arrived, however, they viewed the situation at the border in very different ways. Some framed the crisis in a way that matched the organizational norms, claiming: "You have to filter out the terrorists and the returnees [i.e., European jihadists returning from fighting for ISIL], because they are a threat to society in Europe." To this end, they tried to tackle illegal migration, and stop human smuggling and human trafficking. Even apparent social interactions with refugees, such as handing out sweets, ultimately served intelligence-gathering purposes. The crime-fighting posture and activities of these border guards fitted the preexisting border security norms of their employer closely. Other team members struggled with such norms and shared a mixed motivation to work on Chios: "We've all seen the images of the refugee flow on TV. So yes, maybe you can give a helping hand. Unfortunately, there's also people coming to Europe with other intentions, and to filter them out, that's [necessary for] the safety of your own environment." These border guards challenged border security norms through their practices of helping refugees: "If you go there as a military service member and [present yourself] like, I am a military police officer, then you've got it all wrong, then you shouldn't go there in the first place. You have to do something together. And with what I've seen and experienced, I say: you have to forget everything and just be human. That's very important: to be human." Ultimately, border guards in this latter group followed their own moral inclinations and began to act like humanitarians, feeling a strong moral conviction that this was the right thing to do. With little space in the border protection organization for collective dialogue and reflection on the ethics of border management in this context, neither of the groups of border guards was saved from moral doubts and suffering afterward. It had seemed a straightforward mission to their superiors, but the refugee crisis presented moral dilemmas of such complexity and intensity that one border guard with considerable experience in war zones concluded: "This is tougher than any of the other missions I've been on" (Kalkman & Molendijk, 2021).

5.6 An Ethical Culture

Crisis situations will often present frontline responders with moral dilemmas. There are organizational norms, which help them to make choices in these complex moral contexts under conditions of stress and urgency, but these norms may cause moral distress when responders struggle with the behavioral standards that they are supposed to follow. They might choose to resist or deviate from such norms and follow their inner moral convictions. This will not remove the moral complexities of their work though. Rather, it means that crisis professionals have to resolve moral dilemmas on their own and bear the full weight of moral responsibility. In either case, they risk developing trauma and moral injury. The dilemma features in situations in which frontline responders are torn between following moral standards and acting on their own convictions.

It is important to mention that even though moral distress and dilemmas cannot be prevented altogether from crisis response efforts, the involved organizations can take steps to reduce the number of moral issues for responders. Some of these issues emerge due to the fact that organizations are understaffed and under-resourced (Wolf et al., 2016). Such shortages force employees to make decisions on which victims to help first or make them balance individual and community interests. By increasing slack resources, such as giving responders more time, having enough trained personnel, and deploying sufficient high-quality equipment, morally stressful situations might partially be avoided.

Even with fewer morally stressful situations, responders will face the dilemma between following norms or their own convictions at times. Here, it is useful to move attention from norms to ethical cultures in crisis organizations. Norms are rather static and suggest that, from an organizational point of view, employees can either follow such norms and act morally or deviate from standards and behave immorally. Ethical culture, instead, allows for an open and flexible attitude to moral deliberation and decision-making depending on the specific situation at hand. Moreover, it emphasizes the internalization of moral behavior rather than abiding by organizational norms due to external pressures, such as repercussions after norm violations. An ethical culture is therefore concerned with the moral character and intentions of frontline responders and not solely focused on their actions and the consequences of these actions.

In the crisis response literature, there are already several indications of how an ethical culture can be pursued. A prominent element of an ethical culture is ethics education. Multiple scholars have emphasized the importance of this type of training, because crisis responders are often poorly prepared for facing and resolving moral challenges under stressful situations, while experience and study will help them to assess the moral complexities of a situation and what it means for them (Geale, 2012; Gotowiec & Cantor-Graae, 2017; Gustavsson et al., 2020; Lentz et al., 2021; Löfquist, 2017; Resseguier, 2018). Ethics training, which is characterized by doubts and questions, makes responders aware of the values at stake and their moral responsibilities in a particular situation. It helps responders with developing the ability to independently and critically reflect on complex choice situations. It also enables them to behave capably as moral agents through making, communicating, and implementing their moral judgments as well as accounting for their choices afterward (Wortel & Bosch, 2011). As such, organizational members develop the moral competence that is crucial in frontline response work.

Ethics education will enable crisis responders to develop moral resilience as well. Moral resilience refers to "the capacity of an individual to sustain or restore their integrity in response to moral complexity, confusion, distress, or setbacks" (Rushton, 2016, p. 112). Morally resilient workers pursue meaningful service in complex environments without harm to their moral integrity or causing suffering to themselves. In practice, this requires that they conscientiously analyze their own values and moral views, adopt an attitude of flexible responsiveness in ethical decision-making, live up to their convictions with moral courage, and create meaning in situations that appear senseless. As a consequence, morally resilient crisis professionals face smaller risks of traumatic experiences (Lentz et al., 2021; Rushton, 2016). Yet, an ethical culture should not solely be built at the individual level of frontline responders.

Crisis organizations can take various actions as well. One example is the development of an organizational conscience (Slim, 1997). Rather than sticking to fixed norms, an organizational conscience is developed through the creation of a moral vision for the agency, which demonstrates how it distinguishes right from wrong and which guides its actions in morally complex situations. The formulation of a moral vision is a responsibility of senior management and requires their acceptance and consideration of moral difficulties in frontline work. Managerial involvement can also be useful in specific crisis situations when responders are facing tough moral challenges. Unfortunately, this does not always happen yet. Health-care workers in humanitarian settings suffered from feelings of being silenced and ignored by their organization. The head office and organizational leaders were often located remotely and were perceived to use bureaucracy as an excuse to distance themselves from involvement in ethical challenges, leaving frontline professionals with a sense of helplessness and undermining their loyalty. When their opinions and hardships were taken serious instead, suffering was reduced (Gotowiec & Cantor-Graae, 2017). Hunt (2011) has produced a list of questions that can be used in an organization to support ethical decision-making in such situations. Questions help responders to clarify the ethical issue, the relevant contexts that shape and influence it, explore relevant norms and values, and evaluate decision-making options as well as subsequent implementation. Discussing these questions will lead to a more complete understanding of the moral issue and the selection of a well-considered, defensible choice. When there is little time for elaborate discussion in specific crisis situations, moral exemplars or role models can be particularly helpful in operationalizing the organization's moral vision, serving as an inspiration to responders' rapid moral decision-making (Slim, 1997). Generally, managers need to give due attention to the moral dilemmas of their frontline colleagues by showing that they care about their moral dilemmas, offering tools and resources to support their ethical decision-making, and engaging in sharing and discussing their dilemmas and experiences.

Organizations that pursue an ethical culture would do well to institutionalize an ongoing debate over organizational norms. In that way, organizational ethics becomes an active effort rather than a paper reality. The humanitarian sector, for example, has produced many guidelines and standards with good intentions and widespread support, but there have been concerns that these remain primarily rhetorical statements, while having limited impact on real-world practices (Resseguier, 2018). Instead, crisis organizations would do well to systematically arrange collective deliberation, which reflects a commitment to addressing and debating moral questions (see Löfquist, 2017; Slim, 1997). In addition, it must be possible for frontline personnel to voice their opposition and concern, and be taken seriously. Moral resistance is a key indication that it is crucial to review and potentially revise established organizational norms. This will never be easy, because organizational members are bound to have incongruent views, but actively debating the morality of organizational activities ensures that these actions withstand ethical scrutiny and might reduce moral suffering even if the outcomes are undesirable. An ethical culture might serve both crisis responders and victims, but demands a confrontation throughout the organization with the inevitable moral discomforts of crisis response. It is not easy to be good at doing good.

5.7 Conclusion

The development of an ethical culture is a pathway out of the dilemma of moral behavior in crisis organizations, since responders do not have to choose between either compliance with norms or following their inner convictions. Rather, it opens up moral standards and behaviors for discussion and deliberation. This means that both the organization and the individual have a shared moral responsibility for delivering crisis response in alignment with the highest values.

As crisis organizations are trying to develop an ethical culture, it is useful exploring the differential effects of various types of ethics education, moral visions, and organizational deliberation on ethical decision-making, so good practices can be identified. Moreover, it is important to monitor how the development of an ethical culture affects the psychological well-being of crisis professionals in the long run. Finally, the commitment to ongoing debate and deliberation over moral issues in organizations may produce disagreements among frontline responders or between them and their superiors, so it is useful to know more about how organizations can move beyond these disagreements and still offer guidance for operations in morally complex situations.

Resources for Educators and Professionals

PRACTICAL LESSONS

- Organizational norms offer guidance to frontline responders in stressful situations, but can also produce moral distress if not supported.
- Responders can also rely on their inner convictions, but this produces risks for their psychological well-being as well.
- An ethical culture enables active moral deliberation in crisis organizations through institutionalizing an ongoing debate over moral questions and attending to moral resistance.
- Crisis organizations can formulate a moral vision, ensure managerial involvement, and offer tools and resources to frontline personnel operating in morally complex situations.
- Ethics education helps responders assess the moral complexities of situations, reflect on the values at stake and their responsibilities, and behave capably as moral agents.

QUESTIONS FOR REFLECTION AND DISCUSSION

- What was the last moral dilemma that you faced during a crisis response operation and which considerations motivated your actions?
- How does your organization support frontline decision-making on complicated moral questions and how can it do more to help personnel?
- How often do you talk about the moral dilemmas in your work? What are the reactions in the organization when someone challenges an organizational norm?

---

6 | Emotions
Involvement versus Detachment

Professionalization in the humanitarian sector consists of hiring and training cool-headed and self-controlled aid workers, who do not allow their emotions to get the upper hand or cloud their judgment in the chaotic situations in which they are operating. Humanitarian principles, like impartiality and neutrality, suggest a rational, objective, even technical approach, implying a strict control over altruistic and other virtuous impulses. There are advantages to this, because strong, overpowering emotions may lead to rash decisions and regretful actions that can potentially harm important social relations on the ground. Likewise, cold facts and data are likely to be influential tools in advocacy work, and are more likely to affect political decision-makers than humanitarian observers' feelings. But it is worthwhile asking the question: what do we lose with this turn to the rational, unimpassioned humanitarian? Many of these responders view their work, at least partially, as a vocation and see it as their duty to do well in the world. They are effectively told to suppress such feelings. At the same time, their relations with beneficiaries are reduced to the official, impeding the possibility of bonding or gaining a deeper insight in the lives of the people with and for whom they are working (Carbonnier, 2015; Claire, 2021).

Humanitarians operate in contexts that are rife with human suffering. The victims of conflicts and disasters are likely to experience intense grief, anger, and pain. Relief workers can hardly be insensitive to these feelings. Care and empathy are strongly felt impulses and altruistic motivations are a driving force for many humanitarians and other crisis responders. But there are also good reasons for crisis organizations to prefer frontline personnel to be rational and self-restrained crisis professionals. Clearly, this dilemma goes to the core of their identity: It does not concern what we expect these frontline responders to do, but reflects on the type of persons that we expect them to be. The dilemma results from the fact that there are advantages to both detachment from the situation and emotional involvement in the situation.

6.1 Crisis Response as a Rational Puzzle

Frontline crisis response may sometimes seem like a rational and instrumentalist endeavor, as responders are implicitly assumed to be impassive professionals who seek an optimal outcome in a difficult situation. Typically, crisis response sensemaking, decision-making, and activities are studied from this instrumentalist perspective to analyze whether responders failed or succeeded in producing good crisis response results without heeding responders' experiences of the situation. It seems like the involved individuals are interchangeable entities and their individual lifeworlds are irrelevant. By taking this approach, scholars imply and reproduce an ideal-typical image of responders as unemotional beings, who are concerned with facts and outcomes, but remain insensitive to the suffering or pain they might witness around them.

This is surprising because crises do produce considerable pain and suffering among victims and their loved ones. Research shows that victims experience powerful, mostly negative feelings during a crisis situation. These feelings include fear and concern, surprise, sadness, and regret (O'Connell et al., 2017; Prati et al., 2012). Family and friends of victims may also hasten toward the crisis site and will of course be very worried and likely sentimental (Lois, 2003; Mastracci et al., 2014). Only few studies reflect on the importance or merits of these feelings. In fact, it is not uncommon to imply that people succumb to their emotions and get in the way of the response by acting irrationally and counterproductively. Responders, however, are supposed to keep their cool, even if victims and their relatives do not, to adequately resolve the situation.

The view on responders as cool-headed individuals fits within a tradition in which responders' emotions are treated as mere distractions that only get in the way of their attempts to decisively resolve a crisis. Over the last century, Lois (2003, p. 181) argues, there has been a trend toward the banning of emotions from the public sphere. People are expected to suppress their emotions and need to exercise self-control or will be perceived as socially disruptive. This socio-cultural imperative weighs even more heavily on crisis responders, because their status is increased if they seem unaffected by even the most intense situations. It is a mistake to think that all responders can simply turn off their emotions though.

Recently, some crisis researchers have begun to emphasize the critical role of responders' emotions in crisis response (e.g., Evans, 2019; Mastracci et al., 2014; Wankhade, 2021). Crises produce tragic situations and most frontline crisis professionals are personally affected by their experiences. Research on ambulance work, for instance, shows that the work of call handlers and ambulance crews is emotionally taxing and intense, because of victims' profound fear and grief in combination with the high pace and stakes of emergency medical operations (Granter et al., 2019). An important factor is that this confrontation with emotionally charged situation is highly unpredictable and sudden as well. In emergency medical work, crews shift continuously between extremely tragic and very mundane occupational activities. Likewise, for soldiers, intensely emotional events are just short intervals in long days that are primarily characterized by numbing technical tasks, repetitive training exercises, or extended periods of boredom (e.g., De Rond, 2017). As a result, powerful emotions emerge often rapidly and unexpectedly once responders are alerted or deployed. This makes it crucial to understand how these emotions influence crisis responders and their operations.

In many of the existing studies, scholars have primarily focused on the emotions of responders in the aftermath of crises to find out how they (fail to) cope with the resulting emotional stress. Crises, after all, are extreme contexts, in which the unfolding events may produce significant, even intolerable, psychological consequences for responders in the long run (Hällgren et al., 2018). So far, the role of emotions during crisis response efforts itself has received much less attention, but practice suggests that frontline responders' emotions are very diverse at these moments. The plight of victims causes sadness, worries, and anxiety. Expeditious interventions are likely to result in an adrenaline rush and excitement, and problematic response efforts often lead to frustration, dejection, and anger. But the most important emotion in frontline crisis response is compassion. This lays the foundation for crisis response work and is the most powerful feeling when responders witness the pain and suffering of victims, patients, and colleagues. Compassion, in many ways, is key to the work of frontline responders.

6.2 Emotional Involvement through Compassion

To begin with, compassion is believed to be a driving force for engaging in crisis response work among professionals and volunteers. Emergency services volunteers in Australia, for example, are motivated by an empathetic desire to help people and a wish to improve their welfare (Francis & Jones, 2012). And during the Ebola outbreak, international delegates of the Red Cross volunteered to be deployed in spite of their own and loved ones' fears. They expressed a strong sense of benevolence and emphasized the importance of being there for others in need during the worst times of their lives (McCormack & Bamforth, 2019). Research on compassion organizing also shows that individuals who observe human suffering in their environment are likely to feel and act on a sense of empathetic solidarity with victims. They recognize human suffering (or suffer themselves) after a crisis event, connect with others around them, and coordinate their activities to relieve pain and hardships. Such spontaneous responses unfold both after small incidents (e.g., a house fire) and after major disasters (e.g., a nationwide wildfire) as well as after natural hazards and malevolent actions (e.g., a school shooting), and complement the work of professional crisis organizations (Dutton et al., 2006; Powley, 2009; Shepherd & Williams, 2014). Emotional impulses may not only result in initial benevolent action by frontline personnel but also sustain prosocial actions in the long run. The volunteers helping refugees in the Calais "Jungle" offer an example. Many were determined to go after feeling a strong sense of empathy, but once there, they built relationships with refugees and other frontline responders as a result, which fueled a sense of community and facilitated sustained humanitarian action (Doidge & Sandri, 2019).

Among professional crisis responders, moreover, compassion is reflected in the description of their work as a vocation. This means that their occupational choice is not based on a rational assessment, but results from a strong inclination that induces them to choose a profession that is highly demanding in many respects. At heart, it is an empathetic impulse to help people that brings many firefighters, police officers, paramedics, and other responders to their job (Mastracci et al., 2014). Studies on aid workers show that the vast majority also consider their work deeply meaningful and are strongly devoted to it due to its altruistic nature. They work additional and irregular hours to the extent that it harms their personal relations and adversely affects their private lives (Carbonnier, 2015; Oelberger, 2019). Compassion, in other words, is the primary reason that frontline responders want to work for a crisis organization and the emotion on which our crisis response systems rest as a result.

Emotional involvement through compassion can be helpful during crisis response efforts as well. Compassion produces a sensitivity to victims' emotions, which returns important information to responders. First of all, these emotions can signify the nature or seriousness of the situation. And when individuals suddenly display fear or concern, frontline responders are alerted of a change in their environment that requires their attention (see Maitlis & Sonenshein, 2010). Emergency operators, for instance, are more likely to send help to callers who express (intense) fear, as they take this as a sign that support is acutely needed (Svensson & Pesämaa, 2018). Emotions, clearly, can be used for designing and adapting response efforts (Carbonnier, 2015). And emotional expressions should be recognized as an important source of information to frontline crisis response decision-making as a result.

In a fascinating, six-year ethnographic study on a mountain rescue group, called Peak Search and Rescue, Lois (2003) analyzed group members' motivations to join, their emotional experiences, and the impact of their work on their identities. She found that a crucial skill of rescuers was to grasp and manage the emotions of victims after these had been found. Victims would often rely heavily on the rescue group's efforts to get them out of the area, but their intense emotions might hinder their cooperation with rescuers or even disrupt evacuation attempts. Emotional involvement was helpful in dealing with the most common feelings of victims. In less serious cases, rescuers needed to neutralize the embarrassment of stranded people to help them move beyond excessive apologizing and self-depreciation to opening up about their physical condition and get their cooperation in the evacuation efforts. Oftentimes, victims would also become increasingly anxious as they were waiting to be rescued, potentially hindering their participation once the mountain rescue group arrived (e.g., refusing to be lowered down a cliff on a stretcher). Rescuers had to inspire confidence, provide comfort, and listen to their stories to make them feel secure. In the worst cases, rescuers needed to suppress excessive concerns about the life-threatening condition of victims to avoid them going into shock or paralysis, which would reduce the chances of a successful evacuation. Sensitivity to emotions was therefore widely recognized as crucial to search and rescue operations.

This study also indicates that when responders empathize with the people they are helping, they are more likely to produce customized response efforts. Only responders who bond with victims will be able to grasp their needs and may adjust their actions to provide personalized help. In difficult situations, doctors and police officers are most likely to engage in an integrated response style, characterized not only by empathetic involvement but also by personalized actions. This manifests in a sensitive treatment of clients, such as sincere interpersonal contact and offers of help and support to those on the receiving side, even though such kind gestures are not mandated by the organization (Margolis & Molinsky, 2008). A seasoned emergency nurse explains that high-quality health care requires personal attention and real emotional connection (Wolf et al., 2016). Compassionate caring in emergency nursing does not just leave patients more satisfied, but also builds trust and complements or even facilitates clinical care (Fry et al., 2013; Jeffrey, 2016). While these examples of the use of emotions for crisis response still imply an instrumentalist approach (i.e., emotions are useful for providing better responses), it is worthwhile remarking that compassion is also valuable in its own right to responders and victims alike, and broadly viewed as an important virtue that does not require functional effects to be of merit.

Emotional involvement may seem primarily of relevance to crisis responders in the helping professions and less applicable in other crisis response contexts, such as military operations or extreme expeditions. However, these frontline responders also are emotionally involved in their jobs and feel for one another when things go awry. During the Mount Everest climbing disaster, for instance, climbers had pushed themselves to reach the summit even when this became irrational and dangerous. When a storm did finally cause a disaster, climbers of various expeditions took great risks to save the lives of complete strangers, irrespective of the expedition to which they had originally belonged (Jacobsson & Hällgren, 2016; Tempest et al., 2007). Next, much of the work of soldiers is anything but compassionate and veterans describe that they instead turned off their feelings to engage in combat and kill enemy soldiers. But even among soldiers, who are stereotypically depicted as hardened, unfeeling fighting machines, compassion plays a key role when they open up to their emotions, as many do sooner or later. At these moments, as veterans write, they are overwhelmed by powerful feelings of empathy for comrades and even enemy troops who are suffering through the war. This compassion produces feelings of profound guilt and regret, inspires resistance against war, motivates their risky actions to save fellow soldiers whose lives are in danger, and makes them engage in actions that reduce harm to others (see Remarque, 2004; Sassoon, 2013). Compassion truly has a large influence on the actions and experiences of crisis professionals.

6.3 The Emotional Toll of Empathetic Crisis Response

There are several reasons for scholars' continuing skepticism toward the emotional involvement of frontline responders during crises though. The normative assumption of rational, cool-headed responders is based on the idea that emotions inhibit good decision-making in crises. When responders are overly involved in the suffering of victims, they may be unable to think clearly or, worse, succumb to powerful emotions of fear and panic (see Lois, 2003). It can also prevent them from making inevitable but difficult decisions, such as the decision to rescue only some members of a group or the choice to use a painful medical procedure. In fact, responders sometimes have to make decisions during crises that go against their compassionate inclinations. They will frequently need to postpone giving help to people in need in the interest of the crisis response effort. The first emergency responders to arrive at the scene of a large-scale accident, for instance, are supposed to assess the situation, determine the needs, and guide the response efforts without getting their hands dirty themselves. They feel a strong urge to help, but responders cannot give in to these feelings of empathy or they will derail the response effort, so they have to accept the conflicting feelings (Mastracci et al., 2014).

Next, frontline responders can usually at best alleviate suffering and reduce the worst effects of a crisis situation. Whether it is the response to a car crash, a search and rescue operation, or hurricane relief, responders cannot prevent all the pain and adversity that crises produce. The result of crisis response is therefore always only partly satisfactory, so many first responders are left wondering whether they could have done more or feel frustrated by knowing that they could

not reduce the suffering any further (Wankhade, 2021). Community
first responders, who respond to medical emergencies when an ambulance is still on its way, also report being frustrated that they could not
offer more help during stressful incidents (Kindness et al., 2014). And
emergency nurses identify that an organizational focus on performance
rather than patients, in combination with resource scarcity, means that
patients do not get the help they deserve, leading to feelings of letting
their patients down (Wolf et al., 2016). Sometimes, particularly during
crises of a large scale, the work of responders can even appear marginal. Members of a military medical team in Afghanistan experienced
such feelings. They subscribe to codes in which patient care is prioritized, but the high influx of severely wounded people and very basic
working conditions make it hard to live up to lofty goals. This grim
reality makes one of them ask without apparent irony for a reason to
live, when asked if she needs anything while preparing for surgery. To
these medics, there is no reasonable logic in the events that they witness, inhumane suffering is pervasive, and their efforts to improve the
situation do not seem to make any significant difference. This poses an
existential threat to them and risks negatively affecting their psychological well-being (De Rond, 2017; De Rond & Lok, 2016).

In general, the tough work of frontline crisis responders has consequences for their mental health (e.g., Benedek et al., 2007). Responders
who are emotionally involved may find it harder to let things go. For
instance, research shows that firefighters are likely to face high levels of stress, suffer from heart conditions and addiction, and commit
suicide or die younger due to occupational effects in any case (Evans,
2019). A higher level of empathy worsens these effects, particularly
for posttraumatic stress symptoms, depression, and anxiety (Wagner
et al., 2019). Similar findings have surfaced in research on paramedics, who are more likely to abuse alcohol and need mental health
stress leave after traumatic events (Regehr et al., 2002). Negative
psychological effects after transgressive events, such as trauma or
moral injury, are also postulated to be more likely in individuals
who feel a stronger personal connection with victims (Molendijk,
2021; Ter Heide, 2020). Crisis professional may also come to suffer from compassion fatigue, which occurs when empathetic persons
take care of suffering people and, over time, experience secondary
traumatic stress, while losing their caring abilities as a consequence
(Dominguez-Gomez & Rutledge, 2009; Hunsaker et al., 2015). High

emotional involvement may therefore render frontline personnel vulnerable to psychological suffering.

6.4 Detachment and Emotional Distance

While emotional involvement by frontline responders may benefit the response efforts in various ways, its potential negative implications make scholars skeptical of personal engagement with victims. These scholars argue for emotional labor, which refers to the management of one's emotions (Guy et al., 2013; Mastracci et al., 2014; Wankhade, 2021), and in practice often effectively means that responders have to suppress their feelings. Studies imply that responders will have to keep their cool and remain calm to work efficiently. One firefighter recounted a terrible accident, in which it took a long time to rescue a woman from her car, but he never personalized her, separating himself from the situation to the extent he did not even know what she looked like. Another responder describes it as going seemingly automatically on autopilot during an incident, while a third does breathing exercises and deliberately collects himself to ensure a level-headed approach and avoid infecting others with his nervousness (Mastracci et al., 2014). Such emotional disengagement might also be necessitated by the high workload that renders it impossible for crisis professionals to get overly involved in the lives and challenges of the people they help (Jiang, 2021). The suppression of emotions for the duration of the crisis and resulting dispassionate performances are not rarely viewed as key to good crisis response (see Guy et al., 2013; Regehr et al., 2002).

This depiction of crisis responders matches their ideal-typical image in the public mind, in which they are self-controlled and cool-headed persons that can turn off their emotions. They are supposed to be indifferent to the emotional expressions of victims or bystanders (Svensson & Pesämaa, 2018), and have to remain (or at least appear) unaffected by what they observe themselves. This applies to the wide range of frontline responders, including emergency response personnel (Mastracci et al., 2014), search and rescue team members (Lois, 2003), and high-altitude mountaineers (Swann et al., 2016), but perhaps most of all to soldiers. Soldiers are socialized to show no feeling to their victims, nor to empathize with the local populations whom they are tasked to help and who may often find themselves in a terrible predicament. Among soldiers, emotional detachment is even viewed as an expression of professionalism (Molendijk, 2021). This view also reflects how many frontline crisis professionals are trained in their organization. Traditional, masculine ways of managing emotions are dominant in the US Border Patrol as well. Border patrol agents are taught and encouraged to display stoicism, aggression, and calmness, regardless of the circumstances in which they find themselves. Kindness and caring, instead, are believed to undermine Patrol agents' presence, potentially disrupting the implementation of their official duties (e.g., arrests), and are generally looked down upon within the organization for which they work (Rivera, 2015). The underlying idea is that only the outcome matters and that compassion or other prosocial emotions are either irrelevant or detrimental to reaching that outcome.

Another main reason for emotional distancing during crisis response is that it is believed to protect frontline personnel from psychological suffering once the crisis is over. From this perspective, disengagement can be seen as a form of coping. There are several ways to put this into practice. One is blaming victims for their plight rather than empathizing with them, for instance by referring to their own risky behavior or mistakes that brought them in the precarious situation (Lois, 2003). Another strategy is dehumanizing victims or patients to foreclose compassion, which is particularly potent in a military context and reduces the psychological barriers of soldiers to kill other human beings (Kelman & Hamilton, 1989). When refugees are portrayed as security threats that collaborate with human smugglers, these two strategies are applied by border guards to avoid feeling for refugees and hold them responsible for their own fate (Kalkman, 2019a). A final practice of disengagement is cynical or dark humor that helps frontline personnel to dissociate from the crude reality around them (De Rond, 2017; De Rond & Lok, 2016). Crime scene investigators, for instance, are confronted with very challenging working conditions, such as brutal murders, but still joke around and use humor to reduce emotional tensions and stress, negotiate the emotional burdens of their work, and maintain resilience (Vivona, 2014). These examples illustrate that emotional distancing as a means of a coping is common across crisis contexts.

6.5 Limits of Emotional Detachment

The use of emotional detachment to cope with stressful situations is not flawless. Psychological problems frequently result from the very fact that there are group norms that enforce emotional detachment and punish emotional involvement (Lois, 2003). Indeed, it may be very hard for responders to open up about their feelings and seek external help after a distressing incident in an organization with a culture of emotional suppression. In this way, organizational efforts to promote the control of employees' emotions may initially protect frontline responders against getting overly involved during the crisis, but also hinder the provision of emotional support to personnel when this is still needed after all, thereby increasing risks of adverse psychological consequences, such as trauma (Lennie et al., 2020). In fact, avoiding confrontation with emotions negatively influences responder well-being and increases chances of substance (ab)use (Arble & Arnetz, 2017; Evans, 2019). Likewise, dispatchers who are steered to suppress emotions, for instance through using pre-established scripts, appear more likely to experience emotional exhaustion and burnout (Mastracci & Adams, 2019). Vice versa, the use of one's emotions has been found to increase the psychological well-being of emergency dispatchers (Huard et al., 2021).

It is telling that the border patrol agents, despite working in an organization that promotes emotional detachment, shared that they cannot completely distance themselves from illegal migrants in all cases. Their humanitarian feelings take over when they find people who are in a bad shape, particularly when children are involved. They will enact a "feminine" form of emotional labor by empathizing with victims and offering them material or emotional support. These emotional displays are tainted though, because the organization and colleagues view them as inappropriate, excessive, and objectionable (Rivera, 2015). It is therefore not easy to cope with or act upon these emotions. Likewise, De Rond and Lok (2016) argue that military medics are also not offered the resources to cope with emotionally intense situations. The armed forces have a culture of emotional control and silence signs of emotional stress, while the medical profession emphasizes emotional composure and technical solutions to improve results for patients. Both these social pressures make it difficult for military medics to reach out for help when emotional suppression occasionally fails. Alternative, individual coping mechanisms are attempted but bound to fail, because they are unable to address the roots of the problem. As a result, disengagement mechanisms may cause the emotional troubles that they are supposed to prevent (Table 6.1).

Table 6.1 *The dilemma of emotions*

	Involvement	Detachment
Characteristics	Altruism and compassion	Suppression of feelings
	Crisis response as a vocation	Victims not personalized
		Focus on outcomes
Advantages	Triggers and sustains prosocial action	Efficient operations
	Returns useful information	No distractions
	Customized response	Facilitates coping
Shortcomings	May inhibit decision-making	Incomplete protection against trauma
	Risk of trauma	No organizational support in case of psychological problems

Empirical Example

Military service is extremely demanding as well as dangerous in many respects. Still, soldiers are deeply emotionally involved in their work and are generally very committed to the organization, even so much so that many prove willing to risk or sacrifice their life in missions and operations. But, as veterans describe in their fictional, autobiographical novels, this emotional attachment is put under pressure after their first combat experience, which shatters their expectations of war and what it means to be a soldier. They assumed that war would be meaningful and honorable, and they themselves would engage in a glorious fight. However, none of these expectations come true and they feel betrayed. Seeing and experiencing immense suffering, one soldier in a novel by WWI veteran March states that everything he was "ever taught to believe about mercy, justice, and virtue is a lie." French veteran Barbusse adds the words of another soldier, who with feelings of compassion and guilt concludes: "Heroes? Some sort of extraordinary being? Idols? Rot! We've been murderers. We have respectably followed the trade of hangmen." Soldiers are trained and socialized to emotionally connect to their job as a calling and abstain from feeling for enemy combatants, but over time, the exact reverse may well be the result, as many alienate from their organization while they sympathize with those whom they have killed or hurt. Canadian veteran Harrison offers an illustration: "The image of Karl, he who died on my bayonet, seems to stand before my eyes. The shaking becomes worse. The movements are those of one who is palsied. I begin to sob." Remarque's protagonist, likewise, feels an urge to explain himself to the corpse of a soldier that he killed: "You were only an idea to me before, an abstraction that lived in my mind and called forth its appropriate response." Such traumatic experiences have odd effects. Sometimes, soldiers feel like inhuman machines, or as Remarque put it: "We are insensible, dead men, who through some trick, some dreadful magic, are still able to run and to kill." Turning off their humanity, they are able to continue fighting. At other moments, they are torn by doubt, loneliness, and remorse. These feelings provoke resistance and mutiny against the military organization and its leadership among the troops. Tolstoy writes that, after a battle, "the question arose in every soul: "For what, for whom, must I kill and be killed?" [...] At any moment these men might have been seized with horror at what they were doing and might have thrown up everything and run away anywhere." Veterans' accounts show that these latter emotions become increasingly dominant, as trauma and moral injury develop. Many soldiers experience a strong sense of empathy and guilt, even if these emotions have been suppressed initially and they do not often act upon such feelings during war. Emotional detachment is bound to be ineffective in the long run. Ninh, a Vietnamese veteran, formulated it poetically: "Each of us carried in his heart a separate war" (Kalkman, 2023b).

6.6 Emotion Management

The emotional dilemma for frontline responders is urgent during the response, but also important in the long run, as crises are often potentially traumatic experiences. There seems to be a broad consensus that frontline personnel need to be able to dissociate themselves from the tragedy of the situation, so that their emotions do not impede their decisions or actions, while a detached attitude is also considered the best way to cope with emotionally intense situations and avoid adverse psychological effects. Yet, there are indications that emotional involvement has its advantages as well, because emotions relay important information to responders, fuel their continued involvement in crisis response work, and allow for personalized care to victims and patients. This means that crisis responders face competing pressures with regard to the emotional attitude they should adopt in their work.

It is interesting that emotions are often treated in a uniform manner as either unequivocally problematic or relevant. In practice, emotions can be diversified in two ways. First, there is a broad range of emotional states, some of which may help responders, while others are unhelpful. Feelings of anger and dejection will usually not be very productive, but eagerness and excitement might be more relevant to a fruitful response. When emotions are blamed for impeding crisis response efforts, it is necessary to identify the type of emotion. Second, emotional intensity varies (Catino & Patriotta, 2013; Maitlis & Sonenshein, 2010). Fear, for example, has repeatedly been viewed as causing crisis response failure (Stein, 2004; Weick, 1993). Excessive fear may lead to panic or paralyze frontline responders. Still, some fear may also be a valuable emotion in crisis, because it prevents responders from becoming careless and helps them understand victims' desire for an urgent response to resolve the situation. It is therefore sensible to think in a more nuanced way about the emotional involvement of frontline responders.

By extension, it is clearly appealing to look at negative emotional consequences, when powerful feelings and emotional interactions result in faulty decision-making, overwhelm and paralyze responders, or produce grave psychological injuries. It is important to understand the role of emotions in causing these effects, but it neglects another side of the story. Frontline responders also experience great rewards from helping others in crises. Successful efforts give their work meaning and produce a sense of achievement (Evans, 2019; Hunsaker et al., 2015). An overemphasis on the suppression of feelings in crises also translates to taking emotional rewards and meaning out of crisis work. But positive emotional consequences make the sacrifices of frontline responders worthwhile and need to be granted due attention when evaluating the merits of emotional involvement.

As emotions ultimately enable empathetic crisis responses, it is worthwhile delving a bit further into the concept of empathy (Jeffrey, 2016). Generally, frontline responders are driven by empathy, illustrated by the wish to alleviate the suffering of others through altruistic feelings. Affective empathy refers to subjectively experiencing the feelings of someone else and is associated with emotional contagion. This is often perceived as problematic in current analyses and a reason to reject empathy altogether. Cognitive empathy, however, is about understanding someone's feelings from an objective, analytical distance, combining care and connection with a clear distinction between the self and the victim. It requires taking the perspective of the patient or victim, but not taking over their emotional state. Adopting this latter form of empathy can enable some degree of personalized assistance without responders getting emotionally overwhelmed as a result (see Salvarani et al., 2019). Still, this is no plea to reject affective empathy altogether and only promote cognitive empathy. Responders' empathy can be adjusted to a specific situation through emotion management. While emotion management, for instance in literature on emotional labor, has often effectively been taken to mean that emotions need to be suppressed, it makes better sense to leave it to frontline responders to choose how to get emotionally involved during a particular crisis (see Rivera, 2015). When victims' emotions are dysfunctional, it is sensible to go for cognitive empathy only, but responders can also resort to affective empathy when victims' emotions are useful to the response effort. This indicates that emotions can be managed in such a way that they are useful for crisis response.

Even when emotions are managed for effective use in crisis response, crises will inevitably remain distressing events. Under these circumstances, team and organizational support remain important. For instance, supervisory support renders employees more resilient against developing trauma by creating a safer space for talking about emotions and finding help for traumatized personnel (Bacharach & Bamberger, 2007). Such an organizational climate also allows for mutual care between colleagues with similar experiences. Lower-level leaders can also greatly influence the hardiness of personnel through their words, decisions, and actions. If a leader gives frontline crisis professionals meaningful tasks in highly demanding situations and rewards them appropriately, they will be more likely to view life as meaningful, their own future as controllable, and change as valuable, contributing to their resilience against inevitable pain and stress (Bartone, 2006). Next, crisis organizations can promote self-compassion among personnel, referring to an attitude of mindfulness towards one's one pain and treating oneself with kindness. This protects frontline responders against a range of mental health issues and increases responder resilience further (McDonald et al., 2021). Frontline responders are entitled to such organizational interventions and these may not only help to reduce the impact of tragic events, but also enable them to adopt empathetic approaches in turn. It is clear that the genuine exploration of the constructive role of emotions in crisis response might very well improve crisis organizations' emotion management processes as well as frontline responders' well-being. It is time to open up to responders' emotions.

6.7 Conclusion

The question should not be if emotion has a place in frontline crisis response, but how to ensure emotional involvement in crisis response efforts while reducing potential adverse repercussions. This requires complicating and diversifying frontline responders' emotions in crises, which opens up room for dialogue on how to manage emotions and enables an exploration of appropriate forms of empathy in given situations.

If responders' emotions are going to be used for crisis response, it is useful exploring which emotions are particularly valuable in crisis response operations and studying when emotions are so intense as to become problematic and disruptive. Moreover, it is relevant to find out more about how frontline crisis professionals shift between different forms of empathy and what training programs help them to assess the usefulness of responders' emotions for managing the situation at hand. Finally, there would be merit in researching whether effective forms and degrees of emotional involvement are contingent upon the particular crisis contexts in which responders operate.

Resources for Educators and Professionals

PRACTICAL LESSONS

- Crisis situations are emotional events for both victims and responders.
- Emotions can both impede and facilitate the work of crisis responders, depending on the type and intensity of the emotion.
- Empathy helps responders to take the perspective of the victim and deliver personalized care, but responders should avoid getting overwhelmed as a result.
- Frontline responders can learn and use emotion management skills to decide if and how to get emotionally involved in a particular situation.
- Crisis organizations should build team and organizational support through offering psychological help and by promoting emotional resilience and self-compassion.

QUESTIONS FOR REFLECTION AND DISCUSSION

– Which emotions help you do your work during crisis situations and which emotions are making your work harder? How do you manage your emotions?

– How did you see colleagues' emotions influence their work? Do people openly speak about how a situation affected them in your organization?

– How appropriate and impactful are the emotional support systems of your organization? What initiatives are needed to get more support?

7 | Ties
Cohesion versus Contestation

The life of a soldier is often in the hands of other soldiers. Their decisions and actions mean the difference between life and death. Strong social relations are required before they can entrust their lives to others. Indeed, throughout their training, soldiers form close-knit ties that outweigh almost any other relationship and often come at the cost of alternative social connections. Henri Barbusse (1917), who wrote a fictional account of his time in the French Army during the First World War, described his squad as a flock, a family, and a home. The harsh and dangerous life of the soldiers in his unit created close bonds between these men, even somehow merged them over time, so they began to look alike to the outside observer. External differences in age and background disappeared as they blended into one mass. The general advice, Barbusse counseled, was to avoid trying to be yourself. They did not have their individual identities anymore, but became members of a brotherhood that would take incalculable risks to save each other from danger. Orders and plans fail to stop them from coming to the rescue of a comrade at risk. This account shows team cohesion in its most extreme form.

Crisis organizations, like the armed forces, are known to produce very cohesive teams. This cohesion is widely believed to be an asset, a team characteristic to be proactively pursued and treasured. The soldiers in Barbusse's unit deeply cared about each other, felt strongly committed to their comrades, and would leave no one behind. They would fight for one another, even when losing faith in the purpose of the war. While high levels of cohesion clearly offer military benefits, it may also lead to like-minded soldiers who oversimplify complicated combat situations or avoid engaging in open debate about the best approach in a particular situation for the sake of unity. Such contestation, however, offers valuable insights about the quality of a strategy, but crisis managers fear it may also lead to unit disintegration. In practice, soldiers and other crisis responders face a dilemma resulting from a simultaneous need for cohesion and contestation in their teams.

7.1 Total Institutions

The armed forces are a stereotypical "total institution" (Goffman, 1961). Total institutions have several characteristics. Organizational life is centralized in one location (e.g., barracks) under one authority (e.g., commander). A group of similar individuals participate in the same activities (e.g., training drills). These activities are mandatory and carefully scheduled with limited leisure time (e.g., periods with no weekends). In combination, these activities contribute to the overarching goals of the organization (e.g., combat-ready troops). There is typically considerable distance between organizational levels and formal language is employed when addressing superiors (e.g., salutes and requiring permission to speak). And superiors' instructions and punishments pervade deeply into the personal lives of members beyond what is deemed normal and acceptable outside of the institution.

Organizational interventions do not only determine soldiers' daily lives, but also affect them on a more fundamental level through socialization. Throughout the socialization process, total institutions try to strip recruits of their old identities in an attempt to impose a new identity. Paratroopers' identities, for instance, are not only redefined by imposing physical hardships, but also through informal pressure and power use. Stories about ideal paratroopers set expectations for new recruits, a strong informal culture of peer surveillance and (self-) evaluation ensures abidance with these expectations, and the internalized image of a particular identity fosters a constant pursuit of the aspired self-conception. Thus, members are disciplined and discipline themselves (Thornborrow & Brown, 2009). For many of these organizational members, their lives and selves are subsequently defined by the organization. Members will often be fiercely loyal, view themselves primarily and proudly as a member of the organization, and may be unable to imagine a life outside of the institution (Segal, 1986).

Armed forces offer a clear example, but many crisis organizations show several characteristics of total institutions. Firefighters, for example, aspire to live up to the expectations of others that are reinforced by rituals and stories, develop an idealized image of what it means to be a firefighter, are very proud of their membership once they are accepted, and develop family-like relationships with colleagues (Hallam, 2018). Similarly, expedition crewmembers have a centralized life with mandatory activities. Although there may be more leisure time, it is typically hard to escape the presence (and gaze) of the other crewmembers. A private life is (temporarily) rendered impossible and members are expected to fully dedicate themselves to reaching the expedition's goal, be it to reach a mountain summit or a space mission. Likewise, humanitarian aid workers, operating in volatile settings, usually have long and mentally stressful work lives, might face severe restrictions on movement due to safety hazards, and tend to be very devoted to their work and profession as well. And in search and rescue teams, too, full membership of a team and the recognition as a rescue "hero" are elusive and protected by stringent norms, prescribing self-denial and the development of a group-oriented attitude, which result over time in the growth of special bonds between members (Lois, 2003).

The extensive socialization process explains the near-total commitment of crisis responders to their teams or organizations as manifested in their willingness to face serious danger in their work. Frontline responders in crisis organizations may be seriously harmed and suddenly get injured or even lose their lives. Still, soldiers engage in combat situations, astronauts go on spaceflights, and firefighters enter burning buildings. Likewise, a pandemic will not stop the majority of health workers from doing their job. Over ninety percent of health department personnel in three states in the USA said they would still be willing to provide care if required. Particularly those organizational members with high confidence that they could make a meaningful and effective contribution reported being very likely to show up if asked (Barnett et al., 2009). In other studies, somewhat lower scores are mentioned with sixty to eighty-five percent of crisis professionals reporting willingness to respond, depending on the nature of the crisis (Knezek et al., 2022).

Behavioral studies, however, demonstrate that professionals rarely abandon their role in the majority of disasters and display a greater willingness to respond than they report (Trainor & Barsky, 2011). For instance, when the Great East Japan Earthquake and the subsequent tsunami heavily damaged the Daiichi Nuclear Power Station, top-level political and industry leaders clashed dramatically over how to handle the situation, while hundreds of plant operators, firefighters, and soldiers converged to the site to stabilize the reactors, regardless of a high chances of radiation poisoning and hydrogen explosions (Funabashi & Kitazawa, 2012). Likewise, after the 2011 Christchurch earthquake, staff at the city's emergency department continued working without knowing whether their families were safe or checking how bad their houses were damaged (Dolan et al., 2011). And during the November 2015 Paris attacks, many health-care workers spontaneously came in to help with the emergency medical response, avoiding staff shortages (Ghanchi, 2016). Also, an initial study of the COVID-19 pandemic shows no significant increase in absenteeism of health-care workers (Von Batten, 2020). This acceptance of risks represents not only a considerable sacrifice on responders' part, but will often also be very challenging to their loved ones. Husbands, wives, parents, and children of responders are concerned during their shifts and missions, and the anxiety can be emotionally draining for those at home (Matsakis, 2005). This shows that frontline responders are committed to their work, even when it causes suffering and worry to those who are dear to them. Such organizational membership can even come at the cost of weakened ties with families, friends, and other preexisting affiliations (Segal, 1986).

It is important to emphasize that socialization is decidedly social in nature. It fosters a new member's sense of commitment to the organization or profession, but in many crisis organizations, it does so primarily through promoting strong bonds between organizational members. Unsurprisingly, total institutions are generally the most cohesive organizations, and responders will be particularly likely to take great risks out of loyalty to their team members. Indeed, a sense of obligation to colleagues will increase the likelihood of crisis professionals showing up at work during a crisis (Trainor & Barsky, 2011). Thus, team cohesion in the workplace is a crucial outcome of the extensive socialization efforts in total institutions.

7.2 Cohesion

Team cohesion has often been identified as the single most important characteristic for explaining why groups under immense pressure do not break down, but are able to operate resiliently. Crisis organizations need cohesive teams, because loosely connected teams would easily disintegrate when confronted with danger. To this end, members of crisis organizations typically spend much time in each other's company, suffer hardships together, develop similar identities, and form family-like relations (e.g., "brothers in arms").

In an early study, Shils and Janowitz (1948) argued that close interpersonal relations in Wehrmacht soldiers' primary group (e.g., squad or section) largely explained why they determinedly resisted and continued to risk their lives during WWII, even after ongoing retreats and in the face of seemingly inevitable defeat. Soldiers needed very little in return: satisfaction of their basic needs, affectionate relations with others in the group, and hierarchical relations that met certain conventions. They were not really interested in high-minded ethical considerations or political objectives. A high level of team cohesion sufficed for good morale and a tenacious fighting spirit. For a Wehrmacht soldier, the personal relations were crucial, and "as long as he felt himself to be a member of his primary group and therefore bound by the expectations and demands of its other members, his soldierly achievement was likely to be good" (Shils & Janowitz, 1948, p. 284).

Cohesion is not only a product of informal relations though. In some cases, organizations may aim for future cohesion in the selection process. Space missions, for instance, force small groups of people to spend much time in close proximity under extreme circumstances, so interpersonal compatibility tests are devised to compose a cohesive crew in order to avoid escalating tensions and form a productive team for the duration of the mission (Kanas et al., 2013). If a team has already been selected, participation and proficiency in collective drills is likewise important. Formal training processes are relevant social rituals that contribute to the emergence of comradeship as well (King, 2006). When such teams experience stressful events together, the cohesion will increase even further (Bartone et al., 2002), which explains the extremely high levels of cohesion in military units at war, such as Barbusse's squad. A study on lifeboat workers in the UK and Ireland confirms that a combination of informal ties, formal work practices, shared experiences, and a collective, meaningful purpose cultivate strong and active solidarity in rescue crews operating in risky conditions. This is reflected and reinforced by the social norms that they develop. Lifeboat workers, for instance, adopted the norm that if a team member falls overboard, someone else will directly follow to be with that person, irrespective of the situation. This symbolizes the unconditional solidarity toward one another and builds mutual trust

(O'Toole & Calvard, 2020). Other research shows as well that rescuers will go to great lengths to save a trapped colleague in distress, even tolerating higher risks to themselves to rescue one of their own (Ash & Smallman, 2008)

Such cohesion benefits team performance in various ways. The Wehrmacht soldiers in the study by Shils and Janowitz did not abandon their section, nor did sections disintegrate. Rather, the strong bonds allowed them to continue to perform, regardless of what happened around them. Similar examples abound in military research. US soldiers in the Iraq war were still primarily motivated to fight as a result of unit cohesion and felt responsible for each other to the point they were willing to sacrifice their lives for their comrades. The bonds between soldiers continue to offer a powerful motivation for fighting (Wong et al., 2003). The positive effects of cohesion on performance can also be found in other crisis organizations. Members of these organizations are motivated to show up and do their work, particularly if their organization has a cohesive culture (Trainor & Barsky, 2011). Even emergency service volunteers are more likely to commit to their organization if group cohesion is high (Rice & Fallon, 2011).

Cohesive teams have other advantages as well. Coordination between individuals proves easier and quicker when strong team ties have created interpersonal trust. Godé (2015) conducted research in the French Air Force and found that military personnel had to fully trust each other, since high-pressure activities, particularly in reaction to sudden events, left no space for doubt or double-checks. One navigator compared the squadron even to a tribe, in which trust featured as essential to its culture and performance. Another example of how cohesion enables team coordination comes from the passengers aboard United Airlines Flight 93, hijacked on 9/11. They needed to construct a collective narrative and build a collective identity to develop trust in another before engaging in the risky endeavor to resist the hijackers and try to take back control over the plane. Although the hijackers crashed the plane into the ground, the brave passengers managed to band together and coordinate an effective counter-attack (Quinn & Worline, 2008). In intensive care units, similarly, ties have proven important to coordination. While earlier research mostly looked at individual expertise of team members, a recent study found that strong social relations facilitated rapid task and role distribution. In such teams, members often communicate implicitly and can sense what they are supposed to do. When they are lost, moreover, ICU personnel will rely on people they know rather than those who are most qualified. In this way, tie strengths guide coordination (Rasmussen et al., 2020).

Cohesion can even protect members of crisis teams against workplace injuries, while its absence might produce dangerous situations. In one study, Patterson and colleagues (2016) studied how familiarity between two team members in US emergency medical services affected workplace injuries based on a dataset of over 700,000 shift records. Team cohesion proved key in explaining why some dyads faced lower injury rates than others. Dyads were much less likely to report injuries when they had worked together in shifts before. The authors show that every additional shift reduces the injury rate with an estimated two percent and dyads with more than ten shifts together had the lowest injury numbers. Other studies on volunteer firefighters, humanitarian aid workers, and military personnel demonstrate that it is not just physical safety that may benefit from cohesion, but that camaraderie also proved a good means of protection against psychological strain and burnout among frontline crisis professionals (Ager et al., 2012; Ahronson & Cameron, 2007; Tuckey & Hayward, 2011).

7.3 Dysfunctional Team Dynamics

While there appears to be consensus on the considerable advantages of team cohesion in crisis contexts, some studies have shed doubt on these outcomes. Authors have suggested that the importance of team cohesion has been overstated, since it does not always seem to be needed in frontline crisis teams. Even in a military context, questions have been raised over the need for cohesion in explaining team performance (MacCoun et al., 2006). For instance, the Israel Defense Forces formed ad hoc task forces to conduct specific missions during the Al-Aqsa Intifada without losing effectiveness. Units of various sorts were split and recombined in temporary, loose coalitions for specific tasks during this time period. The emergence of swift trust, rather than strong social bonds, ensured that military performance was not diminished, as soldiers built on assumptions of trustworthiness to cooperate with unfamiliar units (Ben-Shalom et al., 2005). In other crisis contexts, similar findings have been reported. Collectivist orientations in Himalayan mountain climbing teams, for instance, have no significant effects on reaching the summit or safety in homogeneous teams, and collectivism even increases climber deaths in diverse teams (Chatman et al., 2019). Social cohesion does not necessarily reduce accident occurrence among firefighting teams in risky environments either (Fruhen & Keith, 2014). These findings raise questions on why cohesion fails to produce positive results in these cases.

Clearly, strong cohesion may lead to dysfunctional group dynamics as well. One of the most concerning effects of cohesion is the increased likelihood of groupthink. Groupthink refers to the phenomenon in which team members experience social pressures to conform to the perceived group consensus and avoid debate, preventing critical reflection and typically adopting suboptimal decisions (Janis, 1971). When teams are confronted with an external threat, such as during crises, they may be particularly susceptible to groupthink. The over-commitment to consensus in the team and the lack of openness to deviant information are a recipe for disaster. It contributes to sensemaking failures by fostering an oversimplified image of reality and impedes debate on risky decisions. For example, members of the decision-making team, discussing whether to launch the space shuttle Challenger, had gone through the ranks of NASA together and shared a strong sense of loyalty, leading them to censor doubts and concerns of engineers from a private supplier and take the fatal the decision to continue the launch (Moorhead et al., 1991). While most studies on groupthink have focused on top-level, political decision-making, similar dynamics can unfold among frontline personnel. They might feel pressured as well to follow (what they believe to be) the majority viewpoint, prioritizing good relations with teammates over fruitful dialogue.

Strong cohesion in organizations may also lead members to get stuck in their ascribed identity or role, either because this is expected from them by teammates or because they have grown accustomed to a particular position in the team. There are certain disadvantages to having a fixed identity though. One of these disadvantages is that it is hard to view a situation from different perspectives. In general, responders will "see those events they feel they have the capacity to do something about" (Weick, 1988, p. 311). Their capabilities guide their crisis perceptions and define their expectations, narrowing their focus. Seeing some things means not seeing other things, and the more focused one's perceptions, the more (potentially important) information you are missing. A rigid identity also creates troubles when a new understanding or new actions are needed that do not directly validate this identity. A telling example is offered by firefighters facing exploding wild fires, but failing to drop their backpacks, chainsaws, and other tools to save their lives (Weick, 1996). This might seem unreasonable, but it is important to realize that a firefighter's tools are not mere material objects. These tools define firefighters' membership of a social unit, give confidence and meaning to their presence in the area, and are elementary to the shared culture. When an exploding wildfire rapidly approaches, it may feel like a choice between a meaningful identity, derived from strong ties with team members and reflected in the tools, or profound anxiety. It is no wonder that responders have chosen the former. Ideally, responders would have other identities to fall back upon, which may inspire actions that increase their chances of survival in such situations, but this would also undercut team cohesion as members would need to cultivate external social bonds.

Finally, the effects of cohesion are occasionally paradoxical as well. Frequently, a strong sense of cohesion among responders renders them loyal to the team, while at the same time undermining their commitment to the overarching organization. Specifically, team members can be proud about what they achieve, while criticizing others in the same organization for not meeting the same standards or holding them back. Inter-service rivalries in the armed forces are a well-known instance of this. Members of the squad of Barbusse (1917) developed very strong relations with each other, but voiced feelings of deep-seated anger and hatred toward others in the organization who did not share the same experiences or made the same sacrifices. Counterintuitively, team cohesion may reduce responders' involvement in the organization at large.

7.4 Contestation

The idea that contestation in a team, rather than cohesion, is of use to frontline crisis teams might seem puzzling, even if only because we associate cohesion with harmony and friendship, while contestation suggests discord and conflict. Still, these normative associations should not lure us into a simplistic pursuit of team cohesion. Contestation between frontline responders has its merits as well.

First, scholars have tried to unravel why some organizations are highly reliable, even though they operate under significant time pressure and have little leeway for performance variation since any mistake could be disastrous. One of the main ingredients why these organizations do not succumb to the pressure but continue to achieve virtually error-free performance is team heterogeneity. By inviting diversity and skepticism in their crisis organizations, teams are more likely to accept that situations will be complex and deserve to be studied from various perspectives, ensuring mindful operations and reliable performance (Weick & Sutcliffe, 2001). In the absence of such organized diversity, responders may fall prey to a simplified perspective of reality and find themselves unable to adapt when the shared crisis understanding proves misguided. To avoid such situations, it is worthwhile composing groups consisting of members with dissimilar opinions and backgrounds, facilitating open discussions, and organizing doubt (Kramer, 2007; Weick & Sutcliffe, 2001). This was also the experience of Northeast Utilities, a major energy provider in New England, which was shut down by the US Nuclear Regulatory Commission in the 1990s until, among others, it met certain safety requirements. While progress toward a safety conscious work environment was initially slow, the need for drastic change became clear when a new Chief Nuclear Officer reversed the firing of two contract workers who had raised safety concerns. This confronted staff with the problematic culture of silencing disparate views and showcased the urgent need for change. In this organizational change process toward working safely, there was broad and proactive involvement of employees on all levels, with great success. The case demonstrates that a diversity of voices is needed for crisis organizing (Carroll, 2015). In a general sense, cohesive organizations that engage in profound socialization of new employees may create members who think alike and feel strongly connected, but are therefore stuck in their ways and miss important information, while organizational members who nurture their own identities can offer critical input and novel insights.

Second, public administration researchers have studied "bureaucratic politics" or bureaupolitics, referring to the bargaining process through which governmental actors with competing goals reach compromise solutions over public policies and decisions (Allison, 1971). While these scholars initially focused on higher levels of government, similar bureaupolitical processes unfold throughout the public sector. Rosenthal et al. (1991) challenge the predominant assumption of crises as unifying moments in which involved actors rally around the flag

to implement broadly shared response actions by identifying bureau-
politics in crisis response decision-making as well. They argue that
organizational interests continue to play a role during crises, because
the legitimacy and prestige of crisis organizations are at stake. But
first responders may also have limited collaboration experience and
prefer different approaches. In some cases, frontline responders will
come into conflict, simply because they all believe that they can make
a meaningful contribution. The findings of this study are not out of
the ordinary. Similar outcomes are reported in research on Chinese
disaster management (Chen, 2016) and the multi-agency collaboration in US Provincial Reconstruction Teams operating in Afghanistan
(Keane & Wood, 2016). Since no actor can generally impose its will,
choices are compromises. Scholars of this phenomenon hasten to
add that such bureaupolitical tensions, while commonly denounced
as undermining the collective efforts, actually have beneficial consequences, because it introduces checks and balances in decision-making
processes, fosters reflection, and ensures that any decision has sufficient credible support (Rosenthal et al., 1991). Such clear and fair
negotiations are much harder to realize when cohesion is blindly pursued. Very strict ties between like-minded people prevent real discussions over contrasting viewpoints and silence frontline personnel with
alternative ideas for resolving a crisis. In conclusion, bureaupolitical
contestation over competing interests and preferences is of value to
frontline crisis response efforts.

7.5 Team Dissolution

When it becomes clear how contestation in teams benefits crisis
response operations, the question arises why it has such negative connotations. One of the most prominent explanations is that observers
view it as equal to conflict, infighting, and hostile animosity, which are
the most problematic manifestations of team contestation. Research
on isolated and confined teams in extreme contexts (ICE), such as
polar exploration crews and teams of astronauts, provides a few troubling examples. A recurring finding in this research is that tensions rise
and cohesion decreases over time. Interestingly, mutual social support
often gradually drops, as members increasingly withdraw from problems, potentially forming subgroups or engaging in conflicts, which
hamper performance (Golden et al., 2018).

A space mission simulation setting suggests that it is hard for heterogeneous teams in particular to bond and maintain high performance. In the first 110 days of an experiment in a hermetic chamber, two small groups of four were supposed to work together: one all-male Russian group, and one all-male, predominantly Russian group. Collaboration between both groups was fairly unproblematic. In the second 110 days of the experiment, the second group was replaced by an international, mixed-gender group, and this time, the two groups failed to build good working relations. The authors argue that the different cultural and gender composition produced conflicts, manifesting in a couple of incidents. The relationships deteriorated over time to the extent that open conflict interrupted the planned experiments (Gushin et al., 2001). Generally, it is assumed that diverse teams are more likely to face such interpersonal tensions or even hostility and thus make it harder to maintain harmonious, productive working relations (Sandal et al., 2006).

Next, contestation can potentially lead to team disintegration. In this situation, team members do not just fail to collaborate, but are even unable to connect in any meaningful way. Disintegration is a major risk to crisis organizations, because it will almost inevitably result in organizational failure. The psychoanalyst Sigmund Freud (2007), for instance, became interested in why armies sometimes suddenly collapse, even though the external threat does not seem to change noticeably. He arrives at the conclusion that disintegration is the main reason. The crumbling of social support structures leads soldiers to fall victim to overpowering fear, because they feel utterly alone and are unable to withstand the terror of looming death on their own. Other empirical studies support this interpretation. The smokejumpers at Mann Gulch, walking at a considerable distance from each other, never really bonded as a team in the first place. As a result, firefighters went their own way when they were confronted with the exploding wildfire, so that the team effectively ceased to exist, even though its leader still had a plan that would have saved all members' lives (Weick, 1993). Under these circumstances, team members can be viewed as "liminal," which refers to their ambiguous status or identity. Their team membership is fluid at best and does not provide them with meaningful bonds that help them understand their own role in the team and how they relate to other members. The disastrous expedition toward the summit of the Mount Everest in 1996 offers an example. During the expedition, there was a

Table 7.1 *The dilemma of team ties*

	Cohesion	Contestation
Characteristics	Strong social bonds	Team heterogeneity
	Team loyalty	Diversity and skepticism
	Enabled by socialization	Internal negotiations
Advantages	Resilient teams	Mindful operations
	High mutual trust	Fosters reflection
	Improved coordination	Fewer operational errors
	Can reduce workplace injuries	
Shortcomings	Risk of groupthink	Risk of conflict and
	Rigid identity	hostility
	Undermining organizational	Team disintegration
	relations	

culture of individualism, as clients and guides had their own motivations for engaging in the summit attempt and failed to develop a sense of collectiveness. The mountain climbers did not know each other well, nor felt a sense of responsibility for each other's welfare. As a result, there was no mutual care or trust. Being little more than a loose collection of individuals, the participants pushed one another over the edge of their abilities toward tragedy and death (Tempest et al., 2007). Dissolution through conflict and disintegration is therefore looming in frontline crisis response teams that embrace contestation at the cost of cohesion (Table 7.1).

Empirical Example

With the growing role of armed forces in domestic emergency response, Dutch officers have been deployed to local emergency management structures in order to facilitate joint civil-military responses to crisis situations. Response activities include evacuations after floods, fighting wildfires, supporting health services overburdened by COVID-19 patients, and implementing counterterrorism measures. The military officers have years or even decades of work experience in the armed forces and are not used to civilian ways of working. They also do not know their new team members in advance, so their integration in these emergency management teams takes some time. Initially, they will try to familiarize themselves with the emergency management structure to which they are deployed, primarily with the purpose to better carry out their formal role of supporting potential military support missions in case of emergencies. As one officer stated: "And my goal [is] representing the armed forces as well as I can and making the deployment of military means possible and useful." Generally, they adopt a restraint posture and avoid getting involved in crisis response activities that do not directly bear upon their formal responsibilities. In practice, this means that they effectively place themselves outside the team, as exemplified by the words of one officer saying: "I am, and will continue to be, a military person." After a few months, they notice that this attitude will keep them sidelined, so they attempt to better integrate in the team and begin to participate as active members, but also continue to prioritize their formal role: "So I remain that man from the armed forces and that's why I am there in the first place. And occasionally, it's okay that I do things in the general interest which have little to do with the armed forces." Role conflicts and even identity crises are looming in this stage, as officers struggle to combine their official responsibilities with ongoing team integration: "Yeah, if I look at how I spend my time and the location where I am most often, I feel stronger connected to the [emergency management team]. [....] But you shouldn't feel at home too much." Over time, they resolve these tensions by combining social integration (i.e., cohesion) with a functional distance (i.e., contestation). Social integration consists of participating in social activities and investing in interpersonal relations: "Every other week, we do sports at the fire station. If you are there, even if it is only with a few people, it is another step toward joining the team." Next, functional distance means that officers rely on their professional, military expertise and do not hesitate to criticize civilian approaches either: "Based on my background, I do not understand that you are organizing in this way." To avoid professional critique escalating into social conflict, it is important for military officers to be tactful and build trusting relations. Even more: "You have to have a degree of sensitivity to others, a sense of empathy, know when to say something, know when not to say something, be very good at listening to others." As such, military officers are able to contribute to reliable and resilient crisis response operations (Kalkman, 2023b).

7.6 A Safe Space

Frontline crisis responders are facing a challenging conundrum. They need to nurture strong bonds and pursue a cohesive team in order to boost performance in extreme contexts and make sure that they look out for each other in situations where danger is always near. This cohesion may also produce dysfunctional group dynamics, which impair safe and effective operations. Instead, intra-team contestation ensures a thorough review of operational understandings and approaches, preempting disastrous team dynamics and enabling reliable responses. Organizing contestation, however, may in turn result in conflicts and team disintegration, potentially dissolving team ties. Thus, frontline response teams face a dilemma when they need to pursue both cohesion and contestation.

To begin with, it is interesting to reflect on Barbusse's (1917) depiction of his squad as a flock or family, in which soldiers had dropped their individuality and almost fully subjected themselves to their unit. The military literature on this topic is by and large consistent. It emphasizes the merits of profound socialization, a dominant culture of comradeship, and strong team ties. Cohesion is generally interpreted as something positive and worthy of being pursued. The difference with other, critical research on cohesion might well be explained by the nature of the tasks that a team or organization is facing. A high level of cohesion is likely of great use in traditional warfare, in which soldierly activities are relatively straightforward. During World War I, for instance, soldiers in the trenches benefited from a strong sense of unity in carrying out a fairly simple order in a more or less predictable operational context. For frontline tasks like this, cohesion seems advantageous and has fewer negative repercussions. It is when tasks grow complex that cohesion becomes potentially more troublesome. Common belief has it that people should rally around the flag in the event of a crisis, but this type of behavior might make a team less capable to handle complex situations instead.

In these complex tasks, such as contemporary combat operations or peacekeeping missions, it is important to hear diverse viewpoints in open debate. If crises are growing more difficult to understand and manage, contestation becomes increasingly relevant to avoid oversimplified perceptions of reality. At this point, it is important to stress that contestation in crisis teams can range from professional disagreements to interpersonal hostility (Marcinkowski et al., 2021). While personal conflicts are undesirable and will undermine team cohesion and performance, work-related disputes do not necessarily have the same effects. In other words, the nature of the contestation matters, and not every conflict is problematic. Indeed, it is possible to make a distinction between task-related and relationship-related tensions. The former produces reflection on decisions, while the latter are potentially troublesome in disrupting social relations. Although these are analytically distinct, there may be spillover effects. Specifically, contestation over tasks, particularly when intense, might harm social relations between responders. This is precisely why teams suffering from groupthink avoid any and all disagreement. In practice, however, it is crucial for responders to maintain workable social relations, while also keeping their professional distance and enabling their critical reflections on proposed crisis response decisions and actions.

Little research has been conducted on how to achieve cohesive teams that promote intra-team contestation, but some suggestions have been offered. Early on, Weick (1993) has argued that it requires team members' trust in one another and their honesty in sharing observations, combined with respect for all team members' contributions. By extension, this means that team members need to have faith in each other's competencies and skills. Trusting others in crises entails considerable risk, so many crisis organizations have lengthy selection procedures and extensive trainings to ensure that personnel dare to rely on each other. The long induction process can bolster cohesion, because team members have similar experiences that help them to bond. It also facilitates contestation, as members are more likely to attach value to each other's perspectives. Thus, mutual trust in another's capabilities potentially feeds back into cohesion and contestation. In a later elaboration, Weick and Sutcliffe (2001) added that inviting skeptics, even though not always easy, is often crucial for doing well in crisis contexts, while self-importance is a recipe for failure. It is not always easy to operationalize this suggestion, but there are some ways to organize contestation in close-knit crisis teams. One option is to allocate the role of devil's advocate to one member, who has to counter the shared consensus in cohesive teams to protect the team against dysfunctional group dynamics. Another option is to split up the team and have sub-units draw up their approaches separately, before joining again and debating differing opinions and views. When crisis teams organize contestation in these ways, they dissociate the disagreement from the individuals, thereby reducing the chances of interpersonal animosity.

Still, tensions will inevitably emerge under conditions of stress and pressure, so it is also useful to build skills for conflict resolution. In that regard, frontline crisis professionals may benefit from training on how to effectively and constructively engage in high-stake discussions when facing a need for urgent decision-making, which may be particularly relevant in crisis organizations where conformity and obedience are revered norms or where debates have soured relationships in the past. By extension, crisis organizations should develop norms for constructive debate over disagreements by promoting mutual respect as a dominant norm for interactions between frontline responders (Weick, 1993; Weick & Sutcliffe, 2001). Respect does not only materialize in a sensitive attitude toward one another, but also in tactful behaviors and confidence in others' good intentions and skills. These initiatives contribute to the aim of forming frontline teams in which members enjoy strong ties, but are nevertheless willing to disagree and constructively engage in discussions. In general, it means that crisis organizations need to foster a safe space for frontline responders to participate in fruitful debate without their disagreements culminating in hostility or resentment.

7.7 Conclusion

Cohesion and contestation are typically viewed as opposites, in which crisis response teams need to find some uncomfortable middle ground by either promoting interpersonal relations in teams with high levels of social conflict or by introducing diversity and skepticism in highly cohesive crisis units with dysfunctional group dynamics. Yet, cohesion and contestation are not mutually exclusive and both can be pursued in conjunction as long as crisis organizations also invest in fostering mutual trust, respect, and a safe space for debate.

It would be worthwhile to gain more insight into whether particular effects of cohesion and contestation are influenced by the nature of crisis activities or the environments in which crisis teams operate. Moreover, many studies focus on the performance of crisis teams, but individual experiences of team cohesion and contestation have received less attention and may offer valuable information on how to organize and manage frontline crisis teams in ways that fit frontline responders' needs. Finally, it is important to identify best practices in designing training programs for responders on engaging in constructive debates during crises and learn from crisis organizations that manage to offer a safe space for dialogue to their frontline responders.

Resources for Educators and Professionals

PRACTICAL LESSONS

- Crisis organizations often aim to build cohesive teams in which members have strong relations, but contestation in teams also has its advantages.
- While cohesion may work well when crisis teams have to carry out straightforward tasks, the implementation of complex tasks benefits from contestation.
- Task-related contestation leads to more reflection on decisions, but may spill over into relational tensions that are potentially dysfunctional.
- Crisis responders can organize contestation to keep disagreements from damaging social relations.
- Mutual respect is key for constructive debate over disagreements while maintaining strong ties.

QUESTIONS FOR REFLECTION AND DISCUSSION

- Which crisis organizations in your environment have particularly cohesive teams? How well do these teams perform in various crisis situations?
- Are crisis response decisions in your organization immediately accepted by everyone? How do colleagues react when someone questions a decision?
- How important are social relationships in your organization? How do people show (dis)respect to one another?

8 | *Structures*
Organizing versus Disorganizing

When faced with a large or complex incident, frontline responders of the US emergency services organize their activities by using the Incident Command System (ICS). This is a formal structure that integrates and controls all their crisis response capabilities and activities. One of the senior responders is made incident commander and is supported by a command staff reporting directly to her. Other crisis responders are divided into four sections and bear responsibility for operations, planning, logistics, or finance and administration. Within each section, frontline personnel are further subdivided into branches that are tasked with specific operations (e.g., air operations) and operational divisions that are in charge of crisis response operations in a geographical area. Divisions, in turn, consist of strike teams and task forces, which implement the required crisis response activities on the ground. Rules and procedures prescribe the actions of everyone, depending on their role and position in the system. This bureaucratic, standardized structure offers certainty and predictability to frontline responders in situations that are characterized by ambiguity and chaos. The ICS also ensures that frontline actions are implemented in a coordinated way, so crises can be resolved as effectively and efficiently as possible (FEMA, 2018). At the same time, the system leaves little space for alternative ways of operating, even when frontline responders would prefer to have a more loosely organized and flexible structure, so they would have more space for creativity and adaptation in unstable crisis situations.

The example demonstrates that a clear, detailed crisis response structure offers predictability and support to frontline responders, which is particularly welcome in disrupted, stressful crisis situations. It also adds to a widespread belief that an optimal structure can be designed for quick and effective resolutions of crisis situations. Practitioners and researchers alike are searching for the best way to organize crisis response operations. Yet, emergency responders often notice that the formal structure impedes much-needed response actions, so they feel a need to ignore organizational elements in their operations to better manage the incident. The dilemma for responders is therefore that both disorganization and organization may be needed for effective crisis response.

8.1 Organizational Structures for Crisis Response

A crisis response structure is typically designed in advance and remains dormant until a crisis activates it. When such structures are not yet in place, responders will create them in situ to resolve the threatening situation. Adequate crisis response seems therefore to rely on forming the right kind of organizational structure. The ideal structure must both enable a rapid, effective crisis response and should be usable across a range of different crisis situations. Aiming to meet both conditions, emergency services in several Western countries came up with similar Incident Command Systems as the preferred response structure. The quest for the optimal crisis response structure is not limited to emergency services though. In the humanitarian sector, the United Nations Office for the Coordination of Humanitarian Affairs (UNOCHA) has gained a central position in the organization of international responses to a broad range of disasters and other humanitarian crises, while armed forces have undergone repeated organizational changes to create military structures that are more effective in future warfare and other operations.

The common denominator in these developments is that crisis responders search for an adequate crisis structure that can enable a quick, well-organized response and avoid crisis escalation. Latent crisis structures, which are familiar and can be instantly triggered, may indeed end a crisis in an effective and efficient manner. The ICS, for example, is praised for demonstrating "remarkable reliability under a broad range of working conditions, including those marked by extreme uncertainty and instability" (Bigley & Roberts, 2001, p. 1281). The ICS was initially developed by practitioners seeking to improve interagency coordination in response to several California wildfires. The system was subsequently adopted by emergency responders from different states and for various crisis situations, before it became the standard crisis structure for all domestic emergencies in the US. By providing standardized procedures as well as a formal hierarchy, the

ICS is believed to enable the efficient exercise of centralized guidance over collective actions (Bigley & Roberts, 2001; Moynihan, 2009).

The ICS is not uncontested though. It has been criticized for being overly rigid in nature and excessively controlling toward frontline responders. Due to its paramilitary structure, it leaves insufficient room for flexible and adaptive behaviors at the frontline, particularly when crises become more complex. There have also been objections against the fact that a single system was warranted for use during every crisis, regardless of limited evidence in support of it. In practice though, its actual implementation varies widely anyway, so that responders often do not even make use of it in their work (Buck et al., 2006; Jensen & Thompson, 2016). Clearly, there is a tension between the formal, bureaucratic rules and procedures that are central to the ICS and the unanticipated demands of modern-day crises.

Increasingly, adaptive organizational structures have been promoted instead. The identification of so-called High Reliability Organizations (HROs) provides some interesting insights. HROs are organizations that operate in volatile and uncertain contexts with virtually no errors and show resilience in the face of looming failure (Weick & Sutcliffe, 2001). Examples of such organizations are aircraft carriers, intensive care units, and airlines (Roberts & Bea, 2001). Research on these organizations confirms time and again that certain organizing elements, like a sensitivity to operations and deference to (lower-level) experts, are key to continuous high performance (Weick & Sutcliffe, 2001). What is telling, is that high-reliability organizations do not have a fixed division of tasks, roles, or responsibilities, but adopt a flexible attitude to such structuring elements. Other research confirms that adaptive organizing is crucial in response to crises. During disasters, responders need to be enabled to reallocate resources and tasks depending on where the needs are the highest and on who is in the best position to decide or act. They have to reorder relationships to strengthen ties with unofficial and unforeseen partners, so they can gather information from informal sources and coordinate with informal groups. And they should be able to engage in unanticipated behaviors through planning for creative behaviors (Comfort & Kapucu, 2006; Dynes, 1994; Quarantelli, 1997b; Rimstad et al., 2014; Webb & Chevreau, 2006).

In practice, it is possible for both types of organizing to coexist. Faraj and Xiao (2006) studied medical trauma teams and found that they generally follow rather formalized mechanisms for coordinated medical action. Occasionally, however, the state of the patient's health requires a different type of intervention that is not laid down in rules or roles. In those cases, different specialists may intervene beyond their role descriptions, and protocols are broken, because this adaptive way of organizing is believed to be in the patient's interest. Likewise, studying high-speed police pursuits, Schakel and Wolbers (2021) describe how police teams shift between formalized and flexible modes of organizing throughout a pursuit. As teams shift between organizational structures, command switches between various organizational layers, control over resources is rearranged, and the nature of information-sharing changes. The complexity of the operation (i.e., speed, number of involved actors, and area of operations) explains these shifts, with the formal structure sufficing at predictable situations, while flexible organizational modes are much needed when the rapidity, number of responders, or area of operations increases.

At the end of the day, the scientific debate is about how bureaucratic the response structure should be, either in general or during particular crisis response situations. This debate between proponents of a bureaucratic structure and those advocating for a loose structure has continued unabated for decades. The intensity of the discussions might almost blind us to the fact that researchers, regardless of their different viewpoints, build on the same assumption: a well-designed organizational structure is the basis of good crisis response.

8.2 Emergent Organizing

In some crises, such response structures are either absent or failing. When this happens, citizens will usually unite and take matters into their own hands. To this end, they engage in emergent organizing, which refers to the process of structuring tasks, allocating responsibilities, and organizing activities on the ground. Such emergent organizing occurs, for instance, when volunteers gather after a major disaster and organize themselves to guide their spontaneous response efforts. Indeed, new groups are likely to emerge, as people gather and begin to collectively contribute to resolving the crises (Lanzara, 1983; Quarantelli & Dynes, 1977). Such emergent behavior is fairly common in crisis responses. Recent research has demonstrated examples of emergent organizing by volunteers who carried out a maritime evacuation after the attacks of 9/11 (Kendra & Wachtendorf, 2016), reduced suffering after the 2009 Black Saturday bushfires in Australia (Shepherd & Williams, 2014), and even rose up against a terrorist hijacking of their airplane (Quinn & Worline, 2008). The loose structure of these groups enables their ongoing emergent organizing in the early phase of the crisis and allows them to make major contributions to resolving the crisis situation.

Emergent organizing may have other origins as well. Established organizations, faced with their own limitations, can put aside personnel and resources for the construction of new response structures. The COVID-19 crisis, for instance, created a whole new set of demands for which established crisis organizations were insufficiently prepared. Health agencies and supporting military organizations created novel, temporary structures to respond to the pandemic. One example is the formation of a coordination center in charge of redistributing COVID-19 patients over different hospitals to share the burden (Zijderveld & Kalkman, Forthcoming). Likewise, after Hurricane Katrina, local firefighters and police officers improvised search and rescue activities by dividing areas of operations, allocating tasks, using local boats to check flooded buildings, creating a shelter in an abandoned supermarket, and collecting radios to replace failing formal communication means (Rodriguez et al., 2006). In many crisis response operations, emergent coordination between organizations is common as well, because contemporary crises increasingly require the coordinated response of multiple (unfamiliar) organizations (Alvinius et al., 2010; Drabek & McEntire, 2002; Morris et al., 2007). An interesting study by Beck and Plowman (2014) analyzes the aftermath of the Columbia space shuttle disaster. It shows how organizations came together and began to coordinate their efforts to search and recover shuttle material. Although many of the involved organizations were strangers to each other, their concurrent response actions and interactions led to an emergent response structure and produced a successful recovery mission.

Emergent organizations can therefore have different roots, but the results are similar: a novel and flexible organizational structure is created to handle a crisis situation that established organizations cannot effectively put to a halt. As such, emergent organizations reestablish order and normality after an unanticipated disruption. In principle, this subscribes to the general idea that a well-designed organizational structure, even though it is designed emergently during the crisis, is the basis of rapid, coordinated crisis response.

8.3 Crisis and Organization

While crisis researchers have different perspectives on the best way to organize for crisis response, there is a shared and dominant belief that crisis response requires (further) organizing. Implicitly, the words "organization" and "crisis" are viewed as antithetical nouns. Crises are described as moments of chaos and disruption, which can only be brought back to normality through organizing. To resolve the crisis, the responding crisis structure must not subsume to the disorder that characterizes the environment, but stand strong and bring order and stability. There are clear normative undertones in this definition of disorder as the problem and organizing as the solution. It will also come as no surprise that disorganization of the crisis response structure is subsequently perceived as dangerous and disturbing.

One of the problems with disorganization is that it precedes organizational dissolution and thereby harms crisis response performance. Crises can lead to stakeholders or employees withdrawing from the organization, decisions that are no longer supported or followed, and standardized organizational processes grinding to a halt (Pearson & Clair, 1998). When organizations do not unite to control and reverse this dissolution process, organizations are left increasingly weak and powerless. In a network context, such as the humanitarian sector, a lack of structure also poses a major challenge. Disaster relief is notoriously characterized by fierce competition between NGOs, which not only rush to the disaster scene to provide live-saving aid, but also struggle to gain (media) attention for their relief work so they can attract more donations and funding. This rivalry impedes coordination and the resulting humanitarian effort produces suboptimal results.

If the distribution of tasks, allocation of roles, coordination mechanisms, and other structuring elements are abandoned, frontline crisis responders experience little organizational support and have to fend for themselves. Tempest et al. (2007) explain that the 1996 Mount Everest climbing disaster, in which multiple mountain climbers died, can partially be explained by the liminality of team members, who felt no connection to each other and were a group of individuals rather than an actual team. As a result, they had no sense of joint responsibility and lacked mutual understanding, leading them to push each other beyond their abilities in a merciless environment. In extreme contexts, such dissolution may easily lead frontline members to succumb to fear as well. Soldiers, confronted with the enemy, will only stand strong in the company of their comrades. O'Brien (2015, pp. 215–216), a US veteran of the Vietnam War, tells: "at dusk they'd put on their gear and move out single file into the dark. Always a heavy cloud cover. No moon and no stars. It was the purest black you could imagine [...] So pretty soon you'd get jumpy. Your nerves would go. You'd start to worry about getting cut off from the rest of the unit – alone, you'd think – and then the real panic would bang in and you'd reach out and try to touch the guy in front of you, groping for his shirt, hoping to Christ he was still there." In general, soldiers are likely to give in to anxiety and flee when their unit has dissolved and they feel utterly alone (Freud, 2007). Military rituals, including detailed paperwork and unyielding bureaucracy, may therefore gain in importance when a unit is on the verge of surrender or defeat, and serve as a means of coping with fear (Holmes, 1986). A collapse of the organization, from this perspective, is a harbinger of disaster.

Vice versa, organizing efforts are crucial for transforming a situation of chaos and disruption into a calm and manageable situation. By means of these organizing activities, order is "enacted into the event" (Christianson et al., 2009, p. 852). This idea is reflected in many crisis response studies as well as in recent literature reviews on crisis management. One of these reviews described crisis management as a process of "coordinating stakeholders and resources in an ambiguous environment to bring a disrupted system (i.e., organization, community, etc.) back into alignment" (Williams et al., 2017, p. 737). Another emphasizes building relations, information-sharing, collective meaning-construction, and collective actions as crucial to the response effort in the aftermath of emergencies and disruptions (Hällgren et al., 2018). These reviews reiterate the prevailing opinion in research on frontline crisis response, which holds that organizing alone can overcome crises and restore a much-needed state of stability and order, whereas disorganization causes disorder and is problematic and even dangerous.

8.4 Disorganizing for Crisis Response

Disorganization has been identified as the cause of organizational failure and collapse during crises, but the process of disorganizing has received almost no attention from crisis researchers. It should come as no surprise that it is often ignored though. We are being trained to see and study organizing in response to crises, so we might fail to recognize disorganizing, even when it takes place right in front of us. Some scholars, however, have argued that disorganization (or disorder) and organization (or order) are mutually constitutive. From this perspective, when one organizational form replaces another, the latter is necessarily disorganized, which means ordering always simultaneously produces disorder. Disorder will particularly come to the fore in moments of disruption, such as crises, because these situations destabilize stable and seemingly permanent orderings (e.g., Knox et al., 2015). Although these insights offer useful insight into the relationship between organization and disorganization, it risks becoming very abstract and theoretical. Specific organizations, however, may also become more or less structured and add or remove organizational elements. While a bureaucratic, formal organization may do well in very predictable, repetitive work, frontline crisis response typically requires ad hoc, unforeseen, and unique activities. As a result, frontline responders may need to abandon structuring elements and move toward a looser organizational structure, which is a process that can best be described as "disorganizing."

In the practice of frontline crisis response, disorganizing is the opposite of crisis organizing. It is about the disassembly of coordination, relaxing control over people and resources, breaking down routines and roles, keeping or withholding information, and individualizing sensemaking (cf. Christianson et al., 2009; Hällgren et al., 2018; Maitlis & Christianson, 2014; Pearson & Clair, 1998; Weick, 1993; Williams et al., 2017). It constitutes the introduction of uncertainty and disorder into the crisis response.

This may sound puzzling, but to some extent, our strict focus on crisis organizing says more about our imagination than about what we are observing, because disorganizing is quite common in crisis organizations. Organizations, generally, have even been viewed as organized anarchies. Decision-makers, goals, solutions, and problems often come together in an arbitrary way when choices have to be made (Cohen et al., 1972). Retrospectively, we come to see and explain the decision-making process as a rational endeavor, even though the process was messy, uncertain, and ill understood at the time. This also points at a problem of conducting post hoc interviews with frontline crisis responders: they may offer perfectly reasonable explanations for their choices and actions, but their behaviors might have been irrational or random at the moment. Inevitably, however, they will ignore the organizational design with its formal task descriptions, standardized processes, and predefined relations between members. Take the protagonist of Remarque's (2004) *All quiet on the Western Front*, serving at the German frontlines during World War I: He runs and attacks or ducks and hides, but half of the time, he does not understand why he acts in a certain way, nor can he give a justification for his own actions. He simply acts without heeding organizational routines, roles, or instructions. Crisis disorganizing, clearly, is a practical reality.

Disorganizing crisis response structures can resolve the recurring problem of over-organization. In practice, over-organized structures are just as likely as disintegrated structures to fail in crisis response. For example, while analyzing the Tenerife air crash, one can blame the lack of integration among team members in the KLM cockpit that led it to crash into another aircraft (Weick, 1990), but it seems just as convincing to argue that the seemingly fixed allocation of roles and authority hindered the first officer and flight engineer from voicing their safety concerns. And members of the London counter-terrorism police unit were entangled into preplanned frames, scripts, and roles, which led to disastrous confusion and miscommunication instead of an open-minded analysis of the situation (Colville et al., 2013). These risks of over-organization may explain why a few crisis organizations, such as the Red Cross, operate without many structuring elements. Quarantelli and Dynes (1977, p. 31) write that these organizations "have very amorphous boundaries, few clear-cut members, indistinct subunit relationships, vague lines of authority, and global, almost symbolic, rather than instrumental goals." It is a description reminiscent of an organized anarchy. Special operations forces also prefer to avoid over-organization, because sticking to pre-designed organizational structures, mandates, and routines reduces their ability to adapt to the threatening, uncertain environment in which they are operating and thus hinders mission accomplishment (Dalgaard-Nielsen, 2017).

If crises are unique situations, full of uncertainties and surprises, this means that planned structures will necessarily face (potentially fundamental) shortcomings (McConnell & Drennan, 2006). In hospital emergency units, for example, programmed coordination structures fail in situations of high uncertainty about patients' conditions, so non-programmed means of coordination need to be invented by frontline personnel on the spot in these cases (Argote, 1982). To effectively address a crisis nevertheless, frontline responders do not only need to adapt their actions, but also get rid of inhibiting structures. During the crisis, frontline responders have to introduce new roles and routines, while abandoning outdated, pre-crisis task distributions and implementation procedures (see Christianson et al., 2009; Suarez & Montes, 2019; Wolbers et al., 2018). In other words, they need to disorganize and organize at the same time, as traditional structures are (temporarily) overthrown and replaced with new ones that frontline responders believe will better fit the unfolding situation. One example of this dynamic comes from an experiment with nuclear power plant control crews facing a crisis, which demonstrated that more effective teams discarded formalized, routinized interaction patterns during the incidents and resorted to simpler modes of communication to coordinate their actions (Stachowski et al., 2009). Generally, when the crisis structures during a response are adapted or newly invented, there must be simultaneous or preceding disorganizing taking place. The emergence of novel structural elements receives usually more attention than the discarding of the old, but predefined relations, roles, and routines have to be dropped as new structural elements are being introduced to improve the crisis response efforts.

Such disorganizing may even help frontline crisis responders in the implementation of their activities. Task distributions, role allocations, and coordination mechanisms enable efficient performance, but also risk blinding frontline responders to any information beyond their task or role (Weick, 2004). Compartmentalized response structures, which are common in emergency, humanitarian and military contexts, make it hard for individual responders to look and think beyond their specific areas of responsibility and assess the broader impact of their own or their organization's efforts. For instance, high levels of task differentiation made US fighter pilots involved in the Black Hawk shootdown incident in Iraq heedless about their operational environment, drawing them into making a disastrous mistake. They thought their colleagues on the ground had to update

Table 8.1 *The dilemma of organizational structures*

	Organizing	Disorganizing
Characteristics	Designing an optimal structure	Abandoning structuring elements
	Formal or emergent structures	
	Provides order and stability	Moving toward a looser, less ordered structure
Advantages	Resolves chaos and disruption	Avoids over-organization
	Rapid response	Facilitates adaptation and new organizing
	Effective coordination	
Shortcomings	Ineffective operations in uncertain situations	Risk of organizational dissolution
	Inhibits adaptive responses	Lack of support to responders

them about air movements by friendly aircraft, so did not engage in serious sensemaking, but assumed that unidentified helicopters were those of the enemy and shot them down before realizing their mistake (Snook, 2002). Likewise, border guards during the European refugee crisis were more likely to provide humanitarian aid to refugees when they had broadly defined responsibilities rather than very specific task descriptions. Those with specific responsibilities duly implemented their tasks as fingerprinters, document experts, or screeners, but failed to see and address the pressing humanitarian needs in front of them (Kalkman, 2019a). Disorganizing, then, prevents a situation in which people are unable to assess the broader impact of their work and become passive implementers. It activates crisis responders and makes them aware of the crisis organization's goals, while also enabling them to contribute to reaching these ends in a creative, adaptive manner.

Disorganizing is an important process, even, or maybe particularly, in crises. These situations force frontline responders to reconsider fixed structures and potentially abandon preexisting organizational elements that no longer suffice. When role structures or coordination mechanisms falter and fail, clasping to such organizing structures is likely counterproductive. To some extent, responders need to incorporate the disorder of their environments in their operations to be effective (Table 8.1).

Empirical Example

The humanitarian aid mission to the Bahamas by the Dutch, German, and French armed forces after Hurricane Dorian was prepared in detail before arrival in the affected area. The military task force adopted a traditional, organizational approach that consisted of familiar structuring elements. A clear hierarchy was created with top-down command and bottom-up reporting. Officers on all levels started defining their aims and planning their activities. Strict safety standards were set and communicated throughout the task force. Routines for processes like internal communication and resource acquisition were specified. And team ties were emphasized as a means to a fast, coordinated intervention. While these structuring elements were well known and broadly accepted, the operational context made it hard to use this formal, bureaucratic structure in practice. Soldiers on the ground began to view it as an over-organized structure that did not match operational realities and thus started to discard it once they began their relief activities. They took discretionary actions and attached limited value to reporting their activities to their superiors. The general in charge of the relief mission admitted: "We had thought we would be able to control [the mission] to a larger extent, but things developed so rapidly that this proved impossible." Simultaneously, the planning approach was replaced with ad hoc activities by frontline personnel: "They tried to walk through a nice planning process, but if it came down to 'which effects need to be achieved where', they could not make it concrete, which was very logical, because we simply did not have enough information." Safety standards, as well, were widely ignored, as soldiers took considerable risks to deliver as much humanitarian aid as possible in a short time-span, guided by the belief that "necessity knows no law." To give one example, they conducted air operations even though "there was no communication at the airfield, but there was a lot of air traffic without the control tower being staffed. There was no radio network, no safety, nothing, but there were very large air planes." Similarly, routines were discarded, for instance by bypassing formal resource acquisition procedures and shifting to basic communication tools: "WhatsApp was working on the island and it allows you to rapidly distribute information among units, whereas the secure, normal connections of Defense do not." Finally, even team ties were weakened and seemed to dissolve. A visual data analysis of over 200 photographs produced during the mission period of ten days shows that military personnel worked less and less in units and increasingly in dyads or alone. The disorganization of these structuring elements did not lead to a complete dissolution of the organization though. Indeed, a new, temporary organizational form very rapidly emerged. This new structure was more loose and flexible than the preexisting, formal structure, and allowed for an adaptive response by frontline personnel to the disaster for the time being, but it required prior disorganizing before it could emerge (Kalkman, 2023a).

8.5 Reorganizing the Response

When thinking about crisis response, the importance of organizing is fixed in our brains and writings as the normal, necessary, and even the right thing to do. Public leaders and operational managers are expected to create effective crisis structures and if these fail to resolve the crisis, emergent organizations will take their place. Since organizing has become synonymous to creating order, crisis structures are means to transform disorderly situations into normal ones again. Yet, there are indications that disorganizing is not only inevitable in frontline crisis response but also beneficial in many ways. This introduces a dilemma for frontline crisis responders, tasked with constructing a response structure during a crisis, because both organizing and disorganizing might be needed and advantageous.

One solution would be to find the best organizational design for crisis response efforts. This structure would be located somewhere on the axis between over-organization and disorganization. When researchers reflect on the ICS, for instance, they argue that it strikes the right balance (e.g., Bigley & Roberts, 2001), or instead, they state that it is too formal and bureaucratic (i.e., over-organized) (e.g., Dynes, 1994). Here, the type of crisis matters. The ICS, for example, may work well for rather straightforward and predictable incidents, while its performance in crises, which are highly uncertain and urgent, is less overwhelming (Buck et al., 2006). It seems that one fixed response structure cannot adequately address the various crisis situations that it is supposed to resolve.

In some crises, the events will still appear as manageable to frontline responders. Their allocation of responsibilities and coordination of activities might undergo some minor changes, but the organizational structure itself remains intact. Bechky and Okhuysen (2011), for example, studied a special weapons and tactics (SWAT) team of the US police, which was frequently faced with unexpected situations during attempts to arrest risky suspects. The researchers found various adaptive behaviors that enabled team members to continue their work if they faced such a situation. Members of the police team could rapidly switch roles or replace an existing routine with another well-known routine. Flexible organizing ensured good performance. Other crisis scholars also emphasize flexibility, decentralizing coordination, and experimentation as adaptive organizational behavior (Beck & Plowman, 2014; Drabek & McEntire, 2002; Weick, 1993). Creating space for spontaneous behaviors implies some disorganizing, as plans or structures are temporarily put on hold or substituted. Typically, these adaptations are limited and temporary though, such as the replacement of one role structure or coordination mechanism by another.

During uncertain crises, however, drastic changes to the organizational structure are required. The role structure or coordination mechanisms might be abandoned without directly putting an alternative in its place, so that frontline responders can make full use of their own experience and enjoy broad discretionary power or to allow them to slowly construct a more fitting, emergent structure during the response effort. After Hurricane Dorian, the military unit faced a crisis that exceeded responders' imaginations and preparations. Mere adaptive changes could no longer suffice, so disorganizing became virtually inevitable or the crisis response effort would fail. Interestingly, this was a choice made by frontline responders, who loosened ties, dropped plans, and abandoned role structures, without gaining prior approval of their remotely located superiors. Their largely disorganized approach proved to be successful (Kalkman, 2023a).

In both situations, disorganizing takes place, albeit in different ways. In common or predictable crises, disorganizing is a constraint process and serves the clear purpose of getting rid of a structural element in order to replace it with another, more appropriate one. Here, disorganizing is a deliberate decision, as frontline responders take charge of the disorganizing process to ensure that inhibiting elements are dissolved, but the organization does not radically change in character. In uncertain and complex crises, however, disorganizing is more likely to be a far-reaching process and does not serve an immediate goal, nor is an alternative structure instantly available. Disorganizing, in this case, may manifest itself in the deliberate decision to drop structuring elements, but can also be an unmanaged (or even unmanageable) process triggered by the extreme crisis context (i.e., emergent disorganizing).

Some new, emergent structure will have to appear to avoid organizational disintegration, but the nature of the organization will be fundamentally different in any case.

This view on disorganizing suggests that it is a common process in crises, even though it has not received much attention in the academic literature, except as a cause of failure. Disorganizing, in practice, is bound to be experienced as disquieting by frontline responders. Operating under a disorganized structure is highly demanding and often leads to increased anxiety and stress (e.g., Freud, 2007; Weick, 1993). In turn, this means that frontline personnel need to have a certain level of comfort with chaos and uncertainty to avoid succumbing to fear and remain productive when they have to decide and act autonomously and with little organizational support. Research on US Navy Seals shows that this comfort with the uncomfortable enables them to innovate, experiment, and bounce back from failures, even under the most difficult circumstances (Fraher et al., 2017). In addition, frontline personnel need to reflect on how much disorganizing is necessary during a particular crisis and when it is time to revert to the original organizational structures. And even a single crisis may go through various stages, which require various degrees and forms of disorganizing and organizing. Crises, generally, will therefore introduce a constant need for reorganizing.

Reorganizing, from this view, refers to intermittent and simultaneous disorganizing and organizing by frontline crisis responders throughout a crisis situation. Disorganizing can be important in the very early stage of a crisis, when the involved crisis responders are still missing an understanding of the situation, but preexisting structures already prove misinformed and responders feel a need to reorganize. This reorganization can be profound, such as the complete dismantling of the organizational structure and the reconstruction of a new one, or it may be limited to a specific structuring element, such as the modification of coordination mechanisms. Over time, with the crisis waning and entering its more predictable aftermath, familiar response structures can be restored again, unless new unexpected events demand another reorganization of the crisis structure. Ultimately, the crisis and organizational response structure need to develop synchronously. If frontline crisis responders manage to achieve this, the response structure does not determine how a crisis is handled in advance, but it is continuously reorganized in line with emerging demands.

8.6 Conclusion

It is impossible to design a perfect crisis response structure that is effective in every possible crisis scenario, so any organizational structure needs to be reorganized during a crisis by disorganizing structural elements and organizing them anew. This continuous reorganization of the response structure by frontline responders is crucial to construct the appropriate structure for the specific crisis that responders are trying to resolve.

The disorganizing process deserves much more attention in general and it would be interesting to discover why frontline responders decide that dismantling a structuring element is needed and how they proceed next. In addition, there are some indications that disorganizing increases anxiety among frontline personnel, but there are many open questions as to how exactly disorganizing processes influence frontline crisis responders' emotional states. Likewise, reorganizing will inevitably reallocate power and control in the organization, so it may also produce tensions, which is another topic for further research. Finally, we would benefit from additional process analyses of reorganizing dynamics in crisis response structures, so we can improve our understanding of how disorganizing and organizing processes interact and what they produce.

Resources for Educators and Professionals

PRACTICAL LESSONS

- Organizational structures are supposed to help crisis responders bring order in chaos, but disorganizing is beneficial during many crises as well.
- Preexisting crisis response structures generally work well in anticipated incidents when minor changes to organizational structures suffice.
- Complex, uncertain crises require more elaborate dismantling of structuring elements to create space for the construction of a fundamentally new, emergent structure.
- Frontline personnel have to decide how much and what type of disorganizing is necessary in a given situation, but will inevitably face more uncertainty as a result.
- Crisis response structures have to be continuously reorganized to adapt to evolving crises.

QUESTIONS FOR REFLECTION AND DISCUSSION

– During which recent crises did the formal crisis response structure not work well and what were the main reasons?

– What was the most unexpected, complex crisis that you faced in your career and what changes did your crisis organization undergo to manage it? What were the advantages of these changes?

– Are people in your organization prepared for reorganizing the crisis response structure? How would you design the organization in preparation of a very complex, unfamiliar crisis?

9 | Coordination
Integration versus Fragmentation

Hurricane Katrina struck Louisiana and Mississippi on August 29, 2005. In its aftermath, numerous levees and floodwalls failed, leaving New Orleans inundated and producing a catastrophic disaster. As a result, over 1,300 people died and hundreds of thousands were displaced, while the physical destruction made it the most expensive weather-related disaster in US history. The Federal Emergency Management Agency (FEMA) was in charge of coordinating the disaster response effort, but its relations with the armed forces, another main player in the response, were fraught and complex. Indeed, frontline coordination between FEMA and military personnel was complicated. There was a lack of information sharing and communication, mutual unfamiliarity, and no shared control structure. Most military branches pursued integration with FEMA through exchanging liaisons, organizing meetings, and setting up formal collaboration mechanisms, but this took time and the DOD was afterward criticized for slow interagency coordination as well as a delayed response. The US Coast Guard distinguished itself as the only branch of the armed forces that managed to produce a rapid response. Its members were the first to systematically search and rescue survivors after the hurricane. They did so initially without clear agreements with FEMA officials on how to harmonize activities. For instance, there were no procedures for handing over victims to other organizations after they had been rescued. Over time, Coast Guard officials did increase interactions with collaboration partners, but typically on an ad hoc basis and often informally. As a consequence, it was criticized for imperfect coordination and a fragmented, suboptimal crisis response in post hoc evaluations (Morris et al., 2007; Sanial, 2007; United States Congress, 2006).

Coordination between crisis organizations is widely perceived to be essential to operational crisis response. Failing interorganizational coordination was indeed recognized as a major reason for the dramatic response to Hurricane Katrina. Yet, the example also shows that coordination can take different forms. Most military branches tried to be integrated in the collective response network to coordinate their activities with partner organizations, but this coordination was slow to materialize after the hurricane. Alternatively, the Coast Guard simply focused on its own responsibilities and minimized integration as a result, resulting in potentially inefficient and ineffective operations. Military and FEMA personnel, in the example, clearly faced a coordination dilemma: they could try to reach detailed agreements and ensure a harmonization of their activities or choose for a rapid deployment by delineating areas of responsibility and reducing (the need for) interactions. The challenge for frontline responders is that good crisis response requires both speed and an adequate use of scarce resources, while both approaches to coordination seem to achieve either one or the other. This observation raises questions on how to organize interorganizational coordination at the frontline during crises.

9.1 The Need for Coordination

Disasters, such as Hurricane Katrina, require extensive coordination between a variety of organizations, including emergency services, NGOs, private companies, and volunteer groups. Ultimately, hundreds of organizations may get involved and be active at the frontlines of the crisis. To ensure a successful response with this vast number of diverse actors, effective interorganizational communication and collaboration are important (Kapucu, 2006; Waugh Jr & Streib, 2006). When multiple organizations interact to harmonize their frontline activities, they are more likely to efficiently reach their shared objective of resolving the crisis (Drabek & McEntire, 2002).

Such interorganizational coordination is increasingly important due to the changing nature of crises. Contemporary crises are often crossing geographical and functional boundaries, so that professionals from various organizations and different regions will have to participate and collaborate in the transboundary crisis response efforts (Ansell et al., 2010). The 2014 Ebola outbreak in West Africa offers an example, because it led to the involvement of governmental, community, and humanitarian actors across all levels, varying from local religious leaders to the World Health Organization. All shared a collective goal of bringing the epidemic to a halt, but their different backgrounds and approaches complicated coordinated action (Walsh &

Johnson, 2018). After the Columbia shuttle disaster, next, some 25,000 responders of over 130 organizations were participating in the response (Beck & Plowman, 2014). But even regular emergencies may require the involvement of a large group of public and private organizations.

It is worthwhile noting that coordination is a broad term anyway and can apply to many different practices. First, it can refer to mere ad hoc, informal information sharing between two frontline responders on the ground, but it also encompasses a virtual merger of organizations that integrate their activities to such an extent that it becomes hard to distinguish the contributing parties over time. Next, crisis response coordination can take place between two or a few partners in the heat of a crisis, but often also occurs in networks that consist of multiple organizations with a long-term commitment to improving coordination. Some of these coordination efforts, moreover, are mandated when (public) organizations are tasked to work together in particular situations, but for other organizations, coordination is voluntary and therefore likely conditional upon their pragmatic use for it.

There are different mechanisms for organizing coordination between crisis organizations. First, coordination can be imposed through top-down interventions. Such hierarchical structures emerge when there is one organization or individual with a relatively powerful position, who plays a leading role in coordinating the available resources and personnel. The US Incident Command System with its centralized leadership, clear chain of command, and emphasis on formal authority offers an example (Scott & Nowell, 2020). Also, during military missions, civil-military collaboration for reconstruction and conflict resolution may be dominated by well-resourced armed forces that effectively fund and protect civilian partners (Keane & Wood, 2016; Rietjens & Bollen, 2008). Alternatively, in networked forms of collaboration, organizations retain their autonomy and coordinate their activities on a more equal footing through dialogue and negotiation. One example comes from the humanitarian sector, in which NGOs meet and coordinate activities under the auspices of the UNOCHA, but maintain their independence and can withdraw from the coordination efforts at any moment (see Stephenson, 2005).

Crisis researchers do not always agree on how to organize crisis coordination, as some prefer a hierarchical approach, while others advocate for a networked way of working. Still, they are united in the belief that crises require coordination efforts between frontline personnel of responding organizations. In addition, there is broad consensus that coordination often fails in crises. Evaluations of emergency, military, and humanitarian operations frequently lament poor harmonization of activities between involved actors and recommend improvement of interorganizational coordination. Its importance and complexity make coordination one of the most extensively studied themes in crisis response research.

9.2 Integration of the Collective Response Effort

In practice, coordination is usually pursued through attempts to integrate the work of frontline responders from different crisis organizations, either through hierarchical or networked coordination forms. The aim is to incorporate disjointed, independent activities in one collective endeavor. This means that the involved actors come together to ensure that their activities are better harmonized with those of others. Organizations can thus support each other or at least avoid counteracting one another. There are several methods that help to integrate dispersed frontline crisis response efforts.

One way to pursue integration in crisis response is by creating command centers or operations centers, in which representatives of various organizations convene to coordinate their work. This typically takes the form of Emergency Operations Centers (EOCs), which are activated when a crisis unfolds and are positioned near the incident location site or at a predetermined location, depending on whether its members are participating in the response operations or only supporting frontline personnel. In the EOC, involved crisis responders of various agencies regularly meet to harmonize their deployment of available personnel and resources or discuss the collective crisis response approach (Ansell et al., 2010; Beck & Plowman, 2014; Militello et al., 2007; Quarantelli, 1997b). The meeting space allows them to quickly share information that they believe might be of relevance to responders from other organizations and prevent them from getting in each other's way when the response is in progress. As such, the EOC typically functions as a central information and coordination hub during incidents and disasters. The importance of operations centers for integrating multi-organizational efforts is well demonstrated by the response to the 9/11 attacks on the World Trade Centre. The attacks destroyed the physical infrastructure of the EOC, but emergency managers rapidly and successfully improvised a new EOC facility, which at some point hosted about 250 organizations, because frontline responders shared a belief that the EOC was key to response integration and therefore crucial to success (Kendra & Wachtendorf, 2003b).

Colocation of representatives from crisis organizations benefits integrative coordination in another way as well. It breeds familiarity between responders and allows for building social relations that boost collaboration (Beck & Plowman, 2014). Based on a study of interorganizational crisis teams responding to wildfires in the US, Nowell and Steelman (2015) report that representatives from organizations that were already familiar with each other were more likely to communicate and found communication less problematic than representatives without such social ties. Close relations, even friendship, was also identified as the main factor of success in collaboration between the Norwegian police, fire department, and ambulance services (Kristiansen et al., 2019). Even in difficult interorganizational partnerships, such as those between armed forces and humanitarian agencies, familiarity between frontline personnel can build trust and inspire confidence in unlikely crisis partners (Bollen, 2002). Thus, the effectiveness of crisis coordination structures are viewed as conditional upon the quality of interpersonal relations and mutual trust between those who inhabit them, which means that it is important to invest in networking before crises occur (Chang & Trainor, 2018; McEntire, 2002).

Strong relations between crisis responders allow them to transcend the confines of their separate organizations and reach a collective culture, identity, and understandings, coalescing in a common operational repertoire that allows for synchronized actions. This process features prominently in the disaster response effort after the crash of the Columbia space shuttle in 2003. Responders from over 130 organizations were strangers to each other and involved in independent response efforts, but they became part of a coherent, collaborative effort in a period of weeks. Crucial in this process was the creation of a collective identity, which emerged as the disaster response team developed into a united entity and its members started to increasingly identify with the overarching organization rather than only their own organization (Beck & Plowman, 2014). Integration attempts during the Columbia recovery effort brought people together and created a collective out of a number of strangers, whose successful collaboration benefited from their shared vision, common values, and joint planning (see Donahue, 2006). Something similar holds for police officers and ambulance staff in the UK, who share cultural characteristics that facilitate their collaboration. Frontline personnel of both organizations perceive communication as crucial in their work, they have a similar type of humor, and both attach value to storytelling. As such, organizational boundaries can be more easily crossed to produce strong working relations between ambulance and police personnel (Charman, 2015).

When frontline personnel of involved crisis organizations do not have a sense of collectiveness or even lack familiarity, it is useful to appoint liaisons or boundary spanners. They act as representatives on behalf of their organization and can advise others on the resources and capabilities that their organization can deploy in a particular crisis. They also play a key role in scanning for relevant information that might be of use to partner organizations as well as collect and analyze information from the environment that their own colleagues need to know. As such, they play a crucial role in bridging interorganizational gaps and facilitating coordination (Curnin et al., 2014). Research on Swedish military officers, for instance, shows that their collaboration with civilian partners during peace enforcement missions benefits from the work of these liaisons. The liaisons need to understand and smoothly adapt to local cultures, structures, and risky contexts, which requires considerable emotional labor, but if they succeed, they nurture social relations that significantly benefit civil–military collaboration (Alvinius et al., 2014). Liaisons are more likely to improve interorganizational integration when they have sufficient time to build relations with partners and are empathetic to their concerns. They also need the discretion to adapt to the needs of their partners and must have sufficient influence within their organization to steer its approach and actions. And finally, they should have diplomatic or political skills to maneuver in these tense interorganizational environments (Kalkman, 2020a).

9.3 Interorganizational Integration Impediments

These various suggestions to integrate organizational activities and improve coordination between frontline crisis responders imply that integration is far from straightforward or self-evident in crisis response practice. In the public mind, crises may be viewed as events that make people rally around the flag to reach the common goal of ending the crisis, but the reality is different. In fact, there are several reasons why integration in crises remains challenging.

One reason for integration difficulties are technical failures. In some cases, communication devices may be incompatible, so front-line personnel of different agencies cannot interact with each other (Steigenberger, 2016). After large-scale disasters, such as Hurricane Katrina and the Haiti earthquake, other technical barriers to integration have been identified as well (Altay & Labonte, 2014; Day et al., 2009). Response organizations may, for instance, have different data formats and use incompatible measurement tools, so their information cannot easily be transferred or integrated. The data may also be stored in a way that cannot easily be shared (e.g., on paper) or cannot be put to good use by organizations that are using other software or media platforms. Even when information exchange is successful, successful integration is not guaranteed, because information overload is also a challenge in many crises and leave personnel from crisis organizations overwhelmed rather than enabling them to harmonize their activities with other responders.

Another explanation for integration problems is that involved responders have incongruent or even competing priorities during the crisis. The example of the EU refugee crisis is telling: border guards recognized a security crisis with potential threats to EU countries, while frontline personnel from NGOs saw a humanitarian crisis and noticed that refugees were in dire need of aid. Members of both organizations wished to resolve the crisis, but in very different ways. Their antithetical understandings of the situation and diametrically opposed goals impeded integrative coordination attempts (Kalkman, 2019a). Likewise, during humanitarian conflicts, peacekeeping aims may not sit well with humanitarian objectives, because interventions to promote stability sometimes translate to the suspension of essential public services and violation of individual rights (Pramanik, 2015). Still, even in less controversial crises, responders identify different aims. Equipped with a specific goal and mandate, frontline responders prioritize their own objectives over those of others (Ödlund, 2010). During a bomb threat at an elderly care center, for instance, care personnel would be confused about the situation, but know how to best evacuate the building, while police personnel know how to interpret the situation and take control, but have no experience in taking care of the elderly. Their competing priorities render interactions difficult (Danielsson, 2016).

In addition, crisis organizations have their own unique operating styles and distinct cultural characteristics. The fire brigade's action-dominated approach conflicts with the emphasis on communication and storytelling in other emergency services, posing potential hurdles to inter-agency integration (Charman, 2015). Indeed, frontline responders of all crisis organizations develop their own traditions and customs, symbols and artifacts, and language, which differentiate them from other organizations. This binds members to their organization, but also creates a gap between responders from different organizations who will not always grasp or comprehend other responders (Granot, 1997). One notorious example comes from the 1992 Los Angeles riots, during which Marines were deployed to the city to support the local police. During a response to a domestic dispute, one police officer told the Marines to "cover" him. He meant to tell them to point their weapons and be ready for using it, if necessary. However, the term meant very something different to the Marines and they fired over 200 bullets in the house (Delk, 1995). Surprisingly, no one was killed, but it highlighted differences in standard operating procedures and language use. In civil–military coordination during relief and stabilization missions, such operational and cultural differences are very common. Armed forces, using a directive and hierarchical approach, engage in short-term operations to reach predefined goals that are politically mandated and partial. Instead, NGOs use a decentralized and participatory approach to pursue long-term, complex ends in a neutral, independent, and impartial manner. Integrating their activities is complicated as a result (Franke, 2006). Finally, security organizations are often very secretive, a cultural characteristic that signifies lack of trust and impedes information sharing. In practice, it leads to exclusionary practices and problematizes integration with other crisis organizations (Kuipers & Swinkels, 2018).

Crisis response organizations may even purposefully avoid integration. One explanation for this results from the question who should be in charge in a particular situation. All responders may be in favor of coordination in principle, but being coordinated by others is generally received in a much less favorable manner. Integration efforts are supported, but less so when it comes at the cost of autonomy. In addition, there is likely a tension or even open competition between crisis responders with regard to the allocation of responsibilities and tasks, particularly during crises in which new tasks emerge that multiple organizations view as their responsibility and want to put under their control (Quarantelli, 1988). Responders may also want to avoid each other's presence for fear of reputational harm, which is a common occurrence among humanitarians who do not wish to be associated with the armed forces, as this may undermine their carefully crafted image of neutral, independent agencies and even render them potentially vulnerable to violent attacks (Pramanik, 2015). There are other interests at play during crises as well, which problematize integrative coordination. It is not uncommon for managers to think it will boost their reputation, legitimacy, or financial prospects if they are seen as successfully resolving the crisis independently (Rosenthal et al., 1991). For emergency, military, and humanitarian organizations, crises are decisive moments that can mean an increase in funding and public support if they succeed or the opposite when they fail. Integration might lead to a faster and better resolution of the crisis, but this is not the sole (or even primary) interest of organizations and responders during crises. Clearly, there are alternative concerns and interests at play, which are not necessarily conducive to integration attempts.

9.4 Fragmentation of Crisis Response

Most studies on crisis response coordination focus on the tactical or strategic level of interorganizational interactions. Ideal-typically, coordination is realized on these higher organizational levels, where agreements are made to harmonize activities, which frontline responders subsequently implement. The advantage of such centralized coordination is that senior officials in these organizations are believed to have a general overview of the situation and available resources, so they should be able to make informed decisions on how to effectively and efficiently carry out the response activities. Yet, empirical research shows that frontline personnel often have a better, more up-to-date understanding of the situation on the ground and frequently ignore top-down response integration efforts (Groenendaal et al., 2013). Rather, they usually actively minimize or even avoid integration with responders from other organizations. If it is left up to them, frontline personnel tend to choose for fragmentation of the response effort instead.

Fragmentation is an alternative to integration for coordinating crisis response activities. While response integration manifests in attempts to synchronize response activities and merge them in a collective effort, response fragmentation consists of dividing tasks, distributing responsibilities, and allocating activities to specific responders. A coordination approach based on fragmentation aims to reduce the need for spending precious time on harmonizing activities and synchronizing crisis organizations' contributions. Instead, work is assigned to specific organizations, and their frontline responders operate in a fairly autonomous manner, having limited contact with personnel from other organizations. Responders can fully focus on their own, separate areas of responsibility and will only meet again across organizational boundaries when it is absolutely necessary or the time pressure reduces.

One main reason to avoid integration is that it produces interdependencies. Tight couplings between organizations, such as in an integrated response effort, introduce vulnerabilities into the crisis response system (cf. Perrow, 1984). Specifically, if one of the involved crisis organizations fails to deliver, this may impede the work of other organizations that rely on this organization. But when the relations between responders from different organizations are loose instead, crisis organizations are more autonomous and a failure by one organization does not directly threaten the response efforts of the others. Consider the example of civil–military collaboration in which a humanitarian actor depends on a military counterpart to protect it in volatile areas of operation. Their operations are fairly integrated, but the humanitarian agency will be unable to do its work if the military organization is engaged in other missions, withdraws, or deploys too few soldiers. In that case, it might have been better off organizing its own security, even when this constitutes a less efficient use of scarce resources. In fact, this is what often occurs in humanitarian settings, where armed forces and humanitarian aid agencies treasure their independence and wish to evade being controlled or having to justify themselves to other actors in the field. While coordination meetings are common, these are used to inform one another rather than to make firm agreements for which they can be held accountable. Responders continue to work alongside each other in practice (Rietjens & Bollen, 2008; Stephenson, 2005).

Autonomy is indeed highly valued by many crisis responders, as other examples confirm. In their research on frontline emergency response coordination, Berlin and Carlström (2011) find that ambulance, fire brigade, and police personnel are uncertain about the information that other emergency responders have and how they will act on it, leading them to avoid close collaboration. Rather, they often rely on parallelism, a coordination practice in which involved responders briefly negotiate task distribution and work side by side on their own tasks afterward (Berlin & Carlström, 2008). Another coordination practice, sequential collaboration, also relies on fragmenting the work. It consists of carrying out activities in sequence, where frontline responders of different organizations focus on their areas of responsibility and only meet during handovers (Berlin & Carlström, 2011).

A fragmented coordination approach may also be more flexible, and thereby better able to adapt to evolving crisis situations. Agreements to integrate interdependent actions put restrictions on frontline personnel's discretionary behaviors. They are bound by their organization's promises and the expectations of responders from other organizations. This makes it hard to deviate from such agreements, even when the crisis situation has evolved and responders would prefer to change course accordingly. Fragmentation, instead, allows for impromptu work adaptations and unanticipated coordination between various responders (Wolbers et al., 2018). While integrative plans, protocols, and decisions conclude discussions, a fragmented approach to coordination induces ongoing dialogue and improvised collective action.

Fragmenting the crisis response effort through an expertise-based distribution of work before a crisis may also produce a faster response. If areas of responsibility are demarcated in advance, responders of an organization are in control of specific tasks and can rapidly take decisions without first having to ask the permission of others. Often, crisis response personnel prioritize frontline actions over interorganizational communication in the early stages of a crisis anyway. Response integration attempts distract from their core responsibilities and do not produce immediate results (see Altay & Labonte, 2014). A fragmented way of operating, however, in which every organization simply carries out the activities that fit its mandate and background, saves much time and effort. Responders can concentrate their attention on their domain of responsibility and do not have to divide it over all aspects of the response effort (Wolbers et al., 2018). In case of a house fire, the fire brigade makes decisions on how to extinguish the fire and whether to evacuate neighbors, the police cordon off the incident area and keep crowds at a distance, while ambulance personnel decide what type of care victims need and to which hospitals the wounded are transported. Such decisions can be made without wasting precious time on discussing them with others, particularly when responders from one of the services clearly have much more expertise than the others. Clearly, in practice, it often makes sense to fragment the response effort.

9.5 Risks of Fragmentation

Fragmented coordination may be faster and more flexible, but it comes with its own risks. One of these risks is inefficiency. Failure to integrate actions has often resulted in a wasteful use of scarce resources. Personnel of one agency might remain passive, while another organization is overwhelmed. And when organizations do not share information about the crisis or how they are acting in response, it is hard to properly assess victims' needs and prioritize interventions. It can easily lead to a situation where all resources are concentrated in one area, while victims in another area remain underserved. In the Indian Ocean Tsunami response, for instance, aid distribution was sometimes very inefficient, as NGOs distributed resources without integrating knowledge or activities among each other or with government authorities. In Ampara District, Sri Lanka, fishing boats and equipment were distributed to restore the local population's source of food and income, but a large number of recipients had never fished before and were not entitled to a fishing vessel in the first place. In one case, a beneficiary even amassed over thirty boats. At the same time, many actual fishers remained empty handed (Amarasiri de Silva, 2009).

This example also indicates that there is a risk of suboptimal or even counterproductive interventions, because organizations are unaware of what others are doing. When organizations divide responsibilities, they assume that their actions are unrelated to the work of others, but they are still dependent on one another in practice. Fragmented coordination may reduce interdependencies, but crisis responders can rarely operate successfully on their own. During Hurricane Katrina, the Coast Guard rescued victims, but these got stranded and were in serious distress, as there were no other organizations to pick up them from where they were dropped after being rescued, because handovers were not arranged (United States Congress, 2006). Rescue activities were speedy, but are of little use if people are simply left to fend for themselves in a different location.

Moreover, fragmentation can produce (additional) safety risks to frontline responders as well. As crisis organizations are operating autonomously, communication problems are looming and these can have dramatic consequences. If the fire services are focusing on how to handle a safety risk within its area of responsibility (e.g., a toxic cloud of gas) and undervalue interorganizational communication, it takes longer to inform other first responders, even though they are seriously at risk. In another example, a military unit flying with Unmanned Aerial Vehicles during the war in Afghanistan had to share airspace with other units (e.g., helicopters), but were not properly integrated in the military Task Force, so were unable to effectively reduce collision risks, creating dangerous situations (Moorkamp et al., 2016). In short, both frontline crisis professionals and the people they are serving may have reservations about fragmented coordination (Table 9.1).

Table 9.1 *The coordination dilemma*

	Integration	Fragmentation
Characteristics	Harmonizing interorganizational activities Reaching agreements A collective endeavor	Dividing responsibilities and tasks Autonomous organizational operations Limited interactions
Advantages	Good use of scarce resources Access to more information Synchronized actions	Less dependency and uncertainty Flexible operations Rapid responses
Shortcomings	Technical failures Competing priorities Interorganizational differences Organizational interests	Inefficient resource use Suboptimal or counterproductive operations Safety risks

Empirical Example

Emergency response teams consist of professionals from various
emergency services that have their own views and responsibilities. In an
experimental setting, liaisons from the fire brigade, police, emergency
medical services, municipality, and armed forces were faced with two
crisis scenarios, in which possible terrorist attacks were committed
in crowded spaces. As in any other crisis, they needed to coordinate
their activities and make collective decisions about the crisis response
approach. They resorted to two different decision-making pathways.
One pathway was used when one of the professionals, on behalf of
their organization, claimed authority over a specific question and took
decisions individually without asking the others for input, fragmenting
the response operations. For instance, after a possible terrorist attack
in a concert venue, there were rumors that terrorists tried to leave the
scene by taking the train to another city. The police official said in the
first meeting of the emergency response team: "I have already taken
decisions that are of influence for your perception. These are not our
decisions, but they have already been implemented. The most important one is that I stopped the trains. No trains and no busses anymore
within the train station area." Such independent decisions were often
accepted if the decisions were perceived to fall clearly within the sphere
of responsibility of the decision-maker. At other times, when this was
less clear, decisions were disputed, as one of the other professionals believed this needed to be an interorganizational decision. Such
disputes produced mixed results. After a dangerous substance had been
released at a train station in a neighborhood area, the fire commander
informed others he wanted to send out an alert message to tell people
to stay indoors. Another team member suggested an evacuation as an
alternative course of action, to which the fire commander responded
with little patience: "Well, tell them to close windows and doors, and
to turn off the ventilation. Because if we start evacuating, people end
up on the street." This ended the discussion, as all other team members
accepted his authority on this issue. In other situations, decisions
were believed to be of major importance to all involved parties and a
collaborative decision-making pathway was chosen, as representatives
from the different services aimed to reach a consensus, integrating
the response operations. The decision on whether it was safe for
the emergency services to enter the attacked concert venue provides an
example. The fire commander addressed the police officer: "For you,
safety concerns are whether there is a bomb or not. For me, safety is
whether there is a risk of collapse, but if we put those things together,

we can act together." The police representative replied: "'Yes, because we both want to enter the building to exclude some options." Collective decision-making unfolded through repeated and sometimes elaborate discussions, until an agreement was reached. There is merit in using the combination of decision-making pathways. When some decisions are made by one professional alone and other decisions follow a consensus-seeking dialogue, emergency response teams manage to combine speed with deliberation, ensuring that the overall decision-making process is both relatively fast, but also frequently subjected to due reflection (Kalkman et al., 2018).

9.6 Conditional Coordination

While coordination between frontline responders of different organizations is broadly perceived as a necessity to good crisis response, the preferred nature of this coordination remains subject to debate. A majority of scholars emphasizes integrating the work of frontline responders in times of crises by promoting structural and social interventions that bring actors together. This should help them to better understand each other and make it easier to harmonize their actions. Yet, empirical research shows that frontline responders often resort to fragmentation by minimizing their dependence on other crisis organizations and focusing on their own areas of responsibility. This reduces uncertainty in the direct aftermath of a crisis, while boosting the flexibility and speed of the collective response. In turn, it might hamper the efficiency and effectiveness of frontline crisis interventions. Thus, frontline responders face a dilemma, since they are encouraged to pursue both integration and fragmentation as coordination approaches.

There is no simple solution to this dilemma, but it is useful to first reflect on the recurring emphasis on coordination itself. Complex, transboundary crises do indeed require the collective efforts of multiple crisis organizations (Ansell et al., 2010), but coordination has gained such popularity that there is rarely any questioning of whether it should be pursued in a particular crisis. It has become a universal norm rather than a situation-based means to effective crisis response. In many cases, certainly, it will help frontline responders to better resolve crises, but there are also potential downsides and limitations to coordination, which often remain undiscussed. In some crisis situations, for example, the added benefit is marginal, such as in contested crises, during which involved responders will not be able to agree on the nature of the crisis, nor on the required activities. More generally, it is bound to be a time-costly and energy-intensive practice. In the face of urgent needs, even unfamiliar responders might choose to spend their scarce resources on undertaking activities without getting in touch with others. For instance, humanitarian agencies sometimes choose for direct aid provision instead of meeting other organizations to harmonize their actions (Altay & Labonte, 2014; Stephenson, 2005). Coordination, in short, is not by definition the only or even always the preferred course of action for a crisis organization.

Still, in the vast majority of crises, coordination will be of major importance. The coordinated deployment of capabilities and personnel can be lifesaving and significantly alleviate human suffering. Given the limits to top-down control during crises, it makes sense to focus on frontline coordination attempts in particular. Considerable coordination takes place near crisis sites, but it has not always been recognized as such. Even though the on-scene responders cannot always avail of information-sharing and communication channels or the crisis event may have taken these out, coordination is more than organized meetings, agreements on paper, and formal communication. At crisis sites, coordination also emerges as responders observe another's behavior and adapt to it. When first responders from one of the involved organizations call in specific resources or concentrate their resources at one point, other responders gather information from these observations on the nature of the situation, which might inform their actions (Berlin & Carlström, 2008; Groenendaal et al., 2013). Even other organizations' inaction may be a signal that others will use to interpret the crisis situation. For instance, when an NGO or one of the emergency services stays clear of an area or retreats from it out of safety concerns, this serves as a warning to others, even when it is not made explicit. These examples show that frontline responders coordinate among themselves, both with and without instructions to harmonize their activities, in ways that are unique to the operational context.

Structured and systematic ways of coordination remain necessary in many other situations. And frontline crisis responders have to choose whether to integrate or fragment their actions. One relevant factor in their decision-making is the complexity and scale of the crisis, as catastrophic disasters produce more new tasks and overlapping areas of responsibility than minor incidents (see Quarantelli, 1988). When formal areas of responsibility are already divided for familiar incidents, a fragmented approach may suffice and limited organizational investment in integration is needed, but there is likely a need for more extensive communication and synchronization in uncommon crises. So, humanitarians may prefer fragmentation in a disaster when all have clear sectors of expertise and responsibility, but can resort to integrative coordination when a disaster situation invalidates the existing approach and requires renewed harmonization of actions. The nature of the situation is therefore of importance.

There are other reasons for opting for either integration or fragmentation as well, depending on the specifics of the interorganizational relations and the availability of resources. Integrative efforts are particularly helpful when tensions between interdependent crisis organizations turn problematic. When crisis organizations are involved in rivalry, have no history of cooperation, or experience cultural clashes, there are benefits to increasing mutual familiarity and building some sense of community to overcome the excesses of these tensions (Beck & Plowman, 2014; Bollen, 2002). Similarly, when there is a serious shortage of resources or responders of different organizations are continuously counteracting each other and wasting resources, integration is needed to avoid a disastrous waste of investments and capabilities. Alternatively, when speed is the predominant concern, and even more so when ample resources are available, frontline responders can opt for fragmentation by dividing the work and focusing on implementation.

Another important aspect to consider is that integration and fragmentation do not have to be definitive choices at the onset of a crisis response effort. For example, crisis organizations may favor speed in the first hours or days after a crisis before beginning to synchronize their actions. When urgency is less crucial, it might be useful to build a sense of community and meet regularly in an EOC, after which tasks can be increasingly distributed. In a similar vein, especially when response networks grow to include many parties, it can be advisable to integrate actions with some organizations, while fragmenting the work with others. For instance, after a major hurricane or earthquake, emergency service employees benefit from integration with other essential service providers, but might simultaneously choose to give marginal responders very specific tasks that require a bare minimum of contact, such as clearing debris in a particular area. Clearly, this means that coordination will not be an easy or straightforward process, but it might help responders to move between the advantages of either coordination approach. As such, coordination ceases to be a norm with only one accepted interpretation, but becomes conditional upon the crisis at hand.

9.7 Conclusion

Coordination between frontline responders will not be perfected by organizing for full integration and synchronization of activities, nor will it benefit from complete fragmentation through a meticulous specification of areas of responsibility. Instead, coordination practices need to combine elements of integration and fragmentation, and should be selected based on an assessment of the evolving nature of the situation.

More research is needed on the broad variety of coordination practices between frontline responders of different organizations beyond the formal meetings and agreements. It is also worthwhile comparing the effects of different levels of response integration to discover the various consequences of this popular form of coordination and improve our knowledge on the drawbacks or limits of integration attempts. Finally, it would be useful to learn more about how frontline crisis responders move between integration and fragmentation attempts in practice and enact interorganizational coordination during their responses to crisis situations.

Resources for Educators and Professionals

PRACTICAL LESSONS

- Operational coordination can take multiple forms, ranging from merely observing the actions of others to formal and structured meetings.
- Coordination between frontline responders of different organizations is often seen as essential in crises, but this is not necessarily the case.
- Responders can coordinate their response activities through integration or fragmentation.
- Fragmentation of crisis activities ensures a speedy and flexible response, while integration produces a more efficient, synchronized use of resources.

– The nature of the coordination between frontline responders should be conditional on the phase and needs of the crisis as well as the collaboration partner.

QUESTIONS FOR REFLECTION AND DISCUSSION

– When do you feel a need to coordinate your activities with responders from other crisis organizations and when is such coordination not needed?
– Which coordination mechanisms have been prepared? Are these focused on integration or fragmentation? How relevant are these mechanisms in different crisis situations?
– Which other organizations are your most important collaboration partners? How do you coordinate your work with these partners? How does this differ from coordination with less important partners?

10 | Civilians

Inclusion versus Exclusion

On September 11, 2001, a series of terrorist attacks in the United States caused almost 3,000 casualties and triggered a global war on terror. On the day itself, first responders undertook heroic actions to save as many lives as possible and hundreds paid the highest price for their bravery. But ordinary civilians were not just victims that needed to be rescued by professional crisis responders. Many citizens, in fact, became actively involved in the response as well. At the southern waterfront of Manhattan, boat operators and other maritime workers evacuated hundreds of thousands across the Hudson to New Jersey, and quickly began to transport emergency responders and their supplies on their return trips, thereby making a major contribution to the crisis response effort. The emergent, spontaneous aid of these and many other volunteers reduced the crisis impact and alleviated suffering (Kendra & Wachtendorf, 2016). On that same day, passengers and crew of United Airlines Flight 93 realized their airplane was hijacked and decided to fight back. The group of strangers united in a terrifying, unfathomable situation and summoned their courage to make an attempt at retaking control of the aircraft. They made it into the cockpit, but the hijackers crashed the plane in a field, killing all those aboard. Still, their heroic revolt prevented the hijackers from causing further death and destruction on the ground (Quinn & Worline, 2008).

Spontaneous actions by civilians saved many lives that day. When professional frontline responders were still on their way, thoroughly overwhelmed by the situation or otherwise unable to intervene, ordinary people stood up and came to the aid of strangers in need. The vast number of volunteers and their rapid contributions were welcome additions to the official response effort and are rightfully lauded. But it is worthwhile noting that professionals are often critical and distrustful toward spontaneous volunteers and tend to exclude them from official response efforts. The dilemma for crisis responders, therefore, revolves around whether and how to include civilians in crisis response operations.

10.1 Assumptions about Civilian Behavior in Crises

Crisis organizations across the spectrum have long viewed ordinary civilians with considerable skepticism. In the field of emergency management, this view dates back to the early phase of the Cold War, when emergency planning efforts throughout the world were based on military principles. From this perspective, both enemy attacks and disasters are thought to produce social chaos. More specifically, people are expected to display irrational, antisocial behavior after the collapse of control structures. They are predicted to act selfishly and are likely unable to effectively cope with crises on their own. They will, for instance, start to panic and act irrationally or take advantage of the chaos to start looting and plundering. Under these circumstances, it is the government's responsibility to intervene and give aid. A logical solution is to bring disorderly populations back in line by deploying (para-)military organizations that exercise strict control over them and the situation (Dynes, 1994). Military views on human nature, at the roots of this emergency response approach, show signs of Hobbesian thinking, because there is an assumption that crises return people to a state of nature in which all fend for themselves, many suffer as a consequence, and no one can be trusted. A notable example of these assumptions can be seen in the response to the 1906 San Francisco earthquake. In its aftermath, the city was burning to the ground in an ever-expanding conflagration. Brigadier General Funston, however, marched his army into town not to fight the fire but to fight the "mob," treating citizens as enemies by shooting them and keeping them out, thereby suppressing their volunteer firefighting efforts. In the response to this crisis, soldiers were deployed against total demoralization in the city, but interestingly, the military intervention itself contributed to the city's near-total destruction (Solnit, 2010).

In the humanitarian sector, likewise, clients of aid have traditionally been viewed with suspicion and condescension. Often, they were seen as passive victims that needed to be helped, but would do little to help themselves. Not infrequently, communities were diagnosed with "dependency syndrome," which refers to a lethargic mentality of a group, which shows no initiative and does not attempt to solve their own problems or take care of themselves, but choose to apathetically depend on external help (Kibreab, 1993). In practice, victims were usually not given the possibility of providing input or participating in the process either, as they were stereotyped as helpless and ignorant (Ressler, 1978). Even if they were included in the aid delivery process, "beneficiaries" and local partner organizations were eyed with considerable mistrust and were closely monitored to avoid their misuse of resources (Hilhorst, 2018).

In other crisis contexts, a similar perspective on civilians emerged. During the Mount Everest climbing disaster of 1996, professional leaders and guides made crucial mistakes, but clients were being presented as passive or unreasonable and criticized for not contributing to the response. They are accused of making irrational choices by continuing to ascend after the latest turnaround time, waiting with a descent at a dangerous height rather than joining an earlier descent to relative safety, and lacking knowledge of their own limits (Jacobsson & Hällgren, 2016; Tempest et al., 2007). In mountain rescue efforts, similarly, rescuers often find victims frightened, traumatized, and completely dependent. Interestingly, victims are not expected to help make sense of the situation or support in the resolution of the crisis, but are at best not hindering it with their intense, disruptive emotions (Lois, 2003).

To some extent, this dominant perspective on civilians across various crisis contexts matches biological and psychological views on human behavior in situations of danger and stress. Indeed, mammals faced with acute stress typically display a limited set of responses, which serve evolutionary purposes, including freezing, flight, fight, and fright. Humans, specifically, may faint as well under these circumstances (Bracha, 2004). Psychological stress and anxiety in threatening situations are also found to inhibit information processing capabilities of affected people and induce them to resort to familiar actions patterns, regardless of whether these are appropriate in a specific crisis situation (Staw et al., 1981). Early studies on human behavior in crises support these findings. Wallace (1957) claims that it is common for people to become paralyzed and suffer from shock, apathy, and numbness. Victims, in his perception, remain dazed, while those who remained uninjured may free themselves from apathy to some extent and support the response effort, but citizen responses should generally be expected to be minimal. Tyhurst (1957) confirms that some three-quarters of disaster survivors suffer from fear and are otherwise numb. Another ten to twenty-five percent is paralyzed and confused. Overall, social consequences include panic, mass exodus from the affected territory, purposeless activities, social paralysis, and group disintegration. Thus, it seems that people behave in uncontrolled, selfish, and altogether destructive ways when they experience a crisis. Interestingly, this view on human behavior during crises remains enormously popular in fictional books, disaster movies, and in media coverage of disasters. It remains therefore dominant among the general public and policy-makers as well.

10.2 Enduring Myths

Several decades of research by disaster sociologists, however, contradicts this view on human behavior in crises and the idea of people behaving destructively at such moments is rejected by these scholars as a myth. One of the earliest criticisms came from Quarantelli (1960), who countered the negative assumptions about people's actions after crises by arguing that even if people react in distress or shock, this happens only to a small percentage of the population, while these reactions are usually short and local (see also Fritz & Marks, 1954). He argued that disaster research supports a more optimistic view on human nature, because the proactive implementation of disaster response activities is much more common among victims. Other studies provided further support for this alternative perspective. Indeed, people may be frightened at first, but widespread irrational panic is a fiction. It is based on a misreading of concerned people who rapidly, but sensibly, try to leave the scene of the incident and bring themselves and their loved ones to a place of safety. After the disaster, their uncoordinated, spontaneous relief activities are likewise mistaken for chaotic and irrational behaviors, but are actually crucial to providing first aid to victims (Fritz & Williams, 1957).

This also means that people are not apathetically waiting for aid, suffering from the so-called "disaster syndrome," but are usually the very first responders in crises, rescuing others in peril, offering lifesaving first aid, as well as providing shelter and food. In fact, the large number of volunteers (e.g., over a million after the 1985 Mexico City earthquake), which includes uninjured victims themselves, may cause coordination problems, but it also shows that assumptions of victim apathy are simply wrong. People care about one another and will try to help if they can. This also explains why looting, albeit a dominant concern among decision-makers and reported in the media, is very rare in practice. Solnit (2010, p. 131) blames the misguided expectation of selfish behaviors, such as looting, in the aftermath of crises on self-interested elites who rose to power in a competitive society and "see all humanity in their own image." Egotistic self-centeredness may be their reality, but does not reflect the attitudes and behaviors of society at large. As research shows, most people tend to become altruistic after crises and will start reaching out to strangers, while crime rates typically drop (Heide, 2004; Helsloot & Ruitenberg, 2004). Rather than a "fight or flight" reaction, the initial behaviors of people after a crisis follow a 'tend and befriend" pattern, as they engage in caring activities and build social networks (Taylor et al., 2000). Even stronger, many survivors of a large-scale disaster have fond memories of the days and weeks after the event, because it triggered a sense of community between people who did not know each other before. A generous, caring, and creative order is collectively produced by ordinary civilians who are coping with the disaster together and looking after one another (Solnit, 2010).

Interestingly, there is a gap between what people expect of others and how they think they will react to crises themselves. Municipal crisis professionals, for instance, were asked to judge their own and others' reactions in several crisis scenarios. Respondents answered they would probably react in a logical and rational fashion to the crisis, while not being subject to anger, panic, or denial. Their peers were expected to display more of these latter behaviors though. And the general public's reaction would be primarily characterized by fear, emotions, shock, panic, and irrationality (Wester, 2011). Likewise, in a study among citizens of Berlin, some ten percent of respondents expected to react in panic themselves, while sixty percent expected others would. Less than seven percent thought they would be in shock against almost fifty percent thinking others would be in shock. And more than two thirds claimed they would calmly observe the situation and decide what to do, while less than sixteen percent thought others would follow this course of action as well (Lorenz et al., 2018). These numbers show that we have (too) low expectations of other people's behavior in crises.

It is problematic that crisis response professional are not immune to these misconceptions. One study among Japanese crisis professionals found that they were slightly less likely than lay people to expect panic and looting after a disaster, but they were as likely to believe in the disaster syndrome and increased crime rates. In general, they were more likely to believe than disbelieve myths of destructive post-crisis behavior by ordinary people (Nogami, 2018). This has various negative, even deadly, effects on crisis response. Officials who expect panic and shock are late in warning the public about threats (e.g., fires or sinking boats), losing valuable time for evacuations and thereby confronting people with more dangerous situations when they are first informed (Heide, 2004). These myths lead to a waste of scarce resources too. After Hurricane Katrina, crisis professionals were deployed for security provision duties rather than to offer life-saving services, because survivors were being framed and treated as criminals. Rather than food, medicine, and other basic supplies, law enforcement was deployed into the disaster-struck area (Tierney et al., 2006). Finally, a formal crisis response effort based on these myths alienates citizens. By treating survivors as threats rather than victims and precluding volunteer initiatives, crisis organizations do not only create distrust in public institutions and produce an unwillingness among civilians to cooperate with formal response efforts, but they also disrupt enormously beneficial citizen responses.

10.3 Emergence of Civilian Groups in Crisis Response

Citizen initiatives are reported in many crisis situations. It is clear that ordinary people are bound to volunteer out of altruism and will stand up to resolve crises or alleviate suffering, like they did on 9/11 (Kendra & Wachtendorf, 2016; Quinn & Worline, 2008). Volunteers will particularly show up in large disasters and when there are many dead and missing (Iizuka & Aldrich, 2021). They do most of the crisis response work during the "golden hour," the immediate aftermath of the disaster when most lives are saved, and will play a crucial role when formal organizations are absent or overwhelmed (Solnit, 2010). But even during smaller incidents and accidents, bystanders often become first responders. Some of these volunteers have a formal status (e.g., as volunteer firefighters or rescuers), while others employ existing structures, like community groups or businesses, to take on new tasks and contribute to crisis response.

In addition, there are "emergent groups" that will simply enter into existence as volunteers begin to carry out crisis activities and start coordinating their work in an informal manner (Whittaker et al., 2015). These emergent groups are formed by "private citizens who work together in pursuit of collective goals relevant to actual or potential disasters but whose organization has not yet become institutionalized" (Stallings & Quarantelli, 1985, p. 94). In fact, many of these emergent groups are still organizing while they are implementing activities rather than designing a structure before they begin operations (Thompson & Hawkes, 1962). They create ad hoc social structures, with limited attempts at formalization, to carry out non-routine actions with the resources that they have at their disposal. Actions are prioritized over planning or decision-making and membership remains highly ambiguous. Usually, they only stay in existence for a limited time, until the worst effects of the crisis are relieved or formal crisis organizations take over, after which they dissolve (Drabek & McEntire, 2002; Lanzara, 1983; Majchrzak et al., 2007; Twigg & Mosel, 2017), although some will continue their operations for years. Such emergent groups can play a vital role in the response efforts. They will have a better understanding of the local crisis situation and may commence activities well before the police, fire brigade, or other formal response organizations arrive (Quarantelli & Dynes, 1977).

Emergent groups come in many forms and shapes. After the 1980 earthquake in Southern Italy, for instance, a group of students loaded vehicles with relief materials and drove two hours to a hard-hit village for search and rescue activities and to deliver aid. The following day, they began to organize and coordinate the collection, transport, and delivery of relief supplies. After a little over a week, however, the government began to take control and frustrated these operations, leading the emergent group to disband (Lanzara, 1983). On a larger scale, Williams and Shepherd (2016) studied the rise of emergent groups in the aftermath of the 2010 Haiti earthquake and found that some groups established ventures to sustain victims' basic needs by providing food and shelter for years, while other groups aimed to help people recover from the disaster through enabling them to become self-reliant, autonomous, and resilient in the long run. In a very different setting, many volunteers during the EU refugee crisis were also driven by altruistic motives to help others in need and engaged in activities like providing shelter, clothing, and first aid (Chtouris & Miller, 2017; Doidge & Sandri, 2019). And when Malaysian Airlines Flight MH370 went missing, over two million digital volunteers went to a website of a commercial satellite company to join the search by scanning satellite imagery for signs of the crashed airplane. Their interactions were limited to social media posts, but they still experienced a sense of community and purpose in their contribution to the response (Fishwick, 2014).

Such digital volunteering is increasingly common, particularly through crowdsourced online mapping. After the 2010 Haiti earthquake, hundreds of people across the globe downloaded satellite images and helped to record the country's physical infrastructure in a map that could be used by first responders for rescue operations. Volunteers also helped to translate online and text messages from Haitians and geotagged these, so aid organizations and other responders gained a better impression of community needs and could more efficiently organize their relief efforts (Meier, 2011; Zook et al., 2010). As such, affected communities themselves were a main source of information in the construction of these crisis maps. This reflects a broader shift in attitudes toward victims within crisis organizations.

In the humanitarian sector, possibly more than in any other crisis context, affected civilians are less and less viewed as passive, irrational, and selfish, and are increasingly being seen as resilient and resourceful clients who should actively participate in planning and implementing operations (Hilhorst, 2018). Indeed, there is widespread support for a growing role of affected populations in humanitarian relief and other crisis response operations. One reason for this is the normative belief that it is one's moral duty to empower victims of crises by giving them a chance to influence decisions that will mainly affect them and their communities, so engagement is needed in order to respect their rights and dignity. It also makes crisis operations more effective by improving the quality of aid projects, which are more likely to meet clients' needs and wishes. And it has an emancipatory effect through giving voice to marginalized and vulnerable people, increasing their capacities, and addressing inequality or vulnerability at its roots (Brown et al., 2014). Also, research on volunteers who responded to the 9/11 attacks shows that the possibility to participate in the response efforts had therapeutic effects and improved personal healing after the traumatic experience. Finally, volunteers developed a lasting sense of community. As the crisis forced them to reconsider their core values and life choices, many chose to continue participating in volunteer or service work, enhancing community engagement even after the crisis was over (Steffen & Fothergill, 2009). Thus, the direct response and the community's recovery benefited from the inclusion of affected citizens in crisis response operations.

10.4 Exploring the Reluctance to Rely on Civilians

In spite of the growing support for a greater role of ordinary people in crisis response efforts, formal crisis organizations face recurring difficulties with including emergent groups in practice. Indeed, citizen initiatives are often pushed out by formal organizations that leave little room for the activities of emerging organizations. Oftentimes, crisis responders believe that incorporation of emergent groups is not worth the effort. Despite their helpful contributions, volunteers also create new problems that make responders uncertain about whether to include them in the broader crisis response effort (Schmidt, 2019). In response, they regularly revert to their default reaction to push them away from the site of the crisis (Barsky et al., 2007). Cordoning off the area is common in many crises anyway, even though it symbolically and effectively excludes spontaneous volunteers from participating in the response. And when there are no physical barriers, crisis professionals can still produce social exclusion by trying to keep civilians away from core activities (Kvarnlöf & Johansson, 2014). In a way, formal responders and emergent groups are constantly negotiating the boundary of the official response, as volunteers prefer (and proactively try) to be incorporated, while the formal responders are (very) selective in whom they allow to participate (Johansson et al., 2018).

A major reason for crisis professionals to be reluctant about including volunteers is that it distracts from their core focus and activities. For instance, it requires considerable adaptations on their part. They might need to reconsider pre-established task allocations and scripts to synchronize actions with emergent groups (Schmidt, 2019), but they also have to set up channels for communication and information-sharing with an unfamiliar group. These groups, moreover, are often perceived as unmanageable, because they do not have a formal hierarchical structure, so that even their leaders have limited influence over what members do. Under these conditions, formal responders will quickly view coordination with emergent groups as a waste of valuable time and energy. In practice, even humanitarians tend to prioritize getting the job done over doing it in an inclusive manner (i.e., by engaging beneficiaries) in the immediate aftermath of a disaster (Brown et al., 2014). Thus, responders often include only self-reliant volunteers who carry out activities that require little coordination (Kendra & Wachtendorf, 2003b).

Next, reliance on emergent groups introduces new uncertainties in the response (Skar et al., 2016; Twigg & Mosel, 2017). In general, frontline responders of organizations are hesitant to depend on emergent groups for assistance, because they are unsure whether volunteers will converge to the crisis site. During smaller emergencies, particularly, volunteers may stay away and if the formal response relied on spontaneous citizen initiatives, the available resources might not meet the needs of the situation. Vice versa, when plans and scripts assume no contributions by citizens, it is hard to incorporate them if they do arrive to help. And when lots of people converge to a crisis site, even if this is expected, responders worry about losing an overview of the situation. In this case, emergent groups may also obstruct the formal response, particularly when large groups of people block entry into the affected area or unsolicited donations that are of limited use take up much-needed space and time (Whittaker et al., 2015).

Another reason why crisis responders are hesitant to incorporate volunteers is that they often do not know their skills in advance. While there are credentialing systems (Barsky et al., 2007), spontaneous volunteers will often converge with or without having followed trainings in advance. Formal organizations worry about their liability when volunteers, under their supervision, make mistakes and cause safety hazards or do harm to others. Volunteers may also become victims themselves if they are involved in risky interventions without proper instructions or practice (Twigg & Mosel, 2017). After the Mexico City earthquake, for instance, some hundred citizens died while trying to save others (Helsloot & Ruitenberg, 2004). Volunteer organizations have been sued for this reason in the recent past, although this seems to be a rare phenomenon (Sauer et al., 2014; Whittaker et al., 2015). Still, it helps to explain why it is attractive to only involve civilians in safe and marginal processes of the crisis response effort. Armed forces, for example, might use ordinary civilians as potential sources of information for intelligence purposes, but do not trust them with their intelligence reports in turn, let alone include them in the planning or execution of operations. This also points to another obstacle: formal responders do not always have the required skills or staff to interact and make effective use of citizen initiatives (Brown et al., 2014).

But even if they did, there is a final, more fundamental, reason to be reluctant about systematically relying on emergent groups. Crises exacerbate societal inequalities, so that marginalized groups are more vulnerable. These groups may neither have the resources to prepare for disaster, nor the ability to take on a proactive volunteering role. And if they do, they are likely to play a marginal role in emergent groups as well, even though they have specific needs, which risk going unheard and unheeded as a result (Blake et al., 2017; Maguire & Hagan, 2007). This leaves them potentially more marginalized, particularly when formal crisis responders are outsourcing crisis response activities to emergent groups, which might well focus efforts on helping those of their own social group first. Governmental pursuit of social or community resilience sounds like a promising tool for empowering groups, but can also be an excuse for downscaling formal crisis response capabilities without addressing the root causes of marginalized people's vulnerability, thereby rendering them less resilient in the long run (Sudmeier-Rieux, 2014). Clearly, including citizen initiatives in official crisis response operations is far from straightforward (Table 10.1).

Table 10.1 *The dilemma over the role of civilians*

	Involvement	Exclusion
Characteristics	Spontaneous volunteers complement formal response efforts Role for citizen initiatives and emergent groups	Victims as dependent, irrational, and antisocial Little room for volunteering
Advantages	Critical first aid Improved situational understanding Empowering victims	Government responsibility to offer aid in crises Professional crisis interventions
Shortcomings	Distraction from the main task Increases uncertainty Potential lack of skills Risk of exacerbating inequality	Post-crisis human behavior misinterpreted Waste of resources Alienation of citizens

Empirical Example

The military task force that was deployed to provide disaster relief to the Bahamas prepared for close coordination with civilian organizations, such as the local authorities and international aid agencies. Ordinary civilians, however, were not expected to participate in the response. Before arrival, the leadership of the task force had two expectations with regard to the local population. The first was that they would passively await the humanitarian aid provision, leaving the initiative to the task force without undertaking any activities to help themselves. Second, there were rumors about threats of biker gangs and people engaging in criminal behavior: "And there were messages that when Hurricane Dorian passed by, a weapon store was looted. So, there were messages reaching us that weapons were just stolen and that no one knew where they were." As a result, military personnel brought their own weapons ashore for security purposes. As a general explained: "If my people feel threatened because there is looting or because folks think: 'Those pallets, I want to have them'. In that case, they need to be able to offer resistance and that doesn't immediately mean shooting people, but if you are armed, you will have more of a posture than when you are standing there with your hands in your pockets." Both expectations matched the rather negative view on human nature that is predominant in the military organization. Rapidly, however, frontline personnel noticed that their expectations were flawed and that victims of the hurricane were very glad with their presence, posing no threat to them whatsoever. One major of the Marines put it like this: "The only things we got from the local population were hugs and 'thanks for being here'. Not a single threat at all. So, the rifles could be put away and even a Glock was too much." Instead, frontline personnel increasingly began to see the civilian population as a valuable partner in the response efforts. To his own surprise, an officer of the Marines discovered that "every day you see civilians, anywhere you go, you do business with them." Another mentioned: "But what I noticed from the very first day was the enormous resilience of the local population and how, in spite of the fact that everything was destroyed, they had this positive mindset to rebuild everything again." When operations were in full swing, soldiers worked side by side with affected civilians in the response efforts. A great many pictures of the response effort show military personnel and ordinary citizens collaborating. They are discussing progress, go on patrol in empty neighborhoods, transport and distribute basic supplies, and fix broken generators and other machines together. During the second half of the mission, in particular, local civilians played a major role in the task force's selection and implementation of relief activities, and their contributions were widely considered instrumental to success (Kalkman, 2023a).

10.5 Adaptive Incorporation

Ordinary citizens are still often expected to panic or passively wait for help in crisis situations, even though these assumptions have been proven wrong time and again. Civilians form emergent groups that proactively help others in need and are already involved in crisis response activities before formal crisis organizations arrive. As a result, these groups save lives and reduce suffering. Still, crisis responders are likely to exclude them from the official response efforts, because they remain skeptical about the added value of incorporating volunteers. Generally, however, there is a turn toward incorporation, as affected citizens are no longer solely viewed as victims but also as potential collaborators in operational crisis response actions. The dilemma for frontline responders is that they can benefit from including them, but also have an interest in keeping them at arm's length.

In dealing with this dilemma, anticipation and relationship building are key. Anticipation means that frontline crisis responders are prepared for and open to citizen initiatives, and decide on the spot if and how to include and coordinate emergent groups (Skar et al., 2016; Twigg & Mosel, 2017). This demands training and practice on the part of frontline responders to help them make such decisions under stress and pressure. Still, such decentralized volunteer incorporation practices are likely to be more impactful than designing formal, bureaucratic mechanisms (see Waldman et al., 2018). Anticipation also means preparing for changing volunteering habits. Currently, there is a trend toward more flexible and episodic volunteering efforts, people increasingly assist through digital means, and employee volunteer programs are on the rise, so crisis organizations need to prepare for incorporating new types of volunteer contributions in future crises (McLennan et al., 2016). Next, relationship building is very important as well. Frontline crisis responders should not only talk about emergent groups, but also with them. When foreseeing potential roles for an emergent group, they would do well to invite its emerging leaders to find out more about the skills in the group and define its tasks. During an incident or disaster, frontline responders should grant volunteers access to the site, keep them informed, and give them tasks that add value to the response and fit their skills (Scanlon et al., 2014). By building relations, volunteers will feel heard and crisis responders can discover how to make optimal use of their presence during the crisis response effort.

Naturally, the type of crisis matters. It may not come as a surprise that there is virtually no (research on the) involvement of ordinary civilians in the crisis operations of some organizations, such as special forces, emergency trauma teams, and critical infrastructures. There appears to be little room for unsolicited volunteering in the work of these organizations, because the nature of the work is highly specialized, secretive, or dangerous. But even organizations responsible for emergency response or humanitarian aid provision will notice that the specifics of the crisis affect the volunteering dynamics and opportunities, as emergent groups may be more resilient and capable to respond to some situations than others (see Maguire & Hagan, 2007). Spontaneous volunteers will act and be of great importance after flash crises (e.g., traffic accidents) and mass-casualty disasters (e.g., earthquakes). They may even be preregistered and organized for activation in slow-onset disasters (e.g., forest fires, floods, and refugee crises), but may lack expertise, access, or tools for other emergencies (e.g., house fires, air crashes at airports, and crime scenes) (Helsloot & Ruitenberg, 2004; Scanlon et al., 2014). Actual citizen contributions will therefore vary in practice and crisis responders can anticipate roles for volunteers depending on the nature of the crisis.

Next, there are different types of civilians at the site of a crisis. Early research has already suggested that those directly affected will react different from those who have not suffered themselves from the crisis. Typically, the former are taking on a more proactive volunteering role than the latter (Menninger, 1952). However, it is not only helpers who converge to crisis sites. There are also people who are anxious about the fate of loved ones, those who are simply curious about the disaster impact, and those who return to inspect or retrieve their property (Kendra & Wachtendorf, 2003a). These various groups have different degrees of legitimacy and utility to the crisis response, as assessed by frontline responders, and will be treated in different ways (Barsky et al., 2007). Frontline responders will be best positioned to decide during a crisis response effort which citizens may be of use and how they can help. Organized volunteers with some training and credentials who converge to the crisis site to help may be the preferred partners to responders and have most legitimacy in professionals' eyes, but in the direct aftermath of crises, emergent groups and spontaneous volunteers should be expected and their utility to the response deserves to be considered.

There are different degrees of including these citizens. While some emergency response studies take a rather dichotomous perspective by studying if emergent groups are either included or excluded, research on humanitarian aid shows many levels of engagement, ranging from mere information exchange to full-fledged partnerships in which responsibilities are even devolved to local communities (Brown et al., 2014). Using civilians as a vital source of information, the most basic form of inclusion, is broadly accepted, and can manifest in asking those with locally relevant knowledge for information or relying on mapping skills of digital volunteers (Kvarnlöf & Johansson, 2014; Meier, 2011). Still, emergent groups often can and want to do more. Another option is to channel their volunteering efforts, for instance by giving them a specific, usually quite simple task ("segmentation"), but maintaining a distance between them and other responders (Carlson et al., 2017; Nissen et al., 2022). This can include mobilizing civilians to reinforce dykes against floods, search for missing persons in a specific area after the disaster, or transport those with light injuries to hospitals. Even more ambitious is the possibility to include an emergent group as an equal in the response and give it influence in crisis response decisions, which is particularly attractive when the emergent group has indisputable knowledge or expertise pertaining to the crisis. Such a role may be particularly likely in large disasters (e.g., earthquakes and refugee crises) where formal crisis organizations depend on emergent groups to carry out a large quantity of relatively straightforward tasks.

During long-lasting crises, in particular, the role of citizen initiatives may change over time for various reasons. The needs of the crisis response will vary, shifting for instance from search and rescue to the provision of basic resources, and this means that the potential role of emergent groups changes accordingly. Volunteers may also lose interest over time and take up their pre-crisis daily life, while a surge of formal response personnel reduces the need for ordinary civilians as well. While this suggests a declining role of emergent groups, such groups may also professionalize and be coopted in the formal response or formalize to play a role in the recovery phase (Nissen et al., 2022; Scanlon et al., 2014; Williams & Shepherd, 2016). How citizens are incorporated, should therefore not be fixed in advance, but be dynamic (see Johansson et al., 2018). Tasks, roles, and ways of engaging emergent groups will need to be adaptive and flexible (Schmidt, 2019), so frequent reconsideration of civilian contributions has to be part of crisis responders' discussions and decision-making processes.

In spite of the important role that ordinary civilians can play in crisis response, it is important to recognize victimhood as well. Exploring the role of civilians in crisis response is no reason to cut back on formal crisis response efforts. People need and deserve aid in crises and citizen initiatives are a potential means to improve official response efforts, not to replace them. Importantly, the most vulnerable in society may not be well represented in emergent groups, so it is important to avoid reinforcing existing structures of inequality and vulnerability. Ultimately, volunteer inclusion needs to improve the crisis response efforts, so gauging the likely effects on a community is warranted. The resulting assessments may inform various and changing decisions on which volunteers to include and how to use their contributions. Such a deliberate and transparent reflection process would go a long way in the adaptive incorporation of civilians in crisis response efforts.

10.6 Conclusion

Incorporating citizens in the response requires a need for dispelling persistent disaster myths about how people react to crises. This is a precondition for properly valuing the role of emergent groups in crisis response. An adaptive approach to potential contributions of ordinary civilians will enable frontline responders to assess how volunteer inclusion fits the particular crisis situation at hand and can ultimately improve the response efforts.

In the future, it would be interesting to gain more insight in the diversity of civilian reactions to crises by scrutinizing the variety of reactions in different types and phases of crises. Next, it is useful to explore how frontline responders can be trained to optimize their use of ordinary civilians in crisis response efforts. Finally, while the incorporation of civilians in crisis response operations may empower people, it is important to investigate and monitor whether it does not disadvantage marginalized groups or it will be necessary to find a way to correct such undesirable consequences.

Resources for Educators and Professionals

PRACTICAL LESSONS

- Ordinary civilians usually engage in crisis response efforts spontaneously, forcing crisis professionals to consider if and how to include them.
- Diverse groups of people at crisis sites have different degrees of legitimacy and utility in the crisis response effort.
- Reliance on civilians will be higher in the immediate aftermath of a (major) crisis, when emergent groups are formed and formal crisis organizations have yet to mobilize.
- Frontline responders can opt for different forms of inclusion, varying from mere information exchange to full partnerships.
- The adaptive incorporation of civilians requires anticipation and relationship building, but should not come at the cost of support to victims.

QUESTIONS FOR REFLECTION AND DISCUSSION

- What are your experiences with civilians at crisis sites? What is their influence on your crisis response decisions and actions?
- How do you assess the legitimacy and utility of citizens that you encounter during response operations? Under what conditions would you include them in the response effort?
- What role do you anticipate for civilians in specific types of crises? How well is your organization prepared for including and coordinating with them?

---

11 | *Technology*
Early Adoption versus Skepticism

For centuries, armed forces have been at the forefront of technological innovation, as the development of increasingly advanced
weapons, body armor, and means of transportation resulted in
important advantages on the battlefield. It is therefore not surprising that there is a strong faith in modern technology among military personnel. New information and communication technologies
have been welcomed with high expectations and are being viewed as
revolutionary means to enable network-centric warfare, which is a
modern technology-based way of working that should produce better information sharing, faster interventions, and more agile military operations (Alberts et al., 2000; Cebrowski & Garstka, 1998).
Contemporary soldiers, sometimes already called "cyborg soldiers,"
are expected to be helped in their sensemaking, decision-making, and
task implementation by new technological equipment. Yet, practice
shows that reality is more complex. A US drone operating team
faced an overload of information when it was monitoring videos and
communicating with ground troops and analysts. New tools gave
them abundant information, but drowning in this information, they
arrived at the fatal perception that a gathering of Afghan villagers
posed a threat that needed to be eliminated, causing the deaths of
twenty-three civilians (Shanker & Richtel, 2011). A similar incident
had happened before, when Afghan civilians tapping fuel from two
hijacked fuel trucks were killed in an airstrike. It became clear that
live video feeds persuaded the observers into overestimating their
own environmental understanding and led to rash decision-making
with tragic consequences (van Burken, 2013). While drones and other
technologies are intended to help military personnel in their work,
the consequences of these new technologies are not unequivocally
positive and might even be disastrous.

New technologies hold the promise of better frontline operations
in combat situations by improving soldiers' situational understanding

and enabling faster communication. In fast-developing situations, particularly, such technologies should enable military personnel to adapt with greater speed and deliver more targeted interventions, ideally bringing crisis situations under control faster and reducing their impact. This might induce crisis organizations to become early adopters of new technologies. However, both in military and other crisis contexts, technologies often do not have the intended effects, leaving many frontline responders skeptical about the acquisition and incorporation of new technological tools and systems in their operations. Crisis professionals have to ask themselves whether new technological means are a blessing or a curse to their work.

11.1 New Technologies

New technologies have been widely adopted by emergency, humanitarian, and military organizations and are significantly changing the work of frontline crisis responders. These technologies are incorporated in crisis response operations in various ways. First, contemporary information gathering in crisis situations relies on an array of innovative tools and systems. This includes, for instance, Doppler radar for predicting extreme weather conditions and the use of satellites for producing aerial photos of the impact of a disaster (Bennett, 2019). In large disasters, next, geospatial technologies allow for locating infrastructure damage information at an unprecedented scale and the production of impact maps (Kawasaki et al., 2013). Crisis responders' situational awareness can be further improved by using autonomous flying robots, which are specialized in systematically searching for survivors in post-disaster environments, where the mobility of rescue workers is limited and urgency is key. The ability to locate survivors quickly and give an overview of trapped people in an affected area offer critical information to frontline rescuers (Arnold et al., 2018). After found and triaged, victims can be tagged and equipped with automated monitoring devices, so emergency care providers cannot only locate and track patients as they move through the acute care process, but are also able to check on patients in real time (Chan et al., 2004). Crisis data might even be collected by acquiring information from the general public through crowdsourcing, in which the crowd (e.g., affected population) is a key source of crisis-related information (Meier, 2011). Organizations can scan social media to identify reported needs by victims or ask affected people to report their observations and needs directly through everyday technologies, such as by texting or using smartphone applications. These examples of crowdsourcing may considerably improve the "information position" of frontline responders who will have a much more informed understanding of victims' circumstances in particular geographical areas as a consequence. With new information technologies, crisis organizations might have more information on their own crisis response resources too, because these technologies can also be employed to gain insight into the status of their capabilities and personnel, their location at a particular moment in time, and their current operations (Chan et al., 2004; Currion et al., 2007; Turoff et al., 2004).

Second, the analysis of all this information can be facilitated by new technological innovations. For example, it becomes much easier to mobilize large numbers of remotely located people to participate in analyzing the collected data. Digital volunteers have been of great use in scanning large quantities of satellite imagery on potential debris of the missing Malaysian Airlines Flight MH370, but also helped to create detailed maps of disaster areas for use by frontline responders (Fishwick, 2014; Meier, 2011). In other cases, Artificial Intelligence can be employed to predict and contain the spread of a disease outbreak. Or, after a disaster, it can classify social media updates into relevant categories, such as casualty reports or infrastructural damage, and identify which ones are informative to crisis response decision-making by filtering out noisy data (Imran et al., 2014). In combination, improved information gathering and analysis results in a better situational awareness.

Third, crisis organizations share information more easily by using modern communication technology. Importantly, they can more effectively distribute crisis information to the general public. After the information has been analyzed, responders could rapidly reach a broad segment of the population with warning notifications that are being sent out to (nearby) mobile phones or posted on social media. This type of crisis communication might steer people's behavior in a way that is beneficial to the response. Next, information sharing within organizations also benefits from progress in communication technologies, because personnel on different hierarchical levels are enabled to exchange information more rapidly and efficiently.

Frontline personnel can share observations through mobile phones or give their superiors better insight in operations through streaming their activities by means of live, body-worn cameras. In turn, managers may provide analyzed information or instructions through headsets or online platforms. In an interorganizational context as well, information sharing will improve due to the introduction of new technologies. Kapucu (2006) conducted interviews with personnel from organizations involved in the operational response to the 9/11 terrorist attacks and found that common information channels during the response included email, phone, and teleconferencing. A majority of interviewees believed that information technologies contributed to coordination between organizations and respondents recommended further use of information technologies and computerized networks for improving communication in emergency response networks. In another study, contemporary, complex crisis response networks are claimed to be only sustainable and effective in the presence of strong technology-based communication and information-sharing systems. Consistently, high performance by operational crisis response networks is argued to require additional investments in communication technologies (Kapucu & Garayev, 2013). In this regard, crisis response information systems seem particularly promising. Notably, information systems that are accessible and managed by multiple agencies enable improved sharing of relevant data by responders of different organizations (Bennett, 2019). These information systems provide all those involved in the response with graphical, up-to-date information about situational developments, available resources, response decisions, ongoing response activities, and possibly even impact assessments for alternative courses of action (see Bharosa et al., 2010; Comfort et al., 2004; Turoff et al., 2004; Wu et al., 2013). As such, the interorganizational decision-making process is supported by the most up-to-date information, which provides a strong basis for developing shared situational awareness across participating crisis organizations.

Finally, a broad variety of technologies is used in the implementation of crisis response activities. In military operations, this includes high-tech military vehicles, ships, and aircraft with increasingly advanced weapon systems. Autonomous weapons, in particular, are viewed as promising innovations and believed to give a competitive edge on the battlefield. Soldiers make mistakes during operational activities due to intense sensory impressions or the dullness of lengthy, uneventful missions, but autonomous weapon systems are likely better at processing information before implementing highly targeted interventions (Etzioni & Etzioni, 2017). More effective crisis interventions are also facilitated in the emergency response sector by new technology. Prehospital medical technologies, such as defibrillators, bag valve masks, and medications, save many lives on a daily basis and thus result in higher survival rates of patients. Other emergency responders can use robots for remote firefighting when access by firefighters is unsafe, searching and rescuing victims that are hard to reach, as well as inspecting and clearing explosives or other hazardous materials (Schneider & Wildermuth, 2017). In the humanitarian sector, finally, technological innovation creates opportunities for rapid digital cash transfers instead of cumbersome, risky logistical operations to serve affected people. Moreover, humanitarian drones can deliver medical aid or other supplies, while 3D printing allows for the immediate production of much-needed items in a humanitarian response (Arendt-Cassetta, 2021). New technologies, in short, affect crisis information collection, analysis, and sharing as well as the implementation of crisis activities, thereby potentially improving every aspect of frontline crisis response.

11.2 The Promise of New Technologies

Clearly, we have high expectations of these new technologies. To many, technological innovation is synonymous with progress and improvement of crisis response operations. Generally, response activities are believed to be more effective and adaptive as a result of the incorporation of novel technological tools and systems. A main reason for this belief is that it allows for a better operational picture. As responders have more crisis-related information that is better analyzed and can be rapidly communicated, they can adequately make sense of the nature of the situation and rapidly develop shared situational awareness. This line of reasoning is the main premise of the technology-based network-centric warfare approach, which propagates that armed forces should continuously collect and share data, use improved information analysis technologies, and employ modeling and display technologies for presenting data analyses, so as to gain a superior information position. This, in turn, allows for faster decision-making, quicker reactions to situational changes, a disruption of enemy plans and operations, and ultimately more combat power (Alberts et al., 2000; Cebrowski & Garstka, 1998).

In a very different context, a similar relation between crisis technologies and response performance is postulated. Danish medical dispatchers experimented with adding live videos to emergency calls and this technological innovation to emergency calls improved dispatchers' sensemaking. After adding a live video feed to the call, new analyses of patients' condition resulted in a revised and improved response in over a quarter of all cases (Linderoth et al., 2021). Better situational understanding of the crisis clearly facilitated decision-making and effective operations by these responders. Other research supports the idea that a strong situational understanding of operational crisis professionals, due to the use of new information and communication technologies, helps them to make more informed crisis response decisions (Beroggi & Wallace, 1995; Wu et al., 2013). As such, frontline crisis responders operate with increased responsiveness or even anticipate and address crisis situations before these get the chance to escalate (e.g., Alberts et al., 2000; Arendt-Cassetta, 2021). Actions are bound to be more impactful as a result. Altogether, these findings suggest more effective interventions and improved performance by frontline crisis responders.

Apart from improving frontline crisis response, there are additional reasons to use modern technology. An important one is safety. Crisis sites are often dangerous, so physical access is either limited or risky. Combat situations and burning buildings are obvious examples of dangerous operating environments, but so are incidents with hazardous substances and disaster-struck areas with damaged, fragile buildings or poor hygienic circumstances. When there are physical access limitations or safety risks to personnel are high, it is appealing to use advanced technologies instead. Collapsing buildings or falling debris render rescue and search activities dangerous, so robots may take the place of human rescuers and carry out the risky work, so their human operators do not have to risk their lives (Schneider & Wildermuth, 2017). In conflict settings, casualties among military personnel will drop if reconnaissance missions are carried out by autonomous vehicles rather than by units patrolling on foot. Likewise, humanitarian organizations frequently choose to manage humanitarian operations from a remote location, using information and communication technologies to guide and monitor operational activities from the relative safety of a fortified bunker or regional headquarters (Belliveau, 2016; Duffield, 2013).

Some other advantages of technology use in frontline crisis response are worthwhile mentioning as well. Communication technologies enable affected people to give feedback to crisis organizations and speak out against response failures. As such, it enables their meaningful participation and increases the accountability of crisis actors toward the people they are helping, reducing asymmetric power relations (IFRC, 2013). Technology may also cut costs of frontline crisis response. The US Department of Defense calculated that deploying a military robot to a war-zone would be over three times cheaper than deploying a soldier. Over time, unit sizes could therefore be significantly reduced (Etzioni & Etzioni, 2017). This does not only reduce spending, but also allows for more optimal use of personnel, which are in short supply for many crisis organizations, including armed forces. Similar efficiency gains are expected from digitizing information-gathering and analysis processes. In the aftermath of a disaster, Comfort et al. (2004) argue that information systems increase frontline response efficiency by facilitating information exchange between involved actors, thereby not only improving decision-making and coordination in the response effort, but also reducing the time and costs of the intervention. Given all these advantages, it should come as no surprise that the incorporation of modern technology is viewed as a very promising move in many crisis organizations. Early adoption of these new technologies is needed to quickly improve crisis response operations.

11.3 Technological Fix as Fiction

Interestingly, much of the excitement about technological innovation revolves around its potential, while operational experiences are mixed. The benefits ascribed to using modern technology in frontline crisis response are frequently assumed or predicted rather than demonstrated in practice. The enthusiasm about the great possibilities that these innovations offer easily blind us to seemingly inevitable implementation problems (see IFRC, 2013). One sobering example is the conclusion by the United States Congress (2006) that hundreds of millions of funding in crisis management technologies did not contribute to improved interoperability between involved agencies and organizations in the aftermath of Hurricane Katrina. Helicopter crews were unable to get in touch with boat crews, while commanders from the National Guards of Louisiana and Mississippi had to use runners to communicate. Clearly, there are some technological challenges to using modern technology in frontline crisis response.

In some cases, technological systems fail or malfunction, potentially causing disasters rather than helping to solve these. Perrow (1984) famously argued that modern-day technological systems, characterized by tight couplings and complex interactions between different parts, are bound to face accidents (so-called "normal accidents"), which have potentially catastrophic consequences. In his research, Perrow found that small mishaps or failures somewhere in the system tend to have cascading, escalating effects that human operators are unable to fully grasp or resolve, so the incorporation of new technologies in crisis response systems is a potentially perilous endeavor. Basically, it means that unforeseeable failures are more likely to happen when more technologies are integrated in crisis response systems. Case studies, indeed, show that reliance on technology makes some organizations vulnerable and prone to failure. The crew of Air France Flight 447, for example, relied strongly on cockpit automation, which under usual circumstances ensures a safe and comfortable flight. But when speed indications failed due to weather circumstances, the autopilot disconnected and the pilots had to fly manually in a stressful situation with which they had little experience. With failing technological aids, on which they continued to rely, the pilots took the wrong actions, causing a stall, and were unable to make sense of what was happening before crashing the aircraft into the Atlantic Ocean, losing over 200 lives. Advanced technological instruments may simply not work properly in certain situations and provide responders with erroneous cues, but equally problematic is technology's effect of undermining mindful awareness in crisis responders who are unable to bounce back after a small accident. Here, the very technology that usually helped these frontline operators to stay away from dangerous circumstances eroded their ability to understand and control the aircraft when the technology malfunctioned (Berthod & Müller-Seitz, 2018; Oliver et al., 2017).

In other crisis contexts, information and communication technologies may fail not by accident, but because of active attempts to destroy them and weaken the organization that employs them. Military and humanitarian organizations face this threat in conflict settings, when malicious actors attempt to hack into systems, steal data, or use malware and viruses to shut down computers, rendering cyber security increasingly important (Gentry, 2002; Sandvik, 2016). It becomes more and more clear, in the meanwhile, that such technological failures are particularly problematic, because responders are often less prepared for alternative, original ways of doing their job, having grown overly reliant on these technologies. As these examples demonstrate, the adoption of new technologies produces new vulnerabilities as well.

Even if new technologies do not fail, but perform well, there are limits to what these can achieve. Information-gathering and analysis tools, for instance, may offer vastly more information to frontline personnel, but more information is not necessarily better. The presumption that faster and more information will somehow lead to better crisis response interventions is wishful thinking. There is a real risk of information overload, as responders get overwhelmed by details of little relevance. In addition, data quality checks do not always suffice, so that available information is compromised, poor, or convoluted by a lot of "noise." And there are also concerns that communication quality decreases as non-verbal interactions or qualitative information get lost in exchange for the quantifiable, written data that technologies primarily collect and produce (Qadir et al., 2016; Quarantelli, 1997a). Reliance on technology may, moreover, produce a false sense of awareness or understanding, with frontline responders being over-confident that the images or other collected data offer a complete and fully accurate picture of reality rather than a partial snapshot or a specific version (van Burken, 2013). Indubitably, the fog of war is persistent. This is well-exemplified by an anecdote of a technologically advanced, well-trained unit of US Marines dropping 10,000 pounds of bombs on a suspected Iraqi convoy on one night in March 2003, only to discover the next day that it produced some craters but not a single hit, and realizing that they had no clue what happened just a few kilometers from their camp regardless of all their high-tech tools (Betz, 2006). This shows that crisis information is always limited and uncertainty, a defining element of crises, cannot be innovated away.

Moreover, technologies can usually not simply be incorporated in existing crisis organizations, but require changes to routines and ways of working. In fact, adopting new technologies is much more complex than simply giving frontline responders new tools or systems. Sometimes, required changes seem relatively minor, but are still problematic. For instance, emergency call centers in Louisiana did have the technology to reroute calls when overburdened, but failed to organize this, so that many 911 calls remained unanswered after Hurricane Katrina (United States Congress, 2006). In another example, crowdsourced mapping of the 2010 Haiti earthquake was very successful, but the resulting information remained unavailable to onsite responders in the disaster zone, limiting the operational effects on the ground (Kawasaki et al., 2013). And the armed forces have been unable to hire and retain IT professionals for installing and maintaining new tools and systems, stalling the military's information revolution (Gentry, 2002). Since new technologies often mean a need for more (trained) personnel, staffing issues are a recurring obstacle (McCormick, 2016).

In many other situations, technology adoption demands a significant shift in the operational approach of a crisis organization, which is not necessarily broadly supported among personnel for a multitude of reasons, varying from the protection of vested interests to an obstinate commitment to traditional ways of working. By extension, there is a question of what change is required when new technologies are adopted, since this is far from straightforward in many cases. For instance, when the Dutch government introduced a new information technology infrastructure for emergency response, it aimed for a uniform implementation across the country, but ended up with considerable implementation differences across regional crisis management organizations that did not see eye to eye on how the new information technology infrastructure should support their work (Boersma et al., 2012). The effects of technology adoption are not simple, nor always predictable. Information and communication technologies, for instance, may be used to improve the information position of the crisis response leader and increase top-down control (Beroggi & Wallace, 1995). But it might just as well lead to a shift of power to the frontline responders instead who use their improved situational awareness to synchronize their operational activities through discretionary decision-making (Cebrowski & Garstka, 1998). In any case, established ways of working usually have to be revised and the incorporation of new technologies almost inevitably requires (contested) organizational change.

11.4 Technological Skepticism

There are clear reasons to be reluctant about incorporating new technologies in crisis response organizations. At the risk of missing out on opportunities to advance crisis operations, scholars have identified several reasons to doubt whether it is wise to invest in new technologies at all. They argue that, even if all earlier problems are solved, the unintended side effects of the technological tools and systems do more harm than good to the crisis response efforts. Specifically, there are concerns about the emotional, political, and moral effects of new technology adoption.

One of these concerns is that such technologies detach responders from the crisis situation on the ground. New information-gathering tools enable a physical distancing from the crisis site, but this has various repercussions. While remotely managed crisis operations may reduce the physical risks to responders, it is also bound to reduce their situational awareness, because they are unable to experience and understand the crisis situation as richly when they can no longer interact face to face with victims and bystanders, nor register all the sensory impressions as they used to do. In the humanitarian sector, particularly, the technology-mediated approach to aid delivery is criticized for constituting a socioemotional withdrawal of frontline humanitarians from the field of operations and undermining their proximity and empathy with affected populations (Donini & Maxwell, 2013). The growing distance from the field also makes crisis professionals question themselves. Military drone operators, although describing a sense of virtual proximity, question their very identity as soldiers, because they do not travel to the frontline and experience any action themselves (Rauch & Ansari, 2022). Responders' personal involvement in the crisis, in short, is bound to deteriorate due to increased reliance on technological solutions.

Seemingly neutral technological solutions may also have profound political consequences. Most importantly, it may produce a hierarchy of victims, so that some get faster or better help than others. For instance, when social media are used for information-gathering purposes after a large-scale disaster, crisis support might well go to those who make (the best) use of them rather than those who need it the most.

Technology ideally empowers vulnerable and marginalized groups, but it may as likely silence them (Sandvik et al., 2014). Subsequently, crowdsourced information is not directly used for decision-making either, but is translated into data and subjected to analysis, which are processes from which affected populations are typically excluded. In these processes, as research on the Haiti earthquake and the Nepal earthquake shows, existing inequalities are often inadvertently reproduced as well, while an illusion of neutral, rapid situational awareness is maintained (Mulder et al., 2016). The reinforcement of established power structures is a disturbing, but often invisible, result from technology adoption in crisis contexts. When responders rely on face-to-face interactions instead, they may both have a smaller effect on sociopolitical relations and more local political awareness.

Finally, using technologies at the frontlines of crises has moral implications as well. One of these implications is that it transforms the relationship between operational responders and recipients. Importantly, technology-mediated interactions are feared to undermine the dignity of the latter. Victims are treated as data points rather than as humans, undercutting human-oriented treatment that is characterized by inter-personal respect (van Wynsberghe & Comes, 2020). In addition, information gathering and analysis systems do not produce amoral outcomes, but reflect the prejudices of their makers. With an air of superhuman neutrality, such systems legitimize the fundamentally arbitrary interventions at the frontlines of crises. Moreover, in changing the experiences of crisis response work, new moral questions arise as well. Drone operators of the Air Force share feelings of moral distress, since they watch their potential victims for some time, check whether all potential victims fit demographic requirements (i.e., males over twelve years old), fire at their unsuspecting victims, and see whether they are really dead afterward, while never facing any risk themselves. The operators' distant, virtual involvement as well as the questionable decision-making process preceding interventions are perceived as unfair and produce powerful feelings of shame and guilt. As new drone technology drastically changes the morality of military work, some drone operators strongly disidentify and estrange from the armed forces (Rauch & Ansari, 2022). When technology reforms crisis response operations, the changing relation between responders and recipients clearly evokes challenging moral questions (Table 11.1).

Table 11.1 *The technological dilemma*

	Early adoption	Skepticism
Characteristics	Fast incorporation of crisis response innovations Focus on technological promise	Reluctance to incorporate new technologies Avoiding unintended side effects of novel tools and systems
Advantages	Improved information position Faster adaptation Targeted interventions Reduced safety risks	More personal involvement in crisis Local political awareness Closer relations between responder and recipient
Shortcomings	Technological challenges Increased vulnerability Limited achievements Organizational change needed	Missing out on operational improvements

---

Empirical Example

Humanitarian aid workers operate in dangerous contexts and are often threatened, kidnapped, or even killed during the implementation of their work. NGOs, UN agencies, and the Red Cross have adopted various security measures to protect their staff. Specifically, technological tools and systems are increasingly employed to keep them safe. For instance, security information is collected by monitoring social media accounts, while tracking devices are used to geo-locate frontline aid workers when they are on the road. Next, incidents and alerts are shared through online platforms or mobile phones to inform aid workers about evolving risk situations or to warn them about dangerous developments in the field. Humanitarian technologies also enable aid workers to work remotely. Needs assessments, services delivery, and monitoring of projects no longer require a large physical presence in the area of operations, so fewer staff members are required to go in the field and more humanitarians can stay in bunker-like locations or work from abroad. This operating modality, in which more and more aid workers operate from a safe distance, is called "remote management." It is increasingly popular in dangerous operating contexts, relies heavily on new technologies, and is widely believed to minimize security risks to aid workers. Upon reflection, however, the use of humanitarian technologies does not necessarily reduce risks. In some areas, technological tools have military connotations and may be the reason for armed groups to target the aid workers who use them. Also, malevolent actors try to undermine these technologies: "professional hijackers know by now that organizations equip their cars with [vehicle tracking devices], so they use jamming devices or detection equipment to scan such a car." Technologies, clearly, also introduce new vulnerabilities, triggering a need for further innovations to maintain high levels of security. While security threats to aid workers, in general, may still be reduced, the remaining risks are likely to be faced by local staff operating in the field, because expats are the first to be withdrawn to a remote, safe location. As a result, risks are unevenly divided over humanitarians rather than reduced for all of them equally, potentially producing resentment in the organization. It is also important to note that the adoption of humanitarian technologies is not solely guided by neutral, objective needs assessments. Local political actors, such as armed groups and governments, influence which technologies aid agencies can use in a particular area. One country director in Somalia shared that "they know that if they do not allow us to work with cameras and GPS coordinates and those sort of things, (…) we don't work." This basically means that local actors can use humanitarians' reliance on technologies to exercise control over humanitarian operations and it shows that the use of humanitarian technologies itself is inextricably politicized in many crisis contexts. Another political effect of technology adoption is a shift of power to those local staff members or gatekeepers who know how to use them, because they will hold a key position. Overall, there are concerns that grassroots relations decrease, while distrust toward remotely managed projects is often reported, and the legitimacy of technology-mediated operations among local personnel is doubted. The increased reliance on technologies may make humanitarians operations safer for staff, but it also produces a range of new problems for humanitarian organizations (Kalkman, 2018).

11.5 A Prudent Approach

New technologies for crisis information-gathering and analysis, communication, and response implementation are very attractive. They hold a promise of more effective and efficient frontline crisis responses with smaller risks to responders on the ground. It is therefore appealing to follow technological developments closely and incorporate new technologies early. Critics, however, have not hesitated to point out that technologies often do not meet high expectations due to a range of implementation problems, but also because of unanticipated social and organizational problems. In addition, there are frequently undesirable emotional, political, and moral side effects to adopting technological tools and systems in crisis contexts. The dilemma for frontline crisis responders revolves around finding the right attitude and approach toward these new technologies.

It is useful to start by recognizing that technological innovation is a historical inevitability, regardless of the criticisms of crisis scholars. There is no point in refusing to stay up to date with new innovations or to refrain from using new technologies for frontline crisis response altogether. In fact, if organizations do not keep up with recent developments, it will undermine their effectiveness in the long run. Warning signals are often better distributed through mobile phone alerts than outdoor sirens and people will look for information online rather than listen to the radio. Similarly, frontline personnel that aim to communicate with unfamiliar partners after a disaster better use relatively new but familiar platforms, such as WhatsApp, Skype, and Gmail, rather than resort to landlines, fax machines, or satellite phones (Kalkman, 2023a). Crisis organizations should at least keep up with technologies that define their societies or will render themselves outdated and become ineffective. Clearly, there are overwhelming advantages to using some of these new technologies as well. In the past, it could take a long time for news of a crisis to reach responders and thus for them to respond, while first responders may now arrive in a few minutes after an incident and humanitarian goods will fly into affected areas within a day of a catastrophic disaster. Indeed, some of the criticism against crisis technologies is not so much directed at possible technological failures but at organizational failures to make optimal use of them (e.g., Kawasaki et al., 2013; United States Congress, 2006), thereby in fact supporting their use.

This does not mean that crisis organizations necessarily need to be at the forefront of technological progress. There is a tendency to assume that newer technologies are better than the existing ones, but this is a fallacy. New tools and systems are appealing, but should not be adopted for their own sake. Technological innovations only make sense to incorporate when these can actually contribute to resolving a problem or otherwise improve crisis response outcomes. The idea that crisis organizations should only adopt a new technology if it helps them do their work sounds like a truism, but technological solutions are frequently proposed to resolve social or moral problems. Proposing a technological solution to a thorny problem seems a safe way out of a controversial issues, but it is never a real solution and will inevitably fail. For instance, when frontline responders do not trust their superiors or there is animosity between two crisis organizations with incongruent views on the nature of a particular crisis, it does not matter that technology can improve communication and information-sharing, because it will not do so under these circumstances. By extension, a certain technology fetishism may lead to a situation where the (technological) solution is already selected while only waiting for the momentum to be introduced (Cohen et al., 1972), regardless of calls to analyze crisis response problems before choosing (technological) solutions (Gentry, 2002; Quarantelli, 1997a).

Technological innovations, next, are diverse and have widely different applications and consequences. The discussions about advantages and risks, however, are often generic. To some extent, that makes sense. Technologies, generally, may enable safer operations, while all technologies may fail or require organizational adaptions. At the same time, this approach risks blinding us to the differential implications of using specific tools and systems. For instance, some tools or systems may make frontline response less efficient because they are overly complex, while others are highly unlikely to fail because they are very resilient. In addition, some tools and systems (e.g., big data analysis) may be useful after large-scale disasters, but less so during small emergencies. The impact on effectiveness, coordination, and operational costs will likely vary (see Stephenson & Anderson, 1997), but recent research mostly speculates about the broad implications of crisis technologies rather than focuses on the consequences of the adoption of one specific technology in a crisis organization.

It is equally important to study how new technologies are incorporated in crisis organizations. There is a rich body of knowledge on resilience engineering, value sensitive design, and responsible research and innovation, which provides useful insights on safety, ethical, and societal aspects of designing and incorporating new technologies in organizations. These insights appear to be rarely used for the analysis or governance of technology adoption in frontline crisis response, but may help crisis responders to adopt novel technologies in a deliberate and conscientious manner. Recently, crisis scholars have developed some guiding principles for when crisis responders are contemplating the incorporation of a new technology. One of the most important principles is that the technology that is to be used during a crisis should be the same as the one used before the crisis, since frontline responders will resort to the tools and system that they know and trust (Bharosa et al., 2010; Groenendaal & Helsloot, 2021; Turoff et al., 2004). It should also be easy to use and not take up more attention and time than absolutely necessary, because frontline responders are already cognitively overtaxed and overburdened during crises (Bharosa et al., 2010; Turoff et al., 2004). Ideally, therefore, new technologies either replace preexisting ones or are integrated with them (Groenendaal & Helsloot, 2021). To avoid the adoption of new technologies for novelty's sake, there must be a logical fit between a task and a technology, so that every new tool or system serves a clear purpose (Mendonça et al., 2007). And when novel technologies are incorporated, crisis managers should be aware of the limitations of these technologies, such as the fact that sense-making will never be perfect regardless of how much information is collected and the inevitability of frontline improvisation irrespective of how confident leaders are about their situational awareness. This means that technological innovations are misused when they lead to organizational or operational rigidity (see Groenendaal & Helsloot, 2021; Mendonça et al., 2007). These principles reflect the belief that new technologies should serve frontline crisis responders and not the other way around. This also means that if frontline responders are not included in the selection and implementation process, the technology is bound to fail.

Technological progress is exciting and fuels a hope that persistent challenges to frontline crisis response can be reduced or altogether resolved. Better situational awareness and interventions are possible with the adoption of new technologies, but the impact of advanced tools and systems does often not meet the high expectations or even fail altogether. To some extent, this is an inescapable part of the innovation process. Yet, when lives are at stake, as is the case in frontline crisis response, cautious implementation of new technologies is warranted. Both the direct and broader implications of specific technologies are to be considered and principles for their design and implementation are to be observed. In the end, a prudent view on technologies accepts its potential with a combination of hesitation and curiosity.

11.6 Conclusion

New technologies hold great promises for improving frontline crisis response, but past experiences show that these promises do not always materialize and that frontline responders should be concerned about undesirable side effects. A prudent approach toward new tools and systems will help responders to choose those technologies that truly contribute to crisis response operations and incorporate these in an appropriate way.

In the future, evidence-based studies are needed to analyze the diverse effects of specific technologies that are used by crisis organizations. In addition, it is worthwhile comparing implementation processes in crisis organizations to find out more about the organizational changes that new technologies require and trigger. Finally, the guiding principles for technology adoption in crisis contexts need to be tested, so these can be refined and complemented.

Resources for Educators and Professionals

PRACTICAL LESSONS

- New technologies may improve crisis response operations in various ways, but often do not meet high expectations or have unforeseen negative consequences.
- New technologies should not be adopted for their own sake, but need to solve a specific, technical problem.
- The potential direct and broader effects of a new technology should be explored beforehand.
- Crisis organizations need to keep up with popular technological innovations to be able to stay in touch with the communities they serve.
- New technologies should be easy to use, serve a clear purpose, empower responders, and also be used before crises to ensure familiarity.

QUESTIONS FOR REFLECTION AND DISCUSSION

- Which recurrent crisis response problems do you face in your work?
  Which of these can be solved by technological innovations and which
  cannot?
- What technology has changed your work the most since you began
  your career? How has your work changed? Why was this technology
  influential?
- How are new technologies introduced in your crisis organization?
  To what extent is there a clear problem to be solved and are possible
  side effects explored?

12 | Goals
Restoring Order versus
Social Transformation

The 2004 Indian Ocean tsunami caused massive death, destruction, and displacement among numerous coastal communities. Extremely high and destructive waves reached hundreds of meters inland, making it one of the deadliest disasters in recorded history. The humanitarian response was unprecedented and enormous quantities of emergency aid were rushed to the affected areas. While this powerful response was crucial in alleviating suffering, it also attracted considerable criticism. The poor and marginalized were hit hardest by the disaster, but the response efforts often favored social groups that were already better off. In Sri Lanka, for instance, powerful groups benefited more from the aid programs than vulnerable groups, such as poor Muslim fishing communities, so that the humanitarian aid provision exacerbated ethnic tensions and inequality (Amarasiri de Silva, 2009). In multiple affected countries, moreover, women were excluded from relief, because of discriminatory policies or because their specific needs were often simply not considered. Despite the large influx of humanitarian aid in the aftermath of the tsunami, they were therefore left poor, excluded, and marginalized (Akerkar, 2007). The size of the tsunami response effort was impressive, but the outcomes raised important questions about the fairness of humanitarian relief operations.

Many tsunami response efforts appear to have aimed for a speedy return to normality and a restoration of the status quo. Yet, since societies were characterized by discrimination and inequality before the crisis, some groups proved more vulnerable to the tsunami than others. These vulnerabilities were upheld or worsened when responders did not actively try to avoid such effects. Alternatively, frontline responders could have tried to pursue social transformation in an attempt to reduce the vulnerabilities of marginalized groups. Still, this is difficult to achieve even in ordinary times, let alone during the massively uncertain and precarious post-tsunami situation. As such, the tsunami response evokes fundamental questions regarding the effectiveness and performance of crisis response operations. By extension, frontline responders face a dilemma regarding the goal of their operations, as they are simultaneously expected to restore order and promote social transformation through their crisis response efforts.

12.1 Restoring Order

Crises are traditionally viewed as disturbing periods of chaos and turmoil. The goal of frontline crisis responders is therefore to rapidly end the disruption and reestablish normality (Dynes, 1994). Ideally, responders quickly retake control and bring the threatening situation to an end, saving people and property, and allowing for daily life to continue (Comfort, 2007). From this perspective, success is measured by how well responders managed to minimize the interruption and how fast communities could return to the preexisting status quo. Many crisis studies, implicitly, adopt this view. Studies on performance indicators and critical success factors usually focus on the preparations of crisis organizations, the speed with which they arrived at the scene, or the quality of coordination between involved responders, believing these aspects to be necessary for a quick return to the status quo (Abir et al., 2017; Zhou et al., 2011). A discussion of goals or general effects of the crisis response operations is surprisingly absent in this operationalization of crisis response success.

The implicit assumption that a return to order is the main goal of crisis organizations also features in prominent definitions of crisis management. In one influential review, it is defined as the "attempt to bring a disrupted or weakened system at any stage of crisis back into alignment to achieve normal functioning" (Williams et al., 2017, p. 740). Elsewhere, crisis management is described as the "attempt to reduce the likelihood of a crisis, work to minimize harm from a crisis, and endeavor to reestablish order following a crisis" (Bundy et al., 2017, p. 1663). The recurring emphasis on restoring normality, order, and stability is illustrative of the tacit objective to bring things back to how they were before the disruption.

This objective is quite clearly reflected in the operations of crisis organizations as well. When firefighters extinguish a house fire or emergency room physicians are trying to save someone's life, the immediate danger of the crisis situation is being averted and some form of order in people's lives is restored. Similarly, when the police respond to riots or border guards react to a migration crisis, frontline responders literally aim to restore order in a certain location. In a military context, likewise, troops are often deployed to eliminate a threat and bring stability to a country or community that suffers from chaos or conflict. During their deployment, military units protect their area of operations against destabilizing forces and will engage enemy combatants to neutralize the risk they pose to the order that the soldiers seek to bring. Tellingly, military personnel themselves use the restoration of normal life and the creation of relative stability in the mission area as their standards of success for assessing the performance of their frontline operations (Beeres et al., 2010). Finally, many humanitarian organizations provide lifesaving assistance in line with humanitarian principles, such as impartiality and neutrality (ICRC, 2015). These principles allow for the creation of a politics-free "humanitarian space," in which all parties accept that aid workers are purely driven by humanitarian motives, so they can deliver urgent relief without restrictions from political actors (Terry, 2011). Such an apolitical approach means that these humanitarians act as neutral professionals (Fox, 2001), who are simultaneously alleviating suffering and stabilizing the situation.

In this view, thus, crisis response is about restoring order to avert chaos. But when the restoration of order is the primary outcome of crisis response, it also means an implicit acceptance of the status quo. Whether this status quo is fair and worthy of being preserved in the first place is not deemed a relevant question. Rather, frontline responders are neutral professionals who impartially strive to resolve the crisis situation and ensure that everyone can rapidly return to their daily lives.

12.2 Discrimination in Crisis Response

Problematically, a passive acceptance of the status quo might mean that crisis responders enable a preservation of an unjust, morally questionable social order. This unsettling thought is the starting-point of a more critical perspective on crisis response. In this perspective, crises are not seen as chaotic disruptions of normality, but are believed to be primarily characterized by social continuity. Societal structures remain intact during the ordeal and preexisting institutions will determine how organizations and people behave in these situations (see Dynes, 1994). This also means that social systems that are unfair and unjust to certain social groups prior to a crisis forebode inequitable effects of the crisis, because discrimination before a crisis will not magically disappear at the critical moment. In fact, a crisis can even be a manifestation of societal injustice itself, particularly when the marginalization of a group pushes it into harm's way. The 2004 tsunami, for example, struck poor Muslim communities in Sri Lanka very hard, because they were living in vulnerable places and congested housing. In addition, women and girls disproportionally died from the disaster in many countries, as they could not swim, their clothes restricted movement, and they were supposed to save the children first (Amarasiri de Silva, 2009; Enarson et al., 2007).

A vast amount of research on disaster sociology has now demonstrated that some groups are indeed much more vulnerable to crises and will bear the brunt of the effects, as social structures put them at a disadvantage, while prevention and preparation measures are not aimed at improving their chances. This explains why scholars argue that the root causes of these disasters are social (Chmutina & Von Meding, 2019; Tierney, 2007, 2019). But if societies discriminate, there is no reason to expect that crisis organizations, rooted in those societies, stand out as completely neutral and fair actors. From this perspective, crisis response may inadvertently perpetuate marginalized communities' vulnerability to crises. Thus, crisis response in this critical view is potentially an extension of the inequity-producing social order and therefore likely an unfair process in itself.

While the effects of discriminatory social systems on crisis vulnerability and recovery have received due attention, there is less research on discrimination in the crisis response phase. Yet, there are sufficient indications that discriminatory prejudices affect the actions of crisis organizations at this stage as well. One noteworthy and disturbing example comes from the aftermath of the 1985 Mexico earthquake, during which police and soldiers went out to protect elites and their property against looting, while ignoring the desperate cries for help from the disadvantaged workers trapped under the rubble (Solnit, 2010). In crisis studies, there are many similar illustrations of discrimination. Gender, race, and class are three of the main factors that explain why some individuals suffer more from crises than others (Enarson et al., 2007; Fothergill, Maestas, & Darlington, 1999; Morrow & Enarson, 1996; Neumayer & Plümper, 2007; Patel et al., 2020; Tierney, 2019).

Women are often negatively affected by patriarchal response procedures and practices. Across the globe, there are cultural or societal obstacles for women to receive disaster aid. One recurring reason for this is that they do not enjoy equal rights or are excluded from public forums through which aid is distributed (Akerkar, 2007). Assistance checks and other financial compensation is often distributed to men who are seen as heading the household, so that relief repeatedly fails to reach women, who are usually running the household and taking care of its members in practice (Byrne & Baden, 1995; Morrow & Enarson, 1996). In addition, women are given little influence in the crisis response stage, which is problematic, because their specific needs, such as menstrual hygiene products or protection against gender-based violence, are not considered as a result (Enarson et al., 2007). In smaller emergencies, as well, gender disparities are commonplace. Women who report chest pain, for example, are less likely than men with the same symptoms to receive aspirin or be transported with sirens and light by emergency medical services. They are also less likely to be resuscitated in case of out-of-hospital cardiac arrests (Lewis et al., 2019). Even in maritime disasters, where there is supposedly a norm to let women and children depart the sinking ship and enter the lifeboats first, women are in fact more likely to die than men from shipwrecks, making the Titanic's high survival rate of female passengers a rare exception (Elinder & Erixson, 2012).

Racial and ethnic minorities are also facing inequitable treatment in many crisis response operations. A powerful example comes from the notable differences in law enforcement reactions to two protests in Washington DC: a fairly peaceful Black Lives Matter protest on June 1, 2020, faced an excessively forceful intervention to clear Lafayette Square, while during the Capitol riot of January 6, 2021, police officers were outnumbered and reinforcements arrived late (Chason & Schmidt, 2021). Another study on US policing shows significant racial disparity as well, since minorities are much more likely to be subjected to investigatory stops by law enforcement personnel than whites (Epp et al., 2014). In a different context, African Americans were more likely to suffer and die from Hurricane Katrina as well, because evacuation orders did not reach them or seemed untrustworthy to them (Bolin & Kurtz, 2018). Those who stayed were subsequently treated as criminals rather than victims (Tierney et al., 2006). Similarly, systemic racism toward Puerto Ricans explains both the disastrous impact of Hurricane Irma and Hurricane Maria on the island and the underwhelming response by the US federal government compared with responses to disasters on the mainland (Rodriguez-Díaz & Lewellen-Williams, 2020). In smaller incidents, a large study in the United States shows that white patients are most likely to receive pain medication, and black patients in pain are least likely to receive it. Even pediatric patients of racial or ethnic minority backgrounds are less likely to be administered pain medication than white children (Hewes et al., 2018). A similar study of one state in the USA confirms that it was much less common for Hispanic and Asian patients to have their pain assessed and all minority patients had a smaller chance of receiving pain medication by emergency medical services than white patients (Kennel et al., 2019).

Finally, the poor are known to often miss out on emergency response services too. Sometimes, they are simply not on the radar of frontline responders, because they live in unmapped houses or streets, are illiterate, or are distrustful of the government. In addition, media reports after disasters will typically highlight the impact of the crisis on the relatively affluent, guiding response efforts to these fairly well-off neighborhoods rather than those neighborhoods in which people are most needy (Fothergill & Peek, 2004). During Hurricane Katrina, for instance, the poor did not own means of transportation and could not afford the evacuation or they cared for someone who was unable to evacuate, so they stayed behind and were left to fight for themselves by the government that failed to provide even the most basic services (Bolin & Kurtz, 2018). Moreover, there is some evidence from South Korea and the US, which shows that when emergency medical services are called for cardiac arrests, their response times are longer for low-income areas and more often missing benchmarks that ensure rapid medical aid when time is scarce (Hsia et al., 2018; Ramos et al., 2021).

There are other identity markers that render people marginalized and less well-served in crisis response efforts. For instance, lesbian, gay, bisexual, transgender, queer, and other non-heterosexual or non-cisgender communities often face discrimination. People with disabilities, children, and the elderly may also have special needs that responders do not consider. And migration status and caste are additional reasons that leave people underserved in crisis response operations. Importantly, identity markers interact to make individuals potentially more vulnerable (i.e., intersectionality). White, well-off, middle-aged men usually enjoy the best crisis response services across disasters and emergencies. Vice versa, poor women from minority groups are almost always hit the hardest and suffer the longest, as multiple categories of marginalization compound their vulnerability (Enarson et al., 2007; Morrow & Enarson, 1996).

12.3 Discrimination in Crisis Organizations

Structural discrimination does not only affect frontline crisis response activities, but also crisis organizations themselves. In some of these organizations, including fire brigades, armed forces, special police units, and rescue services, there are very prominent masculine, chauvinistic, and elitist norms. It is not uncommon for these organizations to have an organizational culture, which favors a specific type of employee (e.g., ethnic majority, middle or upper class men), while anyone deviating from this ideal-typical image faces obstacles. As a result, these organizations are usually not diverse, nor inclusive to women and minority groups who choose to join their ranks.

First, studies in a broad variety of crisis organizations show that these are almost invariably masculine organizations with persistent barriers to the inclusion and full participation of women. Examples from the fire services are telling. Over a third of women report harassment and sexual advances, while more than five percent were assaulted (Jahnke et al., 2019). Women are told they do not belong in the organization, they are patronized, and their abilities are constantly questioned, while their actions are closely watched (Chetkovich, 1997; Mastracci et al., 2014). Any small mistake, regardless of how common among men, is blamed on women's gender, and their career progress is hampered by assumptions about their lack of interest and availability or simply because of favoritism toward male colleagues. In daily work, men dominate meetings and leaders fail to take notice of women's contributions (Parkinson et al., 2019). The result is that women have to work harder for similar evaluations, face mental challenges, and might leave the organization prematurely (Jahnke et al., 2019). In other crisis organizations, similar situations exist (Alvinius et al., 2021). In one rescue organization, gender stereotypes portrayed men as superior rescuers due to their assumed physical strength, technical inclination, and emotional resilience. Their self-confidence was not even adversely affected by poor performance. Vice versa, women performing well did not experience a boost in self-confidence either. As such, gender stereotypes remained intact (Lois, 2003). In armed forces, as well, masculinity features in almost every organizational aspect. Feminine traits, although crucial in peacekeeping missions, are rejected, while aggressive violence is often glorified. In addition, the uniforms are made for men, stereotypes that portray women as weak and unfit are repeated, and women are blamed for adversely affecting military effectiveness (Heinecken, 2015). There is also a gendered allocation of roles, a use of masculine norms for evaluation of performance, and generally, a reproduction of gender inequality in armed forces, which results in women being excluded from full participation in organizational activities (Alvinius et al., 2018; Sasson-Levy & Amram-Katz, 2007).

Racial and ethnic minorities face similar obstacles to full inclusion when they join crisis organizations. In the post-9/11 US Navy, for instance, black personnel is promoted at a rate of seventy-nine percent and Hispanics at seventy-two percent relative to white service members (Golan et al., 2021). In the UK, minority background personnel makes up 7.6 percent of the armed forces, but are less likely to reach higher ranks, as only 2.4 percent of officers is from a racial or ethnic minority group (Clark et al., 2022). Minority soldiers also get longer sentences in the military justice system, face higher risks of PTSD, and experience more barriers to receiving care through the Veterans Affairs health-care system (Burk & Espinoza, 2012). Sometimes, minority frontline personnel may not perceive the crisis organization in general as discriminatory, but only particular individuals or units in it. In a study on the Oakland fire service, Chetkovich (1997) reports that minority personnel do not fully trust some majority colleagues to have their backs in a risky situation, because they are known to have racist views. Also, some fire stations, dominated by older white officers, are described as traditional and openly antagonistic to minority firefighters. This does not necessarily make these minority firefighters feel excluded, but still makes hazing rituals and career progression harder for them. In the context of extreme expeditions, discrimination against minorities is also apparent. In the 1996 Mount Everest climbing disaster, the Sherpa supported the climbing expedition and engaged in heroic rescue attempts when things went awry, but were silenced in post hoc accounts and if they were mentioned at all, they were primarily blamed for a lack of discipline rather than being submissive to their Western superiors (Elmes & Frame, 2008). Finally, many in the humanitarian sector are well aware of the troubled history of humanitarianism, in which notions of the white man's burden, colonialism, and Western imperialism were mixed with aid efforts. Still, Westerners at international headquarters and expats in regional offices are largely in control over how humanitarian aid is distributed, while local staff mostly implements projects on the ground. There are increasing calls for a decentralization of power, through which local staff gain decision-making responsibilities and are empowered to lead aid projects autonomously (Maietta et al., 2017; Slim, 2021), but these efforts to promote racial and ethnic equity in humanitarian organizations still have to materialize.

Finally, class continues to be an important factor in crisis organizations as well. Sometimes, the effects of socioeconomic inequality are very clear. Take the large gap in humanitarian agencies between well-off expats residing in relative safety (e.g., aid compounds or abroad) and visiting project sites in armored vehicles, while the much poorer local staff frequently operate in risky settings with fewer resources at their disposal. Similarly, in extreme expeditions, wealthy clients require the services of economically disadvantaged guides, putting them on an unequal footing as they enter perilous areas. The armed forces were traditionally a class-based organization as well with aristocrats holding senior officer positions and getting preferential medical treatment over the lower-class soldiers. Still, there is a socioeconomic casualty gap in US military operations. Military personnel from poor families are more likely to die in combat than those that come from richer, high-educated social backgrounds (Kriner & Shen, 2010). Relatedly, the "class ceiling" remains relevant, among others in the UK Navy, where socioeconomic background continues to affect career progression and the most senior ranks are filled by a class-wise homogenous elite (Clark et al., 2022). In Israel, also, the class differentiation is maintained, because the glorified combat role is almost solely accessible to middle-class draftees who use their military service for self-development and career advancement, while lower-class youths are condemned to blue-collar work that marginalizes them. Thus, the armed forces are not a "great equalizer," but underscore and reproduce socioeconomic inequality (Levy & Sasson-Levy, 2008).

Within crisis organizations, too, there are other identity markers that adversely affect some people's ability to join, be fully included, or reach a leadership position. Examples include the LGBTQ+ community, disabled people, and those without proper documentation. They do not fit pervasive norms in these crisis organizations either. Again, intersectionality is important, as some people's identities (e.g., poor women of ethnic minority groups) leave them particularly marginalized, so their voices are even less likely to be heard and taken seriously. Problematically, the exclusion of marginalized groups feeds back into narratives on the exceptionality of members of the dominant social group and can be used by them as justification for their continued discrimination against others. Discriminatory crisis organizations, next, are prone to reinforce societal inequalities through their crisis response operations, as personnel may well view crises as disruptions of the social order to be contained and reversed.

12.4 Crisis as an Opportunity for Change

The marginalization of specific social groups in and by crisis organizations indicates that crisis response is not a neutral, apolitical process. In times of scarcity and need, responders distribute crucial services that can potentially mean the difference between life and death for those affected. Inevitably, it will influence the social relations and distribution of resources in a community or society (Olson, 2000). This also explains why involved actors will try to steer and negotiate the operations of crisis organizations (Hilhorst & Jansen, 2010). Still, this side of crisis response often remains hidden behind a rhetoric of impartial, technocratic professionalism. For instance, official evaluation reports pretend to give a hegemonic account of events and suggest an objective assessment of crisis responders' performance. In reality, however, there are many different ways to measure success and failure, multiple outcomes will be differentially and partially reached, and evaluators are bound to have differing perceptions, so every evaluation is inherently politicized (McConnell, 2011, 2020). When crisis response is recognized as an inherently political activity, frontline responders have good reasons to debate and reconsider their goals (Hilhorst, 2002). If they stick to restoring order as their main goal, crisis response becomes little more than the attempt to minimize the consequences of the crises that the current social order produces by helping those who suffer from them, while doing nothing to challenge the crisis-producing order itself (Barnett, 2005). Frontline responders can choose to be more ambitious though and see a crisis as an opportunity to reform society for the better.

Crises show the failures of the existing order and produce opportunities for much-needed change, because these failures are suddenly very clear for all to see. In any case, this understanding provides a basis for criticizing crisis responses that reproduce inequality. It does not matter if a response was fast and well coordinated: when vulnerable groups are further stigmatized and marginalized after the crisis response phase is over, the response was a failure. For example, the 2004 tsunami response, which left women and minorities (further) marginalized (Akerkar, 2007; Amarasiri de Silva, 2009), deserved a meticulous review to discover the origins of these disappointing consequences and to ensure that similar results are avoided in future operations. Crisis response is a public service that is supposed to be delivered in a fair and accountable manner (Maynard-Moody & Musheno, 2012), but if it fails to do so, crisis organizations need to be held responsible.

More boldly, frontline responders can develop an activist posture and strive to correct discrimination. To this end, crisis organizations should embrace an agenda for societal change that reduces the vulnerability of marginalized groups and increases their resilience. A feminist ethics of care approach provides a basis for such a radical alternative to current crisis response approaches. It is based on a relational logic that prioritizes interpersonal relationships during crises, emphasizes the quality of care, and aims for social transformation toward a better social order (Branicki, 2020). In this line of thinking, frontline crisis response is not just a practical attempt to resolve the crisis and reduce its impact, but an opportunity to address historical inequality and dismantle unjust power structures (Leach & Rivera, 2022). In the pursuit of fair crisis interventions, it makes sense that crisis responders' actions serve those with the highest needs first, which increases societal resilience in the long run. In practice, this means that frontline responders have to compensate for existing societal inequalities by prioritizing the marginalized and vulnerable in their response efforts.

Changing the goal of crisis response from restoring order toward promoting social transformation is not without its risks and challenges though. Frontline crisis responders are professionals with technical expertise in their work and may not want to be activists for social change. Indeed, persistent discrimination within crisis organizations suggests that there will be limited support among personnel,

Table 12.1 *The dilemma of crisis response goals*

	Restoring order	Social transformation
Characteristics	Rapidly ending the disruption Preserving the status quo	Crisis as an opportunity for change Reform society for the better
Advantages	Averting chaos Speedy return to ordinary life Protecting responders' neutral professionalism	Correcting past inequality and discrimination Increasing societal resilience Fair crisis interventions
Shortcomings	Might uphold unjust social order Potential discrimination based on gender, race, and class Perpetuating vulnerabilities	Limited support and disagreement among crisis responders Politicization of crisis response

at least initially. Even if there is support for such a focus in a crisis organization, there will likely be disagreement between organizational members about what social transformation should entail in practice and how it can best be achieved. There is also a risk of politicizing crisis response (see Fox, 2001), opening up space for criticism of front-line response actions on a political basis and potentially impinging on responders' professionalism. Despite these disadvantages, a neutral approach is not only a political choice in itself, but also seems increasingly untenable in an unjust world (Table 12.1).

Empirical Example

During the height of the EU refugee crisis, thousands of refugees arrived in Greece on a weekly basis. In response, a team of Dutch border management officers, stationed at Chios, was tasked with intercepting and apprehending people who illegally crossed the Aegean Sea and had to bring them ashore so they could be interrogated and registered at the reception center. Their mission was to support the Greek authorities in ramping up border protection and stabilizing the situation. Yet, this is not how they viewed their task. Most of them almost instantly rejected the security framing of the crisis and their security-oriented mission. They saw the suffering and hardships of refugees and recounted tragedies with great feeling: "There was one boy of five who died during the passage from malnutrition. He had been on the road for so long. Some sat on the boat for three hours in cold conditions. He was on his way for months from Syria, and he died due to malnutrition. So, a boat arrived with a dead child inside." Another shared: "This deployment was very tough for me yes. I have been deployed eight times in total and have been in war areas [...] but this, with little children, boats capsizing, children falling into the water...." These experiences and emotions motivated the majority of the border officials to reframe the situation as a humanitarian crisis. Interestingly, they even began to make sense of themselves as humanitarians, seeking increasing cooperation with NGOs and volunteers by sharing information and coordinating their actions. By extension, they began taking humanitarian actions themselves. After the death of a Syrian boy, members dug a grave and ensured that the costs were covered, one helped in the washing rituals, and many attended the funeral. In addition, they participated in daily humanitarian activities. One of them said: "I have also been distributing food, serving soup to refugees. [...] If you see that people are needed and you don't have anything to do, why wouldn't you help?" Even though it appears curious that members from a border protection organization sided with refugees against the EU's strict border control policies, one member justified the team's crisis response activities by empathizing with refugees: "What would you do? You would take the gamble. Yes, I'd go with the flow of refugees, maybe I'd succeed and maybe I am able to give my family a future." While their humanitarian actions went against the spirit of their deployment, they felt compelled to adopt a crisis response approach that effectively pursued social transformation. They failed, however, to convince their leadership of this need for change in the crisis response approach, so it was not institutionalized. Later, when they were relieved, teams received clearer instructions and were granted less discretionary space. Members of these subsequent teams became progressively skeptical of immigration, repeating that their main goal was to restore order at the external EU border by adopting a crime-fighting posture and enforcing strict compliance with stringent EU migration policies (Kalkman, 2019a).

12.5 Social Equity

A majority of studies assume that frontline crisis response is aimed at resolving the disruption as quickly as possible and restoring the status quo. This approach defines the goals of crisis response narrowly and does not heed the structural inequalities in society that crises spotlight and intensify. Frontline crisis responders may easily and inadvertently reinforce gender, race, and class inequalities through their operations as a result, unless they recognize that their services (re)distribute important resources and are therefore inherently political. Alternatively, their goals might be formulated in terms of social transformation toward a fairer society, which requires them to do away with the self-image of neutral professionals and to embrace an activist posture. In short, the dilemma of frontline responders is that they are tasked and trained to quickly resolve crises, but also have good reasons to pursue societal transformation.

The goals of crisis response are not usually subjected to scrutiny in crisis management scholarship, and researchers rarely pause to assess and discuss what frontline responders have to achieve. The existing order is usually treated as a given that is not up for debate, but unconsciously accepted as inevitable. Part of the reason that crises are feared in the first place is that they show the weaknesses and fragility of the existing order. Frontline crisis response, to some extent, is a way of suppressing this anxiety by rapidly restoring the status quo. Still, crises may undermine our image of the old order and create windows of opportunity for reconsidering questions of fairness and justice, thereby potentially inspiring the pursuit of social change.

Yet, it is unrealistic to expect that equitable results of crisis response operations will be realized if crisis organizations are unable to stop internal discrimination against employees based on their gender, race, or class. If members of crisis organizations hold prejudiced beliefs, frontline responses will likely reflect these and thus reproduce existing inequalities. Clearly, discriminatory organizations will not deliver social equity, even if crises give them ample opportunity. Masculine, chauvinistic, and elitist norms may be pervasive and persistent across crisis organizations, but they are not inescapable. Reforming crisis response organizations is a challenging task and will most certainly alienate some frontline personnel, but a failure to do so means an acceptance of the status quo and can be interpreted as the legitimation of discriminatory practices. Instead, a diverse and inclusive organization will likely improve crisis response performance. Indicative evidence comes from research on military missions, in which armed forces are found to develop a better intelligence picture, enjoy more credibility among local populations, and benefit from enhanced force protection if women are meaningfully represented in missions (see Dharmapuri, 2011). To build more inclusive crisis organizations, crisis responders have to be trained in self-reflexivity, cultural competence, and social justice in order to increase awareness of discrimination dynamics. This is a first step toward a purposeful contribution to social equity (Mills & Miller, 2015). Advocates may also need to show the importance of an equity focus. One study, for example, showed that frontline personnel did not initially respond favorably to a proposed gender focus in their organization's humanitarian activities, claiming they intended to save lives regardless of someone's gender. The director only garnered support when she made clear that saving lives requires understanding why people die and that gender may be a significant part of the answer (Eklund & Tellier, 2012). Evidently, a change in crisis response operations requires a preceding change within crisis organizations.

Even if crisis organizations become more equitable themselves, our expectations of crisis response contributions to social equity should be modest. Frontline responders cannot be expected to radically resolve deep-rooted societal inequalities overnight, since these are maintained through systemic forces and are embedded in societal structures. A compounding factor is that crisis responses typically need to be fast as well, because only urgent interventions can prevent escalating adversity. Thus, frontline responders have very little time to weigh their options and consider the broader implications of different courses of actions. Still, a modest contribution to social equity is preferable to a dispassionate reinforcement of structural inequality. Frontline crisis responders, moreover, are in a position to make such an impact. Even when government policies and organizational codes of ethics do not specify the pursuit of equity through crisis response operations (Stabile et al., 2022), public policy is made in its implementation by street-level personnel. Humanitarian principles and professional values gain shape and meaning in practice, so crisis responders' stances and actions matter. In fact, normative judgments define the work of frontline crisis responders, even if they do not always recognize it themselves (Maynard-Moody & Musheno, 2012). Crisis organizations should promote open dialogue about fairness and justice between personnel to explicate these normative judgments and discuss them, ensuring that the voices of marginalized groups are given due attention.

A fairly simple initiative that crisis responders can take is conducting a review of their frontline practices and impact. The increased vulnerability of marginalized groups means that they will probably have higher needs and require additional support during crisis operations. Currently, with the self-acclaimed neutral stance, many crisis organizations lack knowledge of the differential effects of their actions on various social groups. Sex-aggregated data can offer much-needed information on why women and men are vulnerable in the first place and provide evidence on the gendered consequences of certain response efforts, which is crucial for steering future crisis operations (Eklund & Tellier, 2012). Similar data on other marginalized social groups needs to be gathered for a comprehensive picture of the situation. Longer-term humanitarian and disaster relief missions can assess such implications for their area of operations, while emergency responders can evaluate the vulnerabilities of the people in their communities and the outcomes of their daily interventions. Such an understanding of vulnerability and coping capacities of various groups is needed as a knowledge base before current response practices can be meaningfully adjusted. At the very least, this should help frontline responders to avoid further marginalization through their crisis interventions. Specifically, properly assessing and incorporating the needs of the most marginalized and vulnerable during crises may not compensate for structural inequalities (Byrne & Baden, 1995), but are examples of crisis response practices that could contribute to social equity nevertheless.

There are many concrete examples of how to achieve this. A research-based toolkit on gender in disasters, for instance, offers useful examples. It shows that special transportation options are needed for pregnant and lactating women during evacuations, medical emergency teams require female doctors and reproductive health specialists, and female victims should be involved in decision-making on shelter, sanitation, and other important disaster relief issues (Chakrabarti & Walia, 2009). Other relevant insights come from an appeal against racism in emergency medicine, which recommends education to become aware of implicit or internalized biases, speaking out against white privilege, and becoming an ally through an active commitment to social justice (Franks et al., 2021). Ideally, it is not only frontline crisis responder who become aware and socially engaged, but vulnerable groups themselves are also empowered to become agents of social change during crisis response operations, enabling them to challenge structural discrimination beyond the crisis response phase (Akerkar, 2007). These social equity-based practices do not only contribute to fairness and social justice, but ultimately improve operational performance in crisis response as well: the needs of more people are better served and the alleviation of suffering is more effective when the most vulnerable, who are generally hit the hardest, are given their fair share of attention and support. In short, functional and moral reasons necessitate the pursuit of social equity in crisis organizations' goals.

12.6 Conclusion

Frontline responders are expected to restore order after a crisis, but their actions might inadvertently uphold and reinforce an unfair status quo as a consequence. To avoid this, they need to embrace social transformation as a goal, which requires diverse, inclusive crisis organizations. Revising crisis response goals will not be a simple process, but is needed to provide equitable crisis response services and change society for the better.

There is a need for comparative analyses between crisis organizations that have formulated different aims to study more systematically how social equity as an explicit goal affects crisis response operations and outcomes in practice. Next, reforming crisis organizations is bound to be contentious, as traditions and values will have to be changed, so good practices need to be learned from successful attempts. Finally, it is useful to explore whether concerns about the politicization of crisis response are justified and scrutinize its effects across crisis contexts.

Resources for Educators and Professionals

PRACTICAL LESSONS

- Crisis response usually aims to restore order and return to the status quo.
- Crises also offer an opportunity for challenging the status quo and pursue social transformation, but expectations of crisis response contributions to social equity should be modest.
- If a crisis organization is not diverse and inclusive, its frontline responders will likely reproduce existing inequalities in their operations.

- Frontline responders can evaluate the effects of their frontline practices to ensure that their operations do not further marginalize vulnerable groups.
- Social equity-based practices ultimately improve operational performance in crisis response.

QUESTIONS FOR REFLECTION AND DISCUSSION

- What are the goals of your crisis organization? What do you think of these goals? Do these goals adequately protect the vulnerable and marginalized in your community?
- What do you personally try to achieve through your work? Do you view yourself primarily as a neutral, impartial professional or as a force for change? What role should crisis professionals play?
- How does your organization reinforce or avoid discrimination against marginalized social groups in its operations? How do diversity and inclusion in your organization influence crisis operations?

13 | *Advancing Research on Frontline Crisis Response*

Emergency responders, soldiers, and humanitarians face persistent dilemmas in their crisis response operations. These dilemmas define their work, but have not yet been subjected to systematic investigation. In this comprehensive overview of research on frontline crisis response, eleven dilemmas were analyzed in depth. The preceding chapters showed how frontline responders try to resolve these dilemmas in different ways and explored the effects of their attempts. This informed reflective thinking about possible crisis response improvements. The final chapter of this book builds on recurring findings and observations in the preceding chapters to formulate a theory of frontline crisis response. This theoretical framework helps to understand, evaluate, and advance crisis response operations. Next, the broader implications of this theory for other organizational contexts are discussed, before promising avenues for further research are identified in a research agenda. The chapter ends with a call for more academic engagement with frontline crisis response.

13.1 A Theory of Frontline Crisis Response

The absence of a theory of frontline crisis response is not surprising. Most studies address only one aspect of the crisis response endeavor, such as leadership or coordination. These studies contribute to our knowledge of the specific issue, but do not aim for a general theory of crisis response. In addition, crisis researchers typically focus on a specific organization and publish in specialized journals, even though cross-fertilization between the literatures on emergency, military, and humanitarian operations is possible and valuable. By systematically analyzing available research on the frontline operations of a variety of crisis organizations, the main components of a theory of frontline crisis response can now be formulated.

Operational dilemmas are central to this theory. Frontline crisis response, indeed, is full of dilemmas. These dilemmas are complex in the best of times, but operational responders face them in threatening and uncertain moments. They do not have the luxury of time and cannot extensively contemplate or debate the right course of action in a particular situation, because the circumstances demand immediate action. Regardless of the challenging dilemmas, frontline personnel of crisis organizations are often remarkably decisive and effective. At the same time, it is not uncommon for them to be criticized in post-crisis inquiries and evaluations. Criticism focuses usually on debatable choices pertaining to these dilemmas. Crisis organizations have been blamed for being too hierarchical, rigidly sticking to protocols, failing to develop a complete situational understanding, unsuccessful integration of organizational activities, and undermining the helpful activities of ordinary civilians (e.g., Andrus, 1994; Bureau d'Enquêtes et d'Analyses, 2012; Independent Police Complaints Commission, 2007; National commission on terrorist attacks upon the United States, 2004; Telford et al., 2006; United States Congress, 2006). Yet, evaluation reports typically fail to reflect on the dilemma that responders faced, nor recognize that alternative resolutions to the dilemma could likewise have caused controversy or will probably lead to failures in future crises. The complexity of frontline crisis response may make any resolution to a dilemma appear questionable in retrospect. This seems like a rather fatalistic view, but it is important to emphasize the persistence and complicated nature of these dilemmas to avoid the appealing adoption of simple solutions. These dilemmas cannot be fully resolved by choosing for either one of the two alternative options. The analyses show that frontline crisis responders typically have to switch, combine, and adapt operational approaches depending on the specific situation that they are facing. To understand why frontline responders act as they do and grasp the complexity of their work, a focus on operational dilemmas in crisis response is therefore essential.

The need for a flexible attitude toward operational dilemmas in crisis response points at the relevance of a contingency theory. This is an alternative to the implicit debate in crisis studies on the transferability of findings. Some crisis scholars suggest that every crisis is unique, so that findings are inextricably linked to a particular context. This explains why crisis research is dispersed over a broad variety of context-specific journals. It also explains why there is virtually no comparative research on crisis organizations, the literature on armed forces is fairly isolated, humanitarian aid and development assistance are studied separately, and there are distinct emergency and disaster research traditions, implying that all these contexts are incomparably different (see also Quarantelli, 2005). While every crisis is new, this viewpoint ignores the fact that frontline response efforts often face considerable similarities as well. A firm commitment to the belief that every crisis is unique would also be problematic, because it prevents learning lessons across cases. Other crisis researchers, instead, apply their findings across crisis contexts and propose definite resolutions to dilemmas. Although all crises indeed display similarities, there is also a risk of over-stating the universality of research findings. This is particularly risky when studies are based on single cases, as is fairly common in crisis research. Case studies often focus on exceptional crises (e.g., Hurricane Katrina, Afghanistan war, COVID-19 pandemic, and the Stockwell shooting), raising questions about the transferability of findings, because the importance of contextual factors is hard to describe. The relevance of crisis context comes to the fore when comparing multiple cases. By juxtaposing a vast amount of studies on crisis response operations, it is evident that frontline responses are contingent upon the nature of the crisis situation, such as its novelty, unexpectedness, impact, ambiguity, and urgency. This view sits between the idea that every crisis is unique and the belief that findings apply across all crisis contexts. There have been indications of the relevance of recognizing situational contingencies in crisis response, as scholars have argued for adapting responses to the complexity, size, and uncertainty of a situation (Argote, 1982; Kenis et al., 2019; Kettl, 2003; Quarantelli, 1997b, 2005). Still, this insight has only been suggested incidentally in crisis response studies and has not been systematically pursued. In this research, however, contingent factors are found to be profoundly important in understanding competing findings in crisis response studies. Operational dilemmas can only be adequately managed when attending to these situational contingencies, which is why it needs to be part of a frontline crisis response theory.

Next, crises are not static events, for which responders need to somehow find the appropriate approach that will serve as a silver bullet to resolving the situation. Instead, one of the defining elements of crises is uncertainty: responders do not know how the situation will evolve, nor can they predict what will be required of them in the next hours or even minutes. As a result, frontline responses to crises cannot be fixed, but need to evolve over time as well. The phase and pace of the crisis inevitably affect the organization and management of the response to the situation. It is therefore important to view crisis response as a longitudinal process, throughout which responders adjust their operations and activities (Williams et al., 2017). This is evidenced, for instance, in medical emergencies and high-risk police operations, where there is a need for switching between coordination practices, roles, and routines in reaction to the evolving situation (Bechky & Okhuysen, 2011; Faraj & Xiao, 2006). In mountain climbing too, team members have to shift between routines, heuristics, and improvised actions (Suarez & Montes, 2019). Currently, studies apply this process perspective primarily to the incubation phase of crises rather than to the response phase (Roux-Dufort, 2007; Turner, 1976; Williams et al., 2017) or view adaptations of the crisis response as rare, unique events rather than a continuous dynamic (see Faraj & Xiao, 2006; Schakel et al., 2016; Weick, 1993). In a more general sense, there is therefore still a tendency to see the crisis response phase in a rather static manner, even though frontline responders have to continuously reassess and change their practices. Frontline personnel can and need to adapt the way they deal with dilemmas in crisis response operations over time. As such, a frontline crisis response theory needs to build on a process perspective.

In formulating a new crisis response theory, it is also necessary to reject a dogmatic approach to organizing and managing crisis response. Many studies still implicitly adopt such dogmatic assumptions by focusing on how frontline personnel of crisis organizations can reach an optimal solution by perfecting their approach. Clearly, recommendations differ considerably and the literature is frequently characterized by dualism, or even antagonism, so definite standards for how to design or implement crisis response are not helpful. This does not only offer little leeway to frontline responders, but also forecloses due attention for conflicting findings and viewpoints. Instead, an action-oriented, pragmatic perspective emphasizes that frontline responders usually work their way out of operational dilemmas to produce a fairly effective and adequate response. A perfect approach, based on optimal operating principles, sounds good in theory, but is completely unrealistic in the messy, chaotic contexts of crises. Such situations require a pragmatic mindset. Pragmatic responders are not concerned with veracity and perfection, but start (en)acting without full information, experiment and make preliminary decisions, acknowledge failures and try again, and heavily rely on their experience while operating in fundamentally uncertain situations (Ansell & Boin, 2019; Isabelle et al., 2012; Weick, 1993, 1995). The dualities of operational dilemmas are occasionally cast aside as well, for instance when plans allow for improvisation and useful improvised actions are retained in heuristics. As such, pragmatism embraces reflection-in-action, in which debate and dialogue accompany ongoing actions and interventions. This way of thinking and operating has demonstrated its relevance in handling almost all of the crisis response dilemmas that were presented in the previous chapters. A pragmatist approach to dealing with operational dilemmas is therefore an essential component of the new theory.

Clearly, frontline crisis responders aim to resolve crisis situations first and foremost, but this instrumentalist goal easily blinds us to the human side of crisis response operations. Frontline responders are not resources or tools to be deployed, but authentic individuals who are emotionally involved in their work. Likewise, patients and victims are not objects or organizational products, but human beings with whom responders interact and for whom they will often feel empathy. The problem with an instrumentalist approach is that it risks losing sight of what is most important to frontline crisis responders themselves. An existentialist view, instead, focuses attention on the lived experiences of responders. Many of them seek a sense of purpose in their job and view their work as a deeply meaningful vocation (Jiang, 2021; Mastracci et al., 2014; McCormack & Bamforth, 2019). Typically, they have also developed a strong professional identity and identify with their employer (Hunniecutt, 2020; Hunt, 2008). And they feel very responsible for the choices that they make and the outcomes of these choices (Gotowiec & Cantor-Graae, 2017). This means that it is problematic, from an existentialist view, if crisis responders' sense of purpose is undermined, personnel disidentify from their organization, or managers ignore issues of individual choice and responsibility. In many ways, crisis situations do not only threaten affected populations, but also pose existential threats to frontline crisis responders, their identities, their normative frameworks, and what they hold dear. Research on the prevalence of trauma and moral injury among emergency responders, soldiers, and humanitarians hints at this, and thereby emphasizes the importance of focusing on the lived experiences of crisis responders. Existentialist authors, from Kierkegaard to Dostoyevsky, highlight how important crises are to shaping our lives, so it would be unforgivable to leave individual experiences out of crisis response research, only because it does not directly link to instrumentalist outcomes. Frontline responders' ways of dealing with the most personal dilemmas in particular benefit from existentialist insights. As a consequence, these insights deserve a place in a new frontline crisis response theory.

Based on these main elements, a new theory of frontline crisis response can be formulated. It begins with the observation that the work of frontline responders is characterized by persistent operational dilemmas, which they try to resolve during crisis situations. There are no universal solutions for these dilemmas, so responders need to adapt their approaches and decisions to the situational contingencies of the crisis. Competent responders continue to adapt their operations during the crisis as the situation evolves, so organizing and managing crisis response is an ongoing process. In this process, they rely on pragmatic principles by rejecting the dogmatic pursuit of perfection in crisis operations and dealing with dilemmas in complex crises through experimentation, experience-based activities, and reflection-in-action. Since crises affect the sense of purpose and identities of operational personnel as well, it is equally important to incorporate an existentialist view on the authentic, lived experiences of operational responders. Thus, this new theory comprises operational dilemmas, situational contingencies, crisis response processes, pragmatic principles, and existentialist views as main components.

Importantly, this theory does not only describe the organization and implementation of frontline crisis response, but also offers a basis for suggesting improvements to practice. Simple, sweeping solutions to operational dilemmas do not suffice. Instead, the elements of the crisis response theory give directions for more reflective ways of handling these dilemmas. Attention for contingencies, processes, pragmatism, and existentialism has been key to identifying these directions for crisis response improvements, as elaborated in each of the previous theme-based chapters (see Table 13.1). As such, the new theory might serve as a foundation for understanding, evaluating, and advancing frontline crisis response operations.

Table 13.1 *Directions for improvement of frontline crisis response*

Themes	Crisis response dilemmas	Directions for improvement
Leadership	Command and control versus decentralization	Co-constructing authority
Sensemaking	Creating clarity versus embracing ambiguity	Plausible sensemaking
Acting	Planned routines versus spontaneous improvisation	Reflective acting
Ethics	Organizational norms versus individual convictions	An ethical culture
Emotions	Involvement versus detachment	Emotion management
Ties	Cohesion versus contestation	A safe space
Structures	Organizing versus disorganizing	Reorganizing the response
Coordination	Integration versus fragmentation	Conditional coordination
Civilians	Inclusion versus exclusion	Adaptive incorporation
Technology	Early adoption versus skepticism	A prudent approach
Goals	Restoring order versus social transformation	Social equity

13.2 Broader Theoretical Relevance

This frontline crisis response theory relies on research in a broad range of crisis contexts and the resulting insights apply to these various contexts in turn. Yet, it is an open question whether findings on frontline crisis response operations can also be generalized to other organizational contexts, including other organizational levels and settings. For instance, strategic crisis management dynamics might be partly similar to response processes on the operational level, but the boundary conditions of this generalization need further attention. More controversial is the question of generalization to non-crisis settings. Some scholars believe that the work of crisis responders cannot be compared to the work of frontline personnel in other organizations and are hesitant to infer lessons for non-crisis contexts. Other researchers, instead, are convinced that findings from crisis contexts have broader relevance. Hällgren and colleagues (2018) found that around eighty-five percent of references to crisis studies were from articles on non-crisis topics and contexts, which led them to argue that theoretical insights from crisis studies contribute to our thinking about organizations and management in general. The main idea is that crises showcase particular processes and experiences that are omnipresent in organizations and teams, but which might remain hidden in less extreme circumstances. This line of reasoning is adopted by Karl Weick (1993), arguably the most influential crisis researcher, who studied crises to draw broader insights for organization and management studies. From this point of view, crisis studies foreground and illustrate common organizational dynamics in a much more accessible and explicit manner. At its most extreme, therefore, findings on frontline crisis response can be generalized to any other organizational context, regardless of level or setting.

A middle course between these perspectives is possible by focusing on how frontline crisis response efforts compare to specific other organizational contexts. These contexts will lack one of the elements of a crisis (i.e., threat, uncertainty, and urgency), so that processes will unfold somewhat differently, but this does not mean that there is no use in looking for similarities across organizational levels and settings. Thus, the question to be pursued is not whether it is possible to generalize, but how to generalize the theoretical insights. This requires a juxtaposition of contexts before beginning a discussion of the transferability of certain research outcomes. Specifically, the frontline crisis response theory, formulated in this book, contributes to literature on strategic crisis management, frontline work in non-crisis settings, reliable organizing in risky contexts, and post-crisis operations.

First, this book has focused on frontline responses to crises in reaction to the predominantly strategic focus in much of the crisis management literature. Previous research in public administration has extensively analyzed the roles and actions of public leaders and politicians during crises by scrutinizing how they deal with leadership challenges, such as meaning making, decision-making, and accountability (Boin et al., 2016). In a similar vein, management scholars have studied the discourses and practices of organizational leaders and management teams during unexpected, rare events and corporate crises (Bundy et al., 2017; James et al., 2011; Mitroff et al., 1987; Pearson & Clair, 1998). Although the intensity of threats and time pressure differ between strategic and operational contexts, individuals at both levels need to make potentially impactful decisions in stressful and uncertain conditions, offering a basis for cross-fertilization of research findings. While the literature on strategic-level crisis response does include references to some of the elements of the frontline crisis response theory (Ansell & Boin, 2019; Hannah et al., 2009; Williams et al., 2017), there are ample opportunities for building more on process perspectives, contingency approaches, and pragmatist insights in strategic crisis management research. With regard to existentialist ideas, moreover, leaders might have to make far-reaching emotional and ethical decisions that may potentially put their subordinates in danger or affect the status quo. Such choices are bound to affect them personally as well. In addition, leaders face some of the same dilemmas in crises as frontline responders. They need to balance clarity with uncertainty in their sensemaking attempts, have to choose how much discretion to give to frontline personnel, and must reflect on whether to involve stakeholders or operate autonomously. As such, this book contributes to the literature on strategic crisis management by shedding light on some dilemmas that leaders face and how they might deal with these dilemmas.

Second, frontline personnel of crisis organizations work in extreme contexts. Other frontline organizational members may not face the same threats to life in their work, but can still experience surprising and unpredictable situations to which they need to quickly adapt. This can range from jazz musicians (Hatch, 1999) and film production crews (Bechky & Okhuysen, 2011) to vocational rehabilitation counselors, teachers (Maynard-Moody & Musheno, 2003), and street-level bureaucrats at large (Raaphorst, 2018). While the importance of threats in crisis contexts cannot be denied, frontline members in various organizations similarly operate in complex work environments, in which top-down orders and preexisting protocols face shortcomings and they struggle practically and emotionally with defining the right course of action (Lipsky, 1983; Margolis & Molinsky, 2008; Maynard-Moody & Musheno, 2012). Operational dilemmas regarding leadership and actions have received their fair share of attention, but other operational dilemmas have not been studied as much in research on frontline work in non-crisis settings. In all these operational contexts, frontline members will likely face dilemmas on themes such as sensemaking, structures, and technology that are similar to those reported in this book. In addition, contingency and process approaches appear to be rare in research on frontline workers, but may tell us more about differential ways of dealing with operational dilemmas across work contexts and over time. The findings of this research might therefore be of relevance to the literature on frontline, street-level work in a more general sense.

Third, this book is restricted to the response phase of crisis management, suggesting that operational dynamics and processes in this stage are unique, but it is useful to consider what the reported findings may add to research on other forms of crisis management. In the pre-crisis stage, for instance, organizations will aim to prevent and prepare for the occurrence of a crisis. This is studied in the literature on risk management and reliable organizing. In this research domain, scholars have identified organizational processes that produce high reliability and processes that lead to an increase in risks and accidents (Vaughan, 1996; Weick, 1990; Weick & Roberts, 1993). Usually, researchers are primarily preoccupied with operational dilemmas on organizational structures, leadership, and sensemaking (Hällgren et al., 2018; Perrow, 1984; Weick & Sutcliffe, 2001), and have limited attention for the other research themes that featured in the preceding chapters, even though these are bound to be of relevance as well. Moreover, chapters in this book sometimes challenge reported findings, such as the emphasis on flexible team composition, which may undermine team cohesion (cf. Hällgren et al., 2018). While pragmatic principles have been used in this literature, contingency and process perspectives are scarce. The findings in this book, however, show that crisis organizations will likely need to adapt the implementation of principles for reliable organizing to the situation at hand. Next, much of the research on risks and reliability is limited to the organizational or team level, and there is less concern for the individual experiences of employees. This book adds to the existing literature by arguing that frontline personnel in the pre-crisis stage also have to deal with persistent dilemmas, including existential questions revolving around ethics, emotions, and goals, that are likely to be of great personal importance to them. Contributions to the literature on risky contexts and reliable organizing can therefore be inferred from the reported research outcomes in this book.

Fourth, the phase that follows the crisis response stage also has its own dynamics. In practice, it is not always easy to delineate between phases, which is clearly visible in the (sometimes problematic) transition from crisis response to recovery. Shifting from humanitarian aid to development assistance, for instance, is not easy (e.g., Hanatani et al., 2018). In a military context, likewise, combat missions are often supposed to create a safe and stable environment for reconstruction operations (Bensahel, 2006), but overlap between these phases is common. In these post-crisis situations, frontline personnel face somewhat less uncertainty and urgency, but threatening situations may flare up again quickly as well. Existing studies reiterate some of the identified operational dilemmas, particularly with regard to leadership, technology, and the role of ordinary civilians in operations (Brown et al., 2014; Cho, 2014). Other research themes have not received due attention though. In practice, recovery processes may stretch out over years or decades, so process and contingency approaches help to better grasp the evolution of post-crisis operations. In addition, organizational activities in the post-crisis stage are often studied from a strategic perspective on mission effectiveness (Fernandez & Ahmed, 2019; Phillips, 2015; Rietjens & Ruffa, 2019), which means that operational experiences and responders' pragmatic ways of working with dilemmas remain by and large unexplored. Likewise, there is a research gap on existentialist themes, apart from stress and trauma, so that we know little about the individual frontline workers who operate in the aftermath of crises. This book lists a few main components of a frontline crisis response theory (i.e., operational dilemmas, situational contingencies, crisis response processes, pragmatic principles, and existentialist views) that can be used and tested in these post-crisis contexts.

13.3 A Research Agenda for Crisis Response Studies

The aim of this book was to provide a comprehensive analysis of frontline crisis response. A broad variety of crisis contexts was chosen on purpose to identify recurring operational dilemmas and ways of dealing with these dilemmas. One of the core assumptions of this research was that the involved frontline members have comparable experiences, even if they face very different circumstances. The actor-oriented perspective in this book has attributed a limited role to the wider social context though. Critics might argue that crisis responders are significantly affected by the wider context, such as institutional factors, resource availability, and cultural values. For instance, Jin and Song (2017) refer to the institutional context of the Korean Coast Guard to explain its rigid, failed response to the Sewol ferry disaster, while a shortage of competent personnel and lack of medical infrastructure plague emergency medical services in India (Garg,

2012). Such variables potentially influence the manifestation of operational dilemmas for involved frontline responders, so it is crucial to study how the broader context affects frontline crisis interventions. By extension, crisis scholarship suffers from a Western-centric fallacy, as Western scholars and conceptual frameworks have gained a hegemonic position in the research domain (Gaillard, 2019). In response, there have been calls to make research on crises more inclusive (Hendriks et al., 2022). Non-Western research shows specific crisis response challenges that have not received due attention. Examples include a lack of training of emergency medical services personnel in Saudi Arabia (Althunayyan et al., 2021), slow response times of fire services in Ghana (Oppong et al., 2017), and a range of disaster management problems in Thailand (Moe & Pathranarakul, 2006). It is important to explore the experiences of non-Western crisis responders who may face even higher stress and threat levels than their Western counterparts, but who may also have developed their own pragmatic ways of dealing with resulting operational dilemmas.

Next, while all dilemmas are persistent and pervasive, some dilemmas are more likely to manifest in particular contexts. Team ties is a major topic of debate in a military context, while extensive discussions on leadership and actions unfold among emergency response scholars, and humanitarian researchers often study ethics and goals. It would be interesting to explore the reasons for these variations. At the same time, the selection of dilemmas may not be exhaustive and other dilemmas can be added for further scrutiny. Relatedly, there is a clear distinction between the operational dilemmas in this book for analytical purposes. By discussing every theme separately, it becomes possible to delve deeply into the intricacies and complexities of every dilemma. As mentioned in the introduction, however, there are relations between these themes. For instance, organizational norms (ethics) may be laid down in protocols (acting) and result from ideas of what responders need to achieve (goals), potentially causing frustration and anger among frontline responders (emotions). This means that suggested resolutions to a dilemma might have repercussions for other operational dilemmas as well. It would be useful to study recurring relations between operational dilemmas and develop a more integrated approach of dealing with dilemmas.

Finally, frontline crisis responses are difficult to study, because crises are unpredictable and uncertain. Even if researchers are near a crisis, it is crucial that frontline responders are not hindered or distracted by their presence. Ethnographies and participatory action research are therefore very rare (cf. Lois, 2003; Njå & Rake, 2008). Instead, most studies on frontline crisis response make use of retrospective interviews, observations at exercises, and evaluation reports (Hällgren & Rouleau, 2018). Yet, it is doubtful whether this data can fully capture the experiences and impressions of frontline responders. Thus, it is useful to experiment with new crisis research methods. Researchers can, for instance, rely on visual data by collecting (online) images or videos of a response. Alternatively, frontline responders can be equipped with unobtrusive cameras that record their words and actions for future analysis (see Christianson, 2019; Groenendaal & Helsloot, 2016). Another possibility is the use of (autobiographical) fiction, which allows responders to share their memories and perceptions without feeling the need to rationalize or sanitize their stories (Kalkman, 2020c). Works of speculative fiction also enable us to study crisis response dynamics that might or could happen (Hällgren & Buchanan, 2020). These alternative methods of data collection need to be further explored and used in order to improve our understanding of how frontline responders deal with operational dilemmas, find pragmatic solutions over time, and personally experience crisis situations.

13.4 A Final Comment

While the politics of crisis management attracts our attention, frontline crisis response saves our lives. Frontline responders alleviate human suffering and provide aid in the worst of times. As such, it is of crucial importance to expand our research on how emergency responders, soldiers, humanitarians, and other frontline personnel operate in crises. This book can therefore also be read as a call to arms. It does not aim to provide a conclusive analysis, but offers a broad overview of crisis response research that may serve as a foundation for future studies. These studies will have enormous practical relevance, potentially helping crisis organizations with their operations in a world that appears to be increasingly beset by crises. As researchers, it is our obligation to affected communities. We also owe it to our frontline responders who make great sacrifices on a daily basis to help people in need.

References

Abir, M., Bell, S. A., Puppala, N., Awad, O., & Moore, M. (2017). Setting foundations for developing disaster response metrics. *Disaster Medicine and Public Health Preparedness, 11*(4), 505–509.

Ager, A., Pasha, E., Yu, G., Duke, T., Eriksson, C., & Cardozo, B. L. (2012). Stress, mental health, and burnout in national humanitarian aid workers in Gulu, Northern Uganda. *Journal of Traumatic Stress, 25*(6), 713–720.

Ahronson, A., & Cameron, J. E. (2007). The nature and consequences of group cohesion in a military sample. *Military Psychology, 19*(1), 9–25.

Akerkar, S. (2007). Disaster mitigation and furthering women's rights: Learning from the tsunami. *Gender, Technology and Development, 11*(3), 357–388.

Alberts, D. S., Garstka, J. J., & Stein, F. P. (2000). *Network centric warfare: Developing and leveraging information superiority*. Washington: Assistant Secretary of Defense.

Alexander, D. E. (2017). *How to write an emergency plan*. Edinburgh: Dunedin Academic Press Ltd.

Allison, G. T. (1971). *Essence of decision*. New York: HarperCollins Publishers.

Altay, N., & Labonte, M. (2014). Challenges in humanitarian information management and exchange: Evidence from Haiti. *Disasters, 38*(s1), S50–S72.

Althunayyan, S., Alhalybah, A., Aloudah, A., Samarkandi, O. A., & Khan, A. A. (2021). The knowledge of triage system in disaster among emergency medical service personnel at Saudi Red Crescent Authority in Riyadh city stations. *International Journal of Emergency Services, 10*(3), 340–350.

Alvinius, A., Danielsson, E., & Larsson, G. (2010). The inadequacy of an ordinary organisation: Organisational adaptation to crisis through planned and spontaneous links. *International Journal of Organisational Behaviour, 15*(1), 87–102.

Alvinius, A., Deverell, E., & Hede, S. (2021). Militarisation, masculinisation and organisational exclusion in the crisis preparedness sector. *Journal of Risk Research, 24*(12), 1544–1557.

Alvinius, A., Krekula, C., & Larsson, G. (2018). Managing visibility and differentiating in recruitment of women as leaders in the armed forces. *Journal of Gender Studies, 27*(5), 534–546.

Alvinius, A., Kylin, C., Starrin, B., & Larsson, G. (2014). Emotional smoothness and confidence building: Boundary spanners in a civil-military collaboration context. *International Journal of Work Organisation and Emotion, 6*(3), 223–239.

Amarasiri de Silva, M. (2009). Ethnicity, politics and inequality: Post-tsunami humanitarian aid delivery in Ampara District, Sri Lanka. *Disasters, 33*(2), 253–273.

Andrus, J. G. (1994). *Aircraft Accident Investigation Board Report: US Army UH-60 Black Hawk Helicopters 87-26000 and 88-26060.* Washington. DC: US Department of Defense.

Ansell, C., & Boin, A. (2019). Taming deep uncertainty: The potential of pragmatist principles for understanding and improving strategic crisis management. *Administration & Society, 51*(7), 1079–1112.

Ansell, C., Boin, A., & Keller, A. (2010). Managing transboundary crises: Identifying the building blocks of an effective response system. *Journal of Contingencies and Crisis Management, 18*(4), 195–207.

Arble, E., & Arnetz, B. B. (2017). A model of first-responder coping: An approach/avoidance bifurcation. *Stress and Health, 33*(3), 223–232.

Arendt-Cassetta, L. (2021). *From digital promise to frontline practice: New and emerging technologies in humanitarian action.* New York: UNOCHA.

Argote, L. (1982). Input uncertainty and organizational coordination in hospital emergency units. *Administrative Science Quarterly, 27*(3), 420–434.

Arnold, R. D., Yamaguchi, H., & Tanaka, T. (2018). Search and rescue with autonomous flying robots through behavior-based cooperative intelligence. *Journal of International Humanitarian Action, 3*(1), 1–18.

Ash, J. S., & Smallman, C. (2008). Rescue missions and risk management: Highly reliable or over committed? *Journal of Contingencies and Crisis Management, 16*(1), 37–52.

Bacharach, S. B., & Bamberger, P. A. (2007). 9/11 and New York City firefighters' post hoc unit support and control climates: A context theory of the consequences of involvement in traumatic work-related events. *Academy of Management Journal, 50*(4), 849–868.

Baker, M., & Fink, S. (2020). At the top of the Covid-19 curve, how do hospitals decide who gets treatment. *The New York Times.* Retrieved from www.nytimes.com/2020/03/31/us/coronavirus-covid-triage-rationing-ventilators.html

Barbusse, H. (1917). *Under fire: The story of a squad*. New York: Dutton.

Barnett, D. J., Balicer, R. D., Thompson, C. B., Storey, J. D., Omer, S. B., Semon, N. L., ... Lanza, K. M. (2009). Assessment of local public health workers' willingness to respond to pandemic influenza through application of the extended parallel process model. *PloS One, 4*(7), e6365.

Barnett, M. (2005). Humanitarianism transformed. *Perspectives on Politics, 3*(4), 723–740.

Barsky, L. E., Trainor, J. E., Torres, M. R., & Aguirre, B. E. (2007). Managing volunteers: FEMA's Urban Search and Rescue programme and interactions with unaffiliated responders in disaster response. *Disasters, 31*(4), 495–507.

Barton, M. A., & Sutcliffe, K. M. (2009). Overcoming dysfunctional momentum: Organizational safety as a social achievement. *Human Relations, 62*(9), 1327–1356.

Barton, M. A., Sutcliffe, K. M., Vogus, T. J., & DeWitt, T. (2015). Performing under uncertainty: Contextualized engagement in wildland firefighting. *Journal of Contingencies and Crisis Management, 23*(2), 74–83.

Bartone, P. T. (2006). Resilience under military operational stress: Can leaders influence hardiness? *Military Psychology, 18*(sup1), S131–S148.

Bartone, P. T., Johnsen, B. H., Eid, J., Brun, W., & Laberg, J. C. (2002). Factors influencing small-unit cohesion in Norwegian Navy officer cadets. *Military Psychology, 14*(1), 1–22.

Batista, M. d. G., Clegg, S., Pina e Cunha, M., Giustiniano, L., & Rego, A. (2016). Improvising prescription: Evidence from the emergency room. *British Journal of Management, 27*(2), 406–425.

Bechky, B. A., & Okhuysen, G. A. (2011). Expecting the unexpected? How SWAT officers and film crews handle surprises. *Academy of Management Journal, 54*(2), 239–261.

Beck, T. E., & Plowman, D. A. (2014). Temporary, emergent interorganizational collaboration in unexpected circumstances: A study of the Columbia space shuttle response effort. *Organization Science, 25*(4), 1234–1252.

Beeres, R., De Waard, E., & Bollen, M. (2010). Ambitions and opportunities for assessing military performance in crisis response operations. *Financial Accountability & Management, 26*(3), 344–366.

Belliveau, J. (2016). Humanitarian access and technology: Opportunities and applications. *Procedia Engineering, 159(1)*, 300–306.

Ben-Shalom, U., Klar, Y., & Benbenisty, Y. (2012). Characteristics of sense-making in combat. In J. H. Laurence & M. D. Matthews (Eds.), *The Oxford handbook of military psychology* (pp. 218–231). Oxford: Oxford University Press.

Ben-Shalom, U., Lehrer, Z., & Ben-Ari, E. (2005). Cohesion during military operations: A field study on combat units in the Al-Aqsa Intifada. *Armed Forces & Society, 32*(1), 63–79.

Benedek, D. M., Fullerton, C., & Ursano, R. J. (2007). First responders: Mental health consequences of natural and human-made disasters for public health and public safety workers. *Annual Review of Public Health, 28(1)*, 55–68.

Bennett, D. (2019). Information and communication technology in crisis and disaster management. In E.K. Stern, D. Fischbacher-Smith, S. Kuipers, A. McConnell, D. Nohrstedt, & T. Preston (Eds.), *The Oxford encyclopedia of crisis analysis*. Oxford: Oxford University Press. https://doi.org/ 10.1093/acrefore/9780190228637.013.1582

Bensahel, N. (2006). Mission not accomplished: What went wrong with Iraqi reconstruction. *Journal of Strategic Studies, 29*(3), 453–473.

Berlin, J. M., & Carlström, E. D. (2008). The 90-second collaboration: A critical study of collaboration exercises at extensive accident sites. *Journal of Contingencies and Crisis Management, 16*(4), 177–185.

Berlin, J. M., & Carlström, E. D. (2011). Why is collaboration minimised at the accident scene? A critical study of a hidden phenomenon. *Disaster Prevention and Management, 20*(2), 159–171.

Berlin, J. M., & Carlström, E. D. (2015). Collaboration exercises: What do they contribute? A study of learning and usefulness. *Journal of Contingencies and Crisis Management, 23*(1), 11–23.

Bernhard, A. (2020). Covid-19: What we can learn from wartime efforts. *BBC*. Retrieved from www.bbc.com/future/article/20200430-covid-19-what-we-can-learn-from-wartime-efforts

Beroggi, G. E., & Wallace, W. A. (1995). Real-time decision support for emergency management: An integration of advanced computer and communications technology. *Journal of Contingencies and Crisis Management, 3*(1), 18–26.

Berthod, O., & Müller-Seitz, G. (2018). Making sense in pitch darkness: An exploration of the sociomateriality of sensemaking in crises. *Journal of Management Inquiry, 27*(1), 52–68.

Betz, D. J. (2006). The more you know, the less you understand: The problem with information warfare. *Journal of Strategic Studies, 29*(3), 505–533.

Bharosa, N., Lee, J., & Janssen, M. (2010). Challenges and obstacles in sharing and coordinating information during multi-agency disaster response: Propositions from field exercises. *Information Systems Frontiers, 12*(1), 49–65.

Bigley, G. A., & Roberts, K. H. (2001). The incident command system: High-reliability organizing for complex and volatile task environments. *Academy of Management Journal, 44*(6), 1281–1299.

Blake, D., Marlowe, J., & Johnston, D. (2017). Get prepared: Discourse for the privileged? *International Journal of Disaster Risk Reduction*, 25, 283–288.

Boersma, F., Wagenaar, P., & Wolbers, J. (2012). Negotiating the 'trading zone'. Creating a shared information infrastructure in the Dutch public safety sector. *Journal of Homeland Security and Emergency Management*, 9(2), Article 6.

Boin, A., & Hart, P. t. (2003). Public leadership in times of crisis: Mission impossible? *Public Administration Review*, 63(5), 544–553.

Boin, A., Hart, P. t., Stern, E., & Sundelius, B. (2016). *The politics of crisis management: Public leadership under pressure.* Cambridge: Cambridge University Press.

Boin, A., & Nieuwenburg, P. (2013). The moral costs of discretionary decision-making in crisis: Hurricane Katrina and the Memorial Hospital tragedy. *Public Integrity*, 15(4), 367–384.

Bolin, B., & Kurtz, L. C. (2018). Race, class, ethnicity, and disaster vulnerability. In H. Rodríguez, W. Donner, & J. E. Trainor (Eds.), *Handbook of disaster research* (pp. 181–203). New York: Springer.

Bollen, M. (2002). *Working apart together: Civiel militaire samenwerking tijdens humanitaire operaties.* Wageningen: Wageningen University.

Borry, E. L., & Henderson, A. C. (2020). Patients, protocols, and prosocial behavior: Rule breaking in frontline health care. *The American Review of Public Administration*, 50(1), 45–61.

Bracha, H. S. (2004). Freeze, flight, fight, fright, faint: Adaptationist perspectives on the acute stress response spectrum. *CNS Spectrums*, 9(9), 679–685.

Brady, M. (2011). Improvisation versus rigid command and control at Stalingrad. *Journal of Management History*, 17(1), 27–49.

Brandrud, A. S., Bretthauer, M., Brattebø, G., Pedersen, M. J., Håpnes, K., Møller, K., … Schreiner, A. (2017). Local emergency medical response after a terrorist attack in Norway: A qualitative study. *BMJ Quality & Safety*, 26(10), 806–816.

Branicki, L. J. (2020). COVID-19, ethics of care and feminist crisis management. *Gender, Work & Organization*, 27(5), 872–883.

Brooks, J., Grugulis, I., & Cook, H. (2021). Unlearning and consent in the UK Fire and Rescue Service. *Human Relations*, 75(12), 2300–2317.

Brown, A. D., Colville, I., & Pye, A. (2015). Making sense of sensemaking in organization studies. *Organization Studies*, 36(2), 265–277.

Brown, D., Donini, A., & Knox Clarke, P. (2014). *Engagement of crisis-affected people in humanitarian action.* London: ALNAP/ODI.

Buck, D. A., Trainor, J. E., & Aguirre, B. E. (2006). A critical evaluation of the incident command system and NIMS. *Journal of Homeland Security and Emergency Management*, 3(3), Article 1.

Bullock, J. A., Haddow, G. D., & Coppola, D. P. (2017). *Introduction to emergency management*. Burlington: Elsevier Butterworth-Heinemann.

Bundy, J., Pfarrer, M. D., Short, C. E., & Coombs, W. T. (2017). Crises and crisis management: Integration, interpretation, and research development. *Journal of Management, 43*(6), 1661–1692.

Bureau d'Enquêtes et d'Analyses. (2012). Final report on the accident on 1st June 2009 to the Airbus A330-203 registered F-GZCP operated by Air France flight AF 447 Rio de Janeiro–Paris. *Paris: BEA*.

Burk, J., & Espinoza, E. (2012). Race relations within the US military. *Annual Review of Sociology, 38*, 401–422.

Buzan, B., Wæver, O., & De Wilde, J. (1998). *Security: A new framework for analysis*. Boulder: Lynne Rienner Publishers.

Byrne, B., & Baden, S. (1995). *Gender, emergencies and humanitarian assistance*. Brighton: Institute of Development Studies.

Canton, L. G. (2011). Emergency plans: Are they really necessary? Five steps to better response operations. *Risk, Hazards & Crisis in Public Policy, 2*(3), 1–4.

Canton, L. G. (2019). *Emergency management: Concepts and strategies for effective programs*. Hoboken: John Wiley & Sons.

Carbonnier, G. (2015). Reason, emotion, compassion: Can altruism survive professionalisation in the humanitarian sector? *Disasters, 39*(2), 189–207.

Carlson, E. J., Poole, M. S., Lambert, N. J., & Lammers, J. C. (2017). A study of organizational reponses to dilemmas in interorganizational emergency management. *Communication Research, 44*(2), 287–315.

Carroll, J. S. (2015). Making sense of ambiguity through dialogue and collaborative action. *Journal of Contingencies and Crisis Management, 23*(2), 59–65.

Catino, M., & Patriotta, G. (2013). Learning from errors: Cognition, emotions and safety culture in the Italian air force. *Organization Studies, 34*(4), 437–467.

Cebrowski, A. K., & Garstka, J. H. (1998). Network-centric warfare: Its origin and future. *US Naval Institute Proceedings, 124*(139), 28-35.

Chakrabarti, P. D., & Walia, A. (2009). Toolkit for mainstreaming gender in emergency response. In E. Enarson & P. D. Chakrabarti (Eds.), *Women, Gender and Disaster: Global Issues and Initiatives* (pp. 337–360). New Delhi: Sage.

Chan, T. C., Killeen, J., Griswold, W., & Lenert, L. (2004). Information technology and emergency medical care during disasters. *Academic Emergency Medicine, 11*(11), 1229–1236.

Chang, R., & Trainor, J. (2018). Pre-disaster established trust and relationships: Two major factors influencing the effectiveness of implementing the ICS. *Journal of Homeland Security and Emergency Management,* 15(4), Article 1.

Charman, S. (2015). Crossing cultural boundaries: Reconsidering the cultural characteristics of police officers and ambulance staff. *International Journal of Emergency Services,* 4(2), 158–176.

Chason, R., & Schmidt, S. (2021). Lafayette Square, Capitol rallies met starkly different policing response. *The Washington Post.* Retrieved from www.washingtonpost.com/dc-md-va/interactive/2021/blm-protest-capitol-riot-police-comparison/

Chatman, J. A., Greer, L. L., Sherman, E., & Doerr, B. (2019). Blurred lines: How the collectivism norm operates through perceived group diversity to boost or harm group performance in Himalayan mountain climbing. *Organization Science,* 30(2), 235–259.

Chen, G. (2016). *The politics of disaster management in China: Institutions, interest groups, and social participation.* New York: Palgrave Macmillan.

Cherry, N. L. (2014). The frontline: A new focus for learning about leadership. *Australian Journal of Emergency Management,* 29(2), 31–34.

Chetkovich, C. A. (1997). *Real heat: Gender and race in the urban fire service.* New Brunswick: Rutgers University Press.

Chmutina, K., & Von Meding, J. (2019). A Dilemma of language: "Natural disasters" in academic literature. *International Journal of Disaster Risk Science,* 10(3), 283–292.

Cho, A. (2014). Post-tsunami recovery and reconstruction: Governance issues and implications of the Great East Japan Earthquake. *Disasters,* 38(s2), s157–s178.

Christianson, M. K. (2019). More and less effective updating: The role of trajectory management in making sense again. *Administrative Science Quarterly,* 64(1), 45–86.

Christianson, M. K., Farkas, M. T., Sutcliffe, K. M., & Weick, K. E. (2009). Learning through rare events: Significant interruptions at the Baltimore & Ohio Railroad Museum. *Organization Science,* 20(5), 846–860.

Chtouris, S., & Miller, D. S. (2017). Refugee flows and volunteers in the current humanitarian crisis in Greece. *Journal of Applied Security Research,* 12(1), 61–77.

Claire, A. (2021). Reason, emotion and solidarity in humanitarian advocacy. *Journal of Humanitarian Affairs,* 3(1), 46–52.

Clark, S. M., Hack-Polay, D., & Bal, P. M. (2022). Social mobility and promotion of officers to senior ranks in the Royal Navy: Meritocracy or class ceiling? *Armed Forces & Society,* 48(1), 92–114.

Clarke, L. (1999). *Mission improbable: Using fantasy documents to tame disaster.* Chicago: University of Chicago Press.

Clarke, P. K. (2013). *Who's in charge here?: A literature review on approaches to leadership in humanitarian operations.* London: ALNAP.

Cohen, M. D., March, J. G., & Olsen, J. P. (1972). A garbage can model of organizational choice. *Administrative Science Quarterly, 17*(1), 1–25.

Colville, I., Pye, A., & Carter, M. (2013). Organizing to counter terrorism: Sensemaking amidst dynamic complexity. *Human Relations, 66*(9), 1201–1223.

Comfort, L. K. (2007). Crisis management in hindsight: Cognition, communication, coordination, and control. *Public Administration Review, 67*(s1), 189–197.

Comfort, L. K., Dunn, M., Johnson, D., Skertich, R., & Zagorecki, A. (2004). Coordination in complex systems: Increasing efficiency in disaster mitigation and response. *International Journal of Emergency Management, 2*(1–2), 62–80.

Comfort, L. K., & Kapucu, N. (2006). Inter-organizational coordination in extreme events: The World Trade Center attacks, September 11, 2001. *Natural Hazards, 39*(2), 309–327.

Cornelissen, J. P., Mantere, S., & Vaara, E. (2014). The contraction of meaning: The combined effect of communication, emotions, and materiality on sensemaking in the Stockwell shooting. *Journal of Management Studies, 51*(5), 699–736.

Curnin, S., Owen, C., & Trist, C. (2014). Managing the constraints of boundary spanning in emergency management. *Cognition, Technology & Work, 16*(4), 549–563.

Currion, P., Silva, C. d., & Van de Walle, B. (2007). Open source software for disaster management. *Communications of the ACM, 50*(3), 61–65.

Dalgaard-Nielsen, A. (2017). Organizing special operations forces: Navigating the paradoxical pressures of institutional-bureaucratic and operational environments. *Special Operations Journal, 3*(1), 61–73.

Danielsson, E. (2016). Following routines: A challenge in cross-sectorial collaboration. *Journal of Contingencies and Crisis Management, 24*(1), 36–45.

Danner-Schröder, A., & Geiger, D. (2016). Unravelling the motor of patterning work: Toward an understanding of the microlevel dynamics of standardization and flexibility. *Organization Science, 27*(3), 633–658.

Day, J. M., Junglas, I., & Silva, L. (2009). Information flow impediments in disaster relief supply chains. *Journal of the Association for Information Systems, 10*(8), Article 2.

De Rond, M. (2017). *Doctors at war: Life and death in a field hospital.* Ithaca: Cornell University Press.

De Rond, M., & Lok, J. (2016). Some things can never be unseen: The role of context in psychological injury at war. *Academy of Management Journal*, 59(6), 1965–1993.

Dean, M. D., & Payne, D. M. (2013). Disaster management: An ethical review and approach. *International Journal of Emergency Management*, 9(2), 113–126.

Dearstyne, B. (2007). The FDNY on 9/11: Information and decision making in crisis. *Government Information Quarterly*, 24(1), 29–46.

Deflem, M., & Sutphin, S. (2009). Policing Katrina: Managing law enforcement in New Orleans. *Policing: A Journal of Policy and Practice*, 3(1), 41–49.

Delk, J. D. (1995). *Fires and furies: The LA riots*. Palm Springs: ETC Publications.

Dharmapuri, S. (2011). Just add women and stir? *The US Army War College Quarterly: Parameters*, 41(1), Article 4.

Dick, P. (2005). Dirty work designations: How police officers account for their use of coercive force. *Human Relations*, 58(11), 1363–1390.

Doidge, M., & Sandri, E. (2019). 'Friends that last a lifetime': The importance of emotions amongst volunteers working with refugees in Calais. *The British Journal of Sociology*, 70(2), 463–480.

Dolan, B., Esson, A., Grainger, P. P., Richardson, S., & Ardagh, M. (2011). Earthquake disaster response in christchurch, New Zealand. *Journal of Emergency Nursing*, 37(5), 506–509.

Dominguez-Gomez, E., & Rutledge, D. N. (2009). Prevalence of secondary traumatic stress among emergency nurses. *Journal of Emergency Nursing*, 35(3), 199–204.

Donahue, A. K. (2006). The space shuttle Columbia recovery operation: How collaboration enabled disaster response. *Public Administration Review*, 66(S1), 141–142.

Donini, A., & Maxwell, D. (2013). From face-to-face to face-to-screen: Remote management, effectiveness and accountability of humanitarian action in insecure environments. *International Review of the Red Cross*, 95(890), 383–413.

Drabek, T. E., & McEntire, D. A. (2002). Emergent phenomena and multiorganizational coordination in disasters: Lessons from the research literature. *International Journal of Mass Emergencies and Disasters*, 20(2), 197–224.

Duffield, M. (2013). *Disaster-resilience in the network age access-denial and the rise of cyber-humanitarianism*. Copenhagen: Danish Institute for International Studies.

Dunbar, R. L., & Garud, R. (2009). Distributed knowledge and indeterminate meaning: The case of the Columbia shuttle flight. *Organization Studies*, 30(4), 397–421.

Dutton, J. E., Worline, M. C., Frost, P. J., & Lilius, J. (2006). Explaining compassion organizing. *Administrative Science Quarterly, 51*(1), 59–96.

Dynes, R. R. (1983). Problems in emergency planning. *Energy, 8*(8–9), 653–660.

Dynes, R. R. (1994). Community emergency planning: False assumptions and inappropriate analogies. *International Journal of Mass Emergencies and Disasters, 12*(2), 141–158.

Edmondson, A. C. (2003). Speaking up in the operating room: How team leaders promote learning in interdisciplinary action teams. *Journal of Management Studies, 40*(6), 1419–1452.

Eklund, L., & Tellier, S. (2012). Gender and international crisis response: Do we have the data, and does it matter? *Disasters, 36*(4), 589–608.

Elinder, M., & Erixson, O. (2012). Gender, social norms, and survival in maritime disasters. *Proceedings of the National Academy of Sciences, 109*(33), 13220–13224.

Elmes, M., & Frame, B. (2008). Into hot air: A critical perspective on Everest. *Human Relations, 61*(2), 213–241.

Emanuel, E. J., Persad, G., Upshur, R., Thome, B., Parker, M., Glickman, A., ... Phillips, J. P. (2020). Fair allocation of scarce medical resources in the time of Covid-19. *The New England Journal of Medicine, 382*(21), 2049–2055.

Enarson, E., Fothergill, A., & Peek, L. (2007). Gender and disaster: Foundations and directions. In H. Rodríguez, E. L. Quarantelli, & R. R. Dynes (Eds.), *Handbook of disaster research* (pp. 130–146). New York: Springer.

Epp, C. R., Maynard-Moody, S., & Haider-Markel, D. P. (2014). *Pulled over: How police stops define race and citizenship*. Chicago: University of Chicago Press.

Etkin, D., & Timmerman, P. (2013). Emergency management and ethics. *International Journal of Emergency Management, 9*(4), 277–297.

Etzioni, A., & Etzioni, O. (2017). Pros and cons of autonomous weapons systems. *Military Review, May-June*, 72–81.

Evans, T. R. (2019). Emotions in the fire service: Decision-making, risk, and coping. In T. R. Evans & G. Steptoe-Warren (Eds.), *Applying occupational psychology to the fire service: Emotion, risk and decision-making* (pp. 13–57). London: Palgrave Macmillan.

Fagel, M. J. (2011). *Principles of emergency management: Hazard specific issues and mitigation strategies*. Boca Raton: CRC Press.

Faraj, S., & Xiao, Y. (2006). Coordination in fast-response organizations. *Management Science, 52*(8), 1155–1169.

FEMA. (2018). *ICS Review Document*. Retrieved from https://training.fema.gov/emiweb/is/icsresource/

Fernandez, G., & Ahmed, I. (2019). "Build back better" approach to disaster recovery: Research trends since 2006. *Progress in Disaster Science, 1,* Article 100003.

Fishwick, C. (2014). Tomnod – the online search party looking for Malaysian Airlines flight MH370. *The Guardian.* Retrieved from www.theguardian.com/world/2014/mar/14/tomnod-online-search-malaysian-airlines-flight-mh370

Fothergill, A., Maestas, E. G., & Darlington, J. D. (1999). Race, ethnicity and disasters in the United States: A review of the literature. *Disasters, 23*(2), 156–173.

Fothergill, A., & Peek, L. A. (2004). Poverty and disasters in the United States: A review of recent sociological findings. *Natural Hazards, 32*(1), 89–110.

Fox, F. (2001). New humanitarianism: Does it provide a moral banner for the 21st century? *Disasters, 25*(4), 275–289.

Fraher, A. L., Branicki, L. J., & Grint, K. (2017). Mindfulness in action: Discovering how US Navy Seals build capacity for mindfulness in high-reliability organizations (HROs). *Academy of Management Discoveries, 3*(3), 239–261.

Francis, J. E., & Jones, M. (2012). Emergency service volunteers: A comparison of age, motives and values. *The Australian Journal of Emergency Management, 27*(4), 27–32.

Franke, V. (2006). The peacebuilding dilemma: Civil-military cooperation in stability operations. *International Journal of Peace Studies, 11*(2), 5–25.

Franks, N. M., Gipson, K., Kaltiso, S.-A., Osborne, A., & Heron, S. L. (2021). The time is now: Racism and the responsibility of emergency medicine to be antiracist. *Annals of Emergency Medicine, 78*(5), 577–586.

Freud, S. (2007). *Group psychology and the analysis of the ego.* Durham: Duke University Press.

Friesen, I. (2021). Humanitarians' ethics: The role of face-to-face experiences for humanitarian aid workers' motivation. *Disasters,* Online first.

Friesendorf, C. (2018). *How western soldiers fight: Organizational routines in multinational missions.* Cambridge: Cambridge University Press.

Fritz, C. E., & Marks, E. S. (1954). The NORC studies of human behavior in disaster. *Journal of Social Issues, 10*(3), 26–41.

Fritz, C. E., & Williams, H. B. (1957). The human being in disasters: A research perspective. *The Annals of the American Academy of Political and Social Science, 309*(1), 42–51.

Fruhen, L. S., & Keith, N. (2014). Team cohesion and error culture in risky work environments. *Safety Science, 65,* 20–27.

Fry, M., MacGregor, C., Ruperto, K., Jarrett, K., Wheeler, J., Fong, J., & Fetchet, W. (2013). Nursing praxis, compassionate caring and interpersonal relations: An observational study. *Australasian Emergency Nursing Journal*, 16(2), 37–44.

Funabashi, Y., & Kitazawa, K. (2012). Fukushima in review: A complex disaster, a disastrous response. *Bulletin of the Atomic Scientists*, 68(2), 9–21.

Gacasan, E. M. P., & Wiggins, M. W. (2017). Sensemaking through cue utilisation in disaster recovery project management. *International Journal of Project Management*, 35(5), 818–826.

Gaillard, J.-C. (2019). Disaster studies inside out. *Disasters*, 43(S1), S7–S17.

Garg, R. H. (2012). Who killed Rambhor?: The state of emergency medical services in India. *Journal of Emergencies, Trauma, and Shock*, 5(1), 49–54.

Geale, S. K. (2012). The ethics of disaster management. *Disaster Prevention and Management*, 21(4), 445–462.

Gentry, J. A. (2002). Doomed to fail: America's blind faith in military technology. *Parameters*, 32(4), 88–103.

Ghanchi, A. (2016). Insights into French emergency planning, response, and resilience procedures from a hospital managerial perspective following the Paris terrorist attacks of Friday, November 13, 2015. *Disaster Medicine and Public Health Preparedness*, 10(5), 789–794.

Giustiniano, L., e Cunha, M. P., & Clegg, S. (2016). The dark side of organizational improvisation: Lessons from the sinking of Costa Concordia. *Business Horizons*, 59(2), 223–232.

Godé, C. (2015). *Team coordination in extreme environments: Work practices and technological uses under uncertainty*. Hoboken: John Wiley & Sons.

Goffman, E. (1961). *On the characteristics of total institutions*. New York: Holt, Rinehart and Winston.

Golan, A., Greene, W. H., & Perloff, J. M. (2021). Does the US Navy's reliance on objective standards prevent discrimination in promotions and retentions? *PloS One*, 16(4), e0250630.

Golden, S. J., Chang, C. H., & Kozlowski, S. W. (2018). Teams in isolated, confined, and extreme (ICE) environments: Review and integration. *Journal of Organizational Behavior*, 39(6), 701–715.

Gotowiec, S., & Cantor-Graae, E. (2017). The burden of choice: A qualitative study of healthcare professionals' reactions to ethical challenges in humanitarian crises. *Journal of International Humanitarian Action*, 2(1), 1–10.

Granot, H. (1997). Emergency inter-organizational relationships. *Disaster Prevention and Management*, 6(5), 305–310.

Granter, E., Wankhade, P., McCann, L., Hassard, J., & Hyde, P. (2019). Multiple dimensions of work intensity: Ambulance work as edgework. *Work, Employment and Society, 33*(2), 280–297.

Grint, K. (2020). Leadership, management and command in the time of the Coronavirus. *Leadership, 16*(3), 314–319.

Groenendaal, J., & Helsloot, I. (2016). A preliminary examination of command and control by incident commanders of Dutch fire services during real incidents. *Journal of Contingencies and Crisis Management, 24*(1), 2–13.

Groenendaal, J., & Helsloot, I. (2021). *Why technology not always adds value to crisis managers during crisis: The case of the Dutch nation-wide crisis management system LCMS*. Paper presented at the ISCRAM 2021 Conference Proceedings – 18th International Conference on Information Systems for Crisis Response and Management, Blacksburg, United States.

Groenendaal, J., Helsloot, I., & Scholtens, A. (2013). A critical examination of the assumptions regarding centralized coordination in large-scale emergency situations. *Journal of Homeland Security and Emergency Management, 10*(1), 113–135.

Gushin, V. I., Pustynnikova, J. M., & Smirnova, T. M. (2001). Interrelations between the small isolated groups with homogeneous and heterogeneous composition. *Human Performance in Extreme Environments, 6*(1), 26–33.

Gustavsson, M. E., Arnberg, F. K., Juth, N., & von Schreeb, J. (2020). Moral distress among disaster responders: What is it? *Prehospital and Disaster Medicine, 35*(2), 212–219.

Guy, M. E., Newman, M. A., & Ganapati, N. E. (2013). Managing emotions while managing crises. *International Journal of Emergency Services, 2*(1), 6–20.

Hallam, S. (2018). *Tradition under fire: Values, role regulation and work identity within the fire and rescue service*. Northampton: University of Northampton.

Hällgren, M., & Buchanan, D. A. (2020). The dark side of group behavior: Zombie apocalypse lessons. *Academy of Management Perspectives, 34*(4), 1–24.

Hällgren, M., & Rouleau, L. (2018). Researching risk, emergency and crisis: Taking stock of research methods on extreme contexts and moving forward. In J. Gephart, Robert P., C. C. Miller, & K. S. Helgesson (Eds.), *The Routledge companion to risk, crisis and emergency management* (pp. 146–161). New York: Routledge.

Hällgren, M., Rouleau, L., & De Rond, M. (2018). A matter of life or death: How extreme context research matters for management and organization studies. *Academy of Management Annals, 12*(1), 111–153.

Hamblin, R. L. (1958). Leadership and crises. *Sociometry, 21*(4), 322–335.

Hanatani, A., Gómez, O. A., & Kawaguchi, C. (2018). *Crisis management beyond the humanitarian-development nexus*. New York: Routledge.

Hannah, S. T., Uhl-Bien, M., Avolio, B. J., & Cavarretta, F. L. (2009). A framework for examining leadership in extreme contexts. *The Leadership Quarterly, 20*(6), 897–919.

Harrald, J. R. (2006). Agility and discipline: Critical success factors for disaster response. *The Annals of the American Academy of Political and Social Science, 604*(1), 256–272.

Harrison, J. (2019). Organisational factors: Impacting on health for ambulance personnel. *International Journal of Emergency Services, 8*(2), 134–146.

Hart, P. t. (1997). Preparing policy makers for crisis management: The role of simulations. *Journal of Contingencies and Crisis Management, 5*(4), 207–215.

Hart, P. t., Rosenthal, U., & Kouzmin, A. (1993). Crisis decision making: The centralization thesis revisited. *Administration & Society, 25*(1), 12–45.

Hatch, M. J. (1999). Exploring the empty spaces of organizing: How improvisational jazz helps redescribe organizational structure. *Organization Studies, 20*(1), 75–100.

Heide, E. A. (2004). Common misconceptions about disasters: Panic, the disaster syndrome, and looting. In M. O'Leary (Ed.), *The first 72 hours: A community approach to disaster preparedness* (pp. 340–380). Lincoln: iUniverse Publishing.

Heinecken, L. (2015). Are women 'really' making a unique contribution to peacekeeping? The rhetoric and the reality. *Journal of International Peacekeeping, 19*(3–4), 227–248.

Helsloot, I., & Ruitenberg, A. (2004). Citizen response to disasters: A survey of literature and some practical implications. *Journal of Contingencies and Crisis Management, 12*(3), 98–111.

Henderson, A. C., & Pandey, S. K. (2013). Leadership in street-level bureaucracy: An exploratory study of supervisor-worker interactions in emergency medical services. *International Review of Public Administration, 18*(1), 7–23.

Hendriks, E., Kmoch, L. M., Mulder, F., & Fuentealba, R. (2022). Guest editorial: Exploring inclusive publishing practices with early career disaster-studies researchers. *Disaster Prevention and Management, 31*(1), 1–9.

Hermann, C. F. (1963). Some consequences of crisis which limit the viability of organizations. *Administrative Science Quarterly, 8*(1), 61–82.

Hewes, H. A., Dai, M., Mann, N. C., Baca, T., & Taillac, P. (2018). Prehospital pain management: Disparity by age and race. *Prehospital Emergency Care*, 22(2), 189–197.

Hilhorst, D. (2002). Being good at doing good? Quality and accountability of humanitarian NGOs. *Disasters*, 26(3), 193–212.

Hilhorst, D. (2018). Classical humanitarianism and resilience humanitarianism: Making sense of two brands of humanitarian action. *Journal of International Humanitarian Action*, 3(1), 1–12.

Hilhorst, D., & Jansen, B. J. (2010). Humanitarian space as arena: A perspective on the everyday politics of aid. *Development and Change*, 41(6), 1117–1139.

Holmes, R. (1986). *Acts of war: The behavior of men in battle*. New York: Free Press.

Hsia, R. Y., Huang, D., Mann, N. C., Colwell, C., Mercer, M. P., Dai, M., & Niedzwiecki, M. J. (2018). A US national study of the association between income and ambulance response time in cardiac arrest. *JAMA Network Open*, 1(7): e185202.

Huard, C., Deschênes, A.-A., & Rioux, C.-A. (2021). Emotional self-efficacy and workplace psychological health in emergency dispatchers. *International Journal of Emergency Services*, 10(2), 276–287.

Hunniecutt, J. (2020). On not seeing myself in the research on veterans. In A. F. Herrmann (Ed.), *The Routledge international handbook of organizational autoethnography* (pp. 117–133). London: Routledge.

Hunsaker, S., Chen, H. C., Maughan, D., & Heaston, S. (2015). Factors that influence the development of compassion fatigue, burnout, and compassion satisfaction in emergency department nurses. *Journal of Nursing Scholarship*, 47(2), 186–194.

Hunt, M. R. (2008). Ethics beyond borders: How health professionals experience ethics in humanitarian assistance and development work. *Developing World Bioethics*, 8(2), 59–69.

Hunt, M. R. (2011). Establishing moral bearings: Ethics and expatriate health care professionals in humanitarian work. *Disasters*, 35(3), 606–622.

ICRC. (2015). *The fundamental principles of the international Red Cross and Red Crescent movement*. Geneva: International Committee of the Red Cross.

IFRC. (2013). *World disasters report*. Geneva: International Federation of the Red Cross.

Iizuka, A., & Aldrich, D. P. (2021). Attracting altruists: Explaining volunteer turnout during natural hazards in Japan. *Disasters*, 46(2), 526–544.

Imran, M., Castillo, C., Lucas, J., Meier, P., & Vieweg, S. (2014). *AIDR: Artificial intelligence for disaster response*. Paper presented at the Proceedings of the 23rd international conference on world wide web, Seoul, South Korea.

Independent Police Complaints Commission. (2007). *Stockwell One: Investigation into the shooting of Jean Charles de Menezes at Stockwell underground station on 22 July 2005*. Retrieved from London: http://policeauthority.org/metropolitan/downloads/scrutinites/stockwell/ipcc-one.pdf

Isabelle, B., Cécile, G., Carole, D.-G., Pascal, L., Jean, N., & François, P. (2012). Coordination practices in extreme situations. *European Management Journal, 30*(6), 475–489.

Jacobsson, M., & Hällgren, M. (2016). Impromptu teams in a temporary organization: On their nature and role. *International Journal of Project Management, 34*(4), 584–596.

Jahnke, S. A., Haddock, C. K., Jitnarin, N., Kaipust, C. M., Hollerbach, B. S., & Poston, W. S. (2019). The prevalence and health impacts of frequent work discrimination and harassment among women firefighters in the US fire service. *BioMed research international, 2019*, Article 6740207.

James, E. H., Wooten, L. P., & Dushek, K. (2011). Crisis management: Informing a new leadership research agenda. *Academy of Management Annals, 5*(1), 455–493.

Janis, I. L. (1971). Groupthink. *Psychology Today, 5*(6), 43–46.

Jeffrey, D. (2016). Empathy, sympathy and compassion in healthcare: Is there a problem? Is there a difference? Does it matter? *Journal of the Royal Society of Medicine, 109*(12), 446–452.

Jensen, J., & Thompson, S. (2016). The incident command system: A literature review. *Disasters, 40*(1), 158–182.

Jetly, R., Vermetten, E., Easterbrook, B., Lanius, R., & McKinnon, M. (2020). Going to "war": Military approach as the antidote to defeating COVID-19. *Military Behavioral Health, 8*(3), 243–247.

Jiang, W. Y. (2021). Sustaining meaningful work in a crisis: Adopting and conveying a situational purpose. *Administrative Science Quarterly, 66*(3), 806–853.

Jin, J., & Song, G. (2017). Bureaucratic accountability and disaster response: Why did the Korea Coast Guard fail in its rescue mission during the Sewol ferry accident? *Risk, Hazards & Crisis in Public Policy, 8*(3), 220–243.

Johansson, R., Danielsson, E., Kvarnlöf, L., Eriksson, K., & Karlsson, R. (2018). At the external boundary of a disaster response operation: The dynamics of volunteer inclusion. *Journal of Contingencies and Crisis Management, 26*(4), 519–529.

Jordan, S. (2010). Learning to be surprised: How to foster reflective practice in a high-reliability context. *Management Learning, 41*(4), 391–413.

Kalkman, J. P. (2018). Practices and consequences of using humanitarian technologies in volatile aid settings. *Journal of International Humanitarian Action, 3*(1), Article 1.

Kalkman, J. P. (2019a). *Focus on the frontline: Civil-military collaboration in domestic and European crisis management.* Amsterdam: VU University.

Kalkman, J. P. (2019b). Sensemaking questions in crisis response teams. *Disaster Prevention and Management, 28*(5), 649–660.

Kalkman, J. P. (2020a). Boundary spanners in crisis management. *International Journal of Emergency Services, 9*(2), 233–244.

Kalkman, J. P. (2020b). Frontline workers in crisis management. In E. K. Stern, D. Fischbacher-Smith, S. Kuipers, A. McConnell, D. Nohrstedt, & T. Preston (Eds.), *The Oxford Encyclopedia of Crisis Analysis.* Oxford: Oxford University Press. https://doi.org/10.1093/acrefore/9780190228637.013.1582

Kalkman, J. P. (2020c). Sensemaking in crisis situations: Drawing insights from epic war novels. *European Management Journal, 38*(5), 698–707.

Kalkman, J. P. (2022). Mindful Members: Developing a Mindset for Reliable Performance in Extreme Contexts. *Journal of Management Inquiry,* Online first. https://doi.org/10.1177/10564926221082487

Kalkman, J. P. (2023a). Adaptive organizing in response to unexpected events: Military relief operations after Hurricane Dorian. *Academy of Management Discoveries,* Online first. https://doi.org/10.5465/amd.2020.0213

Kalkman, J. P. (2023b). The lived experience of organizational disidentification: How soldiers feel betrayed, dissociate, and suffer. *Culture and Organization, 29*(1), 1-18.

Kalkman, J. P., & Groenewegen, P. (2019). On frontline workers as bureau-political actors: The case of civil–military crisis management. *Administration & Society, 51*(7), 1148–1170.

Kalkman, J. P., Kerstholt, J. H., & Roelofs, M. (2018). Crisis response team decision-making as a bureau-political process. *Journal of Contingencies and Crisis Management, 26*(4), 480–490.

Kalkman, J. P., & Molendijk, T. (2021). The role of strategic ambiguity in moral injury: A case study of Dutch border guards facing moral challenges. *Journal of Management Inquiry, 30*(2), 221–234.

Kanas, N., Sandal, G. M., Boyd, J. E., Gushin, V. I., Manzey, D., North, R., … Fiedler, E. R. (2013). Psychology and culture during long-duration space missions. *Acta Astronautica, 64*(7–8), 659–677.

Kapucu, N. (2006). Interagency communication networks during emergencies: Boundary spanners in multiagency coordination. *The American Review of Public Administration, 36*(2), 207–225.

Kapucu, N., & Garayev, V. (2013). Designing, managing, and sustaining functionally collaborative emergency management networks. *The American Review of Public Administration, 43*(3), 312–330.

Karunakaran, A. (2021). Status–authority asymmetry between professions: The case of 911 dispatchers and police officers. *Administrative Science Quarterly, 67*(2), 423–468.

Kawasaki, A., Berman, M. L., & Guan, W. (2013). The growing role of web-based geospatial technology in disaster response and support. *Disasters, 37*(2), 201–221.

Kayes, D. C. (2004). The 1996 Mount Everest climbing disaster: The breakdown of learning in teams. *Human Relations, 57*(10), 1263–1284.

Keane, C., & Wood, S. (2016). Bureaucratic politics, role conflict, and the internal dynamics of US provincial reconstruction teams in Afghanistan. *Armed Forces & Society, 42*(1), 99–118.

Kelman, H. C., & Hamilton, V. L. (1989). *Crimes of obedience: Toward a social psychology of authority and responsibility.* New Haven: Yale University Press.

Kendra, J. M., & Wachtendorf, T. (2003a). Elements of resilience after the world trade center disaster: Reconstituting New York City's Emergency Operations Centre. *Disasters, 27*(1), 37–53.

Kendra, J. M., & Wachtendorf, T. (2003b). Reconsidering convergence and converger legitimacy in response to the World Trade Center disaster. In L. Clarke (Ed.), *Terrorism and disaster: New threats, new ideas* (pp. 97–122). Bingley: Emerald Group Publishing Limited.

Kendra, J. M., & Wachtendorf, T. (2016). *American Dunkirk: The waterborne evacuation of Manhattan on 9/11.* Philadelphia: Temple University Press.

Kenis, P., Schol, L. G., Kraaij-Dirkzwager, M. M., & Timen, A. (2019). Appropriate governance responses to infectious disease threats: Developing working hypotheses. *Risk, Hazards & Crisis in Public Policy, 10*(3), 275–293.

Kennel, J., Withers, E., Parsons, N., & Woo, H. (2019). Racial/ethnic disparities in pain treatment: Evidence from Oregon emergency medical services agencies. *Medical Care, 57*(12), 924–929.

Kettl, D. F. (2003). Contingent coordination: Practical and theoretical puzzles for homeland security. *The American Review of Public Administration, 33*(3), 253–277.

Kibreab, G. (1993). The myth of dependency among camp refugees in Somalia 1979–1989. *Journal of Refugee Studies, 6*(4), 321–349.

Kim, H. (2013). Improving simulation exercises in Korea for disaster preparedness. *Disaster Prevention and Management, 22*(1), 38–47.

Kindness, P., Fitzpatrick, D., Mellish, C., Masthoff, J., O'Meara, P., & McEwan, M. (2014). An insight into the demands and stressors experienced by Community First Responders. *Journal of Paramedic Practice,* 6(7), 362–369.

King, A. (2006). The word of command: Communication and cohesion in the military. *Armed Forces & Society, 32*(4), 493–512.

Klein, G. A. (1993). A recognition-primed decision (RPD) model of rapid decision making. In G. A. Klein, J. Orasanu, R. Calderwood, & C. E. Zsambok (Eds.), *Decision making in action: Models and methods* (pp. 138–147). New York: Ablex Publishing.

Klein, G. A., Ziegert, J. C., Knight, A. P., & Xiao, Y. (2006). Dynamic delegation: Shared, hierarchical, and deindividualized leadership in extreme action teams. *Administrative Science Quarterly, 51*(4), 590–621.

Knezek, E. B., Vu, T., & Lee, J. (2022). Emergency responder willingness to respond during disasters: A literature review. *Journal of Contingencies and Crisis Management, 30*(1), 71–81.

Knox, H., O'Doherty, D. P., Vurdubakis, T., & Westrup, C. (2015). Something happened: Spectres of organization/disorganization at the airport. *Human Relations, 68*(6), 1001–1020.

Kramer, E.-H. (2007). *Organizing doubt: Grounded theory, army units and dealing with dynamic complexity.* Copenhagen: Copenhagen Business School Press.

Kriner, D. L., & Shen, F. X. (2010). *The casualty gap: The causes and consequences of American wartime inequalities.* Oxford: Oxford University Press.

Kristiansen, E., Johansen, F. H., & Carlström, E. (2019). When it matters most: Collaboration between first responders in incidents and exercises. *Journal of Contingencies and Crisis Management, 27*(1), 72–78.

Kuipers, S., & Swinkels, M. (2018). Peak performance: Collaborative crisis management before and during international summits. *International Journal of Emergency Management, 14*(4), 344–363.

Kvarnlöf, L., & Johansson, R. (2014). Boundary practices at incident sites: Making distinctions between emergency personnel and the public. *International Journal of Emergency Services, 3*(1), 65–76.

Landgren, J. (2005). Supporting fire crew sensemaking enroute to incidents. *International Journal of Emergency Management, 2*(3), 176–188.

Lanzara, G. F. (1983). Ephemeral organizations in extreme environments: Emergence, strategy, extinction. *Journal of Management Studies, 20*(1), 71–95.

LaPorte, T. R., & Consolini, P. M. (1991). Working in practice but not in theory: Theoretical challenges of "high-reliability organizations." *Journal of Public Administration Research and Theory*, 1(1), 19–48.

Leach, K., & Rivera, J. D. (2022). Dismantling power asymmetries in disaster and emergency management research: Another argument for the application of critical theory. *Risk, Hazards & Crisis in Public Policy*, 13(4), 337-355.

Leader, N. (1998). Proliferating principles, or how to sup with the devil without getting eaten. *The International Journal of Human Rights*, 2(4), 1–27.

Lee, S. H., & Olshfski, D. (2002). Employee commitment and firefighters: It's my job. *Public Administration Review*, 62(SI), 108–114.

Lei, Z., Waller, M. J., Hagen, J., & Kaplan, S. (2016). Team adaptiveness in dynamic contexts: Contextualizing the roles of interaction patterns and in-process planning. *Group & Organization Management*, 41(4), 491–525.

Lennie, S.-J., Sarah, E. C., & Sutton, A. (2020). Robocop – The depersonalisation of police officers and their emotions: A diary study of emotional labor and burnout in front line British police officers. *International Journal of Law, Crime and Justice*, 61, Article 100365.

Lentz, L. M., Smith-MacDonald, L., Malloy, D., Carleton, R. N., & Brémault-Phillips, S. (2021). Compromised conscience: A scoping review of moral injury among firefighters, paramedics, and police officers. *Frontiers in Psychology*, 12, Article 639781.

Levy, G., & Sasson-Levy, O. (2008). Militarized socialization, military service, and class reproduction: The experiences of Israeli soldiers. *Sociological Perspectives*, 51(2), 349–374.

Lewis, J. F., Zeger, S. L., Li, X., Mann, N. C., Newgard, C. D., Haynes, S., ... McCarthy, M. L. (2019). Gender differences in the quality of EMS care nationwide for chest pain and out-of-hospital cardiac arrest. *Women's Health Issues*, 29(2), 116–124.

Linderoth, G., Lippert, F., Østergaard, D., Ersbøll, A. K., Meyhoff, C. S., Folke, F., & Christensen, H. C. (2021). Live video from bystanders' smartphones to medical dispatchers in real emergencies. *BMC Emergency Medicine*, 21(1), 1–10.

Lipsky, M. (1983). *Street-level bureaucracy: The dilemmas of the individual in public service*. New York: Russell Sage Foundation.

Löfquist, L. (2017). Virtues and humanitarian ethics. *Disasters*, 41(1), 41–54.

Lois, J. (2003). *Heroic efforts: The emotional culture of search and rescue volunteers*. New York: New York University Press.

Lorenz, D. F., Schulze, K., & Voss, M. (2018). Emerging citizen responses to disasters in Germany. Disaster myths as an impediment for a collaboration of unaffiliated responders and professional rescue forces. *Journal of Contingencies and Crisis Management*, 26(3), 358–367.

Lu, X., & Xue, L. (2016). Managing the unexpected: Sense-making in the Chinese emergency management system. *Public Administration*, 94(2), 414–429.

Lundberg, J., & Rankin, A. (2014). Resilience and vulnerability of small flexible crisis response teams: Implications for training and preparation. *Cognition, Technology & Work*, 16(2), 143–155.

MacCoun, R. J., Kier, E., & Belkin, A. (2006). Does social cohesion determine motivation in combat? An old question with an old answer. *Armed Forces & Society*, 32(4), 646–654.

Macpherson, A., Breslin, D., & Akinci, C. (2021). Organizational learning from hidden improvisation. *Organization Studies*, 43(6), 861–883.

Magnussen, L. I., Carlstrøm, E., Sørensen, J. L., Torgersen, G.-E., Hagenes, E. F., & Kristiansen, E. (2017). Learning and usefulness stemming from collaboration in a maritime crisis management exercise in Northern Norway. *Disaster Prevention and Management*, 27(1), 129–140.

Maguire, B., & Hagan, P. (2007). Disasters and communities: Understanding social resilience. *The Australian Journal of Emergency Management*, 22(2), 16–20.

Maietta, M., Kennedy, E., & Bourse, F. (2017). *The future of aid: INGOs in 2030*. Retrieved from https://reliefweb.int/report/world/future-aid-ingos-2030

Maitlis, S., & Christianson, M. (2014). Sensemaking in organizations: Taking stock and moving forward. *Academy of Management Annals*, 8(1), 57–125.

Maitlis, S., & Sonenshein, S. (2010). Sensemaking in crisis and change: Inspiration and insights from Weick (1988). *Journal of Management Studies*, 47(3), 551–580.

Majchrzak, A., Jarvenpaa, S. L., & Hollingshead, A. B. (2007). Coordinating expertise among emergent groups responding to disasters. *Organization Science*, 18(1), 147–161.

Marcinkowski, M. A., Bell, S. T., & Roma, P. G. (2021). The nature of conflict for teams in isolated, confined, and extreme environments. *Acta Astronautica*, 181, 81–91.

Margolis, J. D., & Molinsky, A. (2008). Navigating the bind of necessary evils: Psychological engagement and the production of interpersonally sensitive behavior. *Academy of Management Journal*, 51(5), 847–872.

Mastracci, S. H., & Adams, I. (2019). Emotional labor in emergency dispatch: Gauging effects of training protocols. *Annals of Emergency Dispatch & Response, 7*(3), 5–10.

Mastracci, S. H., Guy, M. E., & Newman, M. A. (2014). *Emotional labor and crisis response: Working on the razor's edge.* New York: Routledge.

Matsakis, A. (2005). *In harm's way: Help for the wives of military men, police, EMTs, and firefighters.* Oakland: New Harbinger Publications.

Maynard-Moody, S. W., & Musheno, M. C. (2003). *Cops, teachers, counselors: Stories from the front lines of public service.* Ann Arbor: University of Michigan Press.

Maynard-Moody, S., & Musheno, M. (2012). Social equities and inequities in practice: Street-level workers as agents and pragmatists. *Public Administration Review, 72*(s1), S16–S23.

McCann, L., & Granter, E. (2019). Beyond 'blue-collar professionalism': Continuity and change in the professionalization of uniformed emergency services work. *Journal of Professions and Organization, 6*(2), 213–232.

McConnell, A. (2011). Success? Failure? Something in-between? A framework for evaluating crisis management. *Policy and Society, 30*(2), 63–76.

McConnell, A. (2020). Evaluating success and failure in crisis management. In E. K. Stern, D. Fischbacher-Smith, S. Kuipers, A. McConnell, D. Nohrstedt, & T. Preston (Eds.), *The Oxford Encyclopedia of Crisis Analysis.* Oxford: Oxford University Press. https://doi.org/10.1093/acrefore/9780190228637.013.1582

McConnell, A., & Drennan, L. (2006). Mission impossible? Planning and preparing for crisis. *Journal of Contingencies and Crisis Management, 14*(2), 59–70.

McCormack, L., & Bamforth, S. (2019). Finding authenticity in an altruistic identity: The "lived" experience of health care humanitarians deployed to the 2014 Ebola crisis. *Traumatology, 25*(4), 289.

McCormick, S. (2016). New tools for emergency managers: An assessment of obstacles to use and implementation. *Disasters, 40*(2), 207–225.

McDonald, M. A., Meckes, S. J., & Lancaster, C. L. (2021). Compassion for oneself and others protects the mental health of first responders. *Mindfulness, 12*(3), 659–671.

McEntire, D. A. (2002). Coordinating multi-organisational responses to disaster: Lessons from the March 28, 2000, Fort Worth tornado. *Disaster Prevention and Management, 11*(5), 369–379.

McEntire, D. A., Kelly, J., Kendra, J. M., & Long, L. C. (2013). Spontaneous planning after the San Bruno gas pipeline explosion: A case study of anticipation and improvisation during response and recovery operations. *Journal of Homeland Security and Emergency Management, 10*(1), 161–185.

McLennan, B., Whittaker, J., & Handmer, J. (2016). The changing landscape of disaster volunteering: Opportunities, responses and gaps in Australia. *Natural Hazards, 84*(3), 2031–2048.

Meier, P. (2011). New information technologies and their impact on the humanitarian sector. *International Review of the Red Cross, 93*(884), 1239–1263.

Mendonça, D., Jefferson, T., & Harrald, J. (2007). Collaborative adhocracies and mix-and-match technologies in emergency management. *Communications of the ACM, 50*(3), 44–49.

Menninger, W. C. (1952). Psychological reactions in an emergency (flood). *American Journal of Psychiatry, 109*(2), 128–130.

Merkus, S., Willems, T., Schipper, D., van Marrewijk, A., Koppenjan, J., Veenswijk, M., & Bakker, H. (2017). A storm is coming? Collective sensemaking and ambiguity in an inter-organizational team managing railway system disruptions. *Journal of Change Management, 17*(3), 228–248.

Meshkati, N., & Khashe, Y. (2015). Operators' improvisation in complex technological systems: Successfully tackling ambiguity, enhancing resiliency and the last resort to averting disaster. *Journal of Contingencies and Crisis Management, 23*(2), 90–96.

Militello, L. G., Patterson, E. S., Bowman, L., & Wears, R. (2007). Information flow during crisis management: Challenges to coordination in the emergency operations center. *Cognition, Technology & Work, 9*(1), 25–31.

Mills, J. T., & Miller, D. S. (2015). Educating the next generation of emergency management and homeland security professionals: Promoting racial and ethnic understanding via cultural competence and critical race theory. *Journal of Applied Security Research, 10*(4), 466–480.

Mitroff, I. I., Shrivastava, P., & Udwadia, F. E. (1987). Effective crisis management. *Academy of Management Perspectives, 1*(4), 283–292.

Moe, T. L., & Pathranarakul, P. (2006). An integrated approach to natural disaster management: Public project management and its critical success factors. *Disaster Prevention and Management, 15*(3), 396–413.

Molendijk, T. (2021). *Moral injury and soldiers in conflict: Political practices and public perceptions.* New York: Routledge.

Moorhead, G., Ference, R., & Neck, C. P. (1991). Group decision fiascoes continue: Space shuttle Challenger and a revised groupthink framework. *Human Relations, 44*(6), 539–550.

Moorkamp, M., Wybo, J.-L., & Kramer, E.-H. (2016). Pioneering with UAVs at the battlefield: The influence of organizational design on self-organization and the emergence of safety. *Safety Science, 88,* 251–260.

Morris, J. C., Morris, E. D., & Jones, D. M. (2007). Reaching for the philosopher's stone: Contingent coordination and the military's response to Hurricane Katrina. *Public Administration Review*, 67(S1), 94–106.

Morrow, B. H., & Enarson, E. (1996). Hurricane Andrew through women's eyes. *International Journal of Mass Emergencies and Disasters*, 14(1), 5–22.

Moynihan, D. P. (2008). Combining structural forms in the search for policy tools: Incident command systems in US crisis management. *Governance*, 21(2), 205–229.

Moynihan, D. P. (2009). The network governance of crisis response: Case studies of incident command systems. *Journal of Public Administration Research and Theory*, 19(4), 895–915.

Mulder, F., Ferguson, J., Groenewegen, P., Boersma, F., & Wolbers, J. (2016). Questioning big data: Crowdsourcing crisis data towards an inclusive humanitarian response. *Big Data & Society*, 3(2).

National Commission on Terrorist Attacks Upon the United States. (2004). *Final report of the national commission on terrorist attacks upon the United States*. Washington: Government Printing Office.

Neal, D. M., & Phillips, B. D. (1995). Effective emergency management: Reconsidering the bureaucratic approach. *Disasters*, 19(4), 327–337.

Neitzel, S., & Welzer, H. (2012). *Soldaten – On fighting, killing and dying: The secret Second World War tapes of German POWs*. New York: Simon & Schuster.

Neumayer, E., & Plümper, T. (2007). The gendered nature of natural disasters: The impact of catastrophic events on the gender gap in life expectancy, 1981–2002. *Annals of the Association of American Geographers*, 97(3), 551–566.

Nilsson, S., Sjöberg, M., Kallenberg, K., & Larsson, G. (2011). Moral stress in international humanitarian aid and rescue operations: A grounded theory study. *Ethics & Behavior*, 21(1), 49–68.

Nissen, S., Carlton, S., & Wong, J. H. (2022). Gaining 'authority to operate': Student-led emergent volunteers and established response agencies in the Canterbury earthquakes. *Disasters*, 46(3), 832–852.

Njå, O., & Rake, E. L. (2008). An essay on research methodology: An alternative approach to incident command research through participatory action research. *Journal of Contingencies and Crisis Management*, 16(2), 91–100.

Nogami, T. (2018). Disaster myths among disaster response professionals and the source of such misconceptions. *Journal of Contingencies and Crisis Management*, 26(4), 491–498.

Nowell, B., & Steelman, T. (2015). Communication under fire: The role of embeddedness in the emergence and efficacy of disaster response communication networks. *Journal of Public Administration Research and Theory*, 25(3), 929–952.

O'Brien, T. (2015). *The things they carried*. London: Fourth Estate.

O'Connell, E., Abbott, R. P., & White, R. S. (2017). Emotions and beliefs after a disaster: A comparative analysis of Haiti and Indonesia. *Disasters*, 41(4), 803–827.

O'Keefe, P., Westgate, K., & Wisner, B. (1976). Taking the "Naturalness" out of "Natural Disaster." *Nature*, 260(15), 566–567.

O'Toole, M., & Calvard, T. (2020). I've got your back: Danger, volunteering and solidarity in lifeboat crews. *Work, Employment and Society*, 34(1), 73–90.

Ödlund, A. (2010). Pulling the same way? A multi-perspectivist study of crisis cooperation in government. *Journal of Contingencies and Crisis Management*, 18(2), 96–107.

Oelberger, C. R. (2019). The dark side of deeply meaningful work: Work-relationship turmoil and the moderating role of occupational value homophily. *Journal of Management Studies*, 56(3), 558–588.

Oliver, N., Calvard, T., & Potočnik, K. (2017). Cognition, technology, and organizational limits: Lessons from the Air France 447 disaster. *Organization Science*, 28(4), 729–743.

Olson, R. S. (2000). Toward a politics of disaster: Losses, values, agendas, and blame. *International Journal of Mass Emergencies and Disaster*, 18(2), 265–287.

Olsthoorn, P., & Schut, M. (2018). The ethics of border guarding: A first exploration and a research agenda for the future. *Ethics and Education*, 13(2), 157–171.

Oppong, J. R., Boakye, K., Edziyie, R., Owusu, A. Y., & Tiwari, C. (2017). Emergency fire response in Ghana: The case of fire stations in Kumasi. *African Geographical Review*, 36(3), 253–261.

Orton, J. D., & O'Grady, K. A. (2016). Cosmology episodes: A reconceptualization. *Journal of Management, Spirituality & Religion*, 13(3), 226–245.

Parkinson, D., Duncan, A., & Archer, F. (2019). Barriers and enablers to women in fire and emergency leadership roles. *Gender in Management*, 34(2), 78–93.

Patel, J., Nielsen, F., Badiani, A., Assi, S., Unadkat, V., Patel, B., ... Wardle, H. (2020). Poverty, inequality and COVID-19: The forgotten vulnerable. *Public Health*, 183, 110–111.

Patterson, P. D., Weaver, M. D., Landsittel, D. P., Krackhardt, D., Hostler, D., Vena, J. E., ... Yealy, D. M. (2016). Teammate familiarity and risk of injury in emergency medical services. *Emergency Medicine Journal*, 33(4), 280–285.

Pearce, A. P., Naumann, D., & O'Reilly, D. (2021). Mission command: Applying principles of military leadership to the SARS-CoV-2 (COVID-19) crisis. *British Medical Journal, 167*(1), 3–4.

Pearson, C. M., & Clair, J. A. (1998). Reframing crisis management. *Academy of Management Review, 23*(1), 59–76.

Perrow, C. (1984). *Normal accidents: Living with high risk technologies.* Princeton: Princeton University Press.

Perry, R. W. (2004). Disaster exercise outcomes for professional emergency personnel and citizen volunteers. *Journal of Contingencies and Crisis Management, 12*(2), 64–75.

Perry, R. W., & Lindell, M. K. (2003). Preparedness for emergency response: Guidelines for the emergency planning process. *Disasters, 27*(4), 336–350.

Phillips, B. D. (2015). *Disaster recovery.* Boca Raton: CRC Press.

Powley, E. H. (2009). Reclaiming resilience and safety: Resilience activation in the critical period of crisis. *Human Relations, 62*(9), 1289–1326.

Pramanik, R. (2015). Challenges in coordination: Differences in perception of civil and military organizations by comparing international scientific literature and field experiences. *Journal of Risk Research, 18*(7), 989–1007.

Prati, G., Catufi, V., & Pietrantoni, L. (2012). Emotional and behavioural reactions to tremors of the Umbria-Marche earthquake. *Disasters, 36*(3), 439–451.

Qadir, J., Ali, A., ur Rasool, R., Zwitter, A., Sathiaseelan, A., & Crowcroft, J. (2016). Crisis analytics: Big data-driven crisis response. *Journal of International Humanitarian Action, 1*(1), Article 12.

Quarantelli, E. L. (1960). Images of withdrawal behavior in disasters: Some basic misconceptions. *Social Problems, 8*(1), 68–79.

Quarantelli, E. L. (1985). *Organizational behavior in disasters and implications for disaster planning.* Newark: Disaster Research Center, University of Delaware.

Quarantelli, E. L. (1988). Disaster crisis management: A summary of research findings. *Journal of Management Studies, 25*(4), 373–385.

Quarantelli, E. L. (1997a). Problematical aspects of the information/communication revolution for disaster planning and research: Ten non-technical issues and questions. *Disaster Prevention and Management, 6*(2), 94–106.

Quarantelli, E. L. (1997b). Ten criteria for evaluating the management of community disasters. *Disasters, 21*(1), 39–56.

Quarantelli, E. L. (2005). Catastrophes are different from disasters: Some implications for crisis planning and managing drawn from Katrina. Retrieved from https://items.ssrc.org/understanding-katrina/catastrophes-are-different-from-disasters-some-implications-for-crisis-planning-and-managing-drawn-from-katrina/

Quarantelli, E. L., & Dynes, R. R. (1977). Response to social crisis and disaster. *Annual Review of Sociology, 3*(1), 23–49.

Quinn, R. W., & Worline, M. C. (2008). Enabling courageous collective action: Conversations from United Airlines flight 93. *Organization Science, 19*(4), 497–516.

Raaphorst, N. (2018). How to prove, how to interpret and what to do? Uncertainty experiences of street-level tax officials. *Public Management Review, 20*(4), 485–502.

Rake, E. L., & Njå, O. (2009). Perceptions and performances of experienced incident commanders. *Journal of Risk Research, 12*(5), 665–685.

Ramos, Q. M. R., Kim, K. H., Park, J. H., Do Shin, S., Song, K. J., & Hong, K. J. (2021). Socioeconomic disparities in rapid ambulance response for out-of-hospital cardiac arrest in a public emergency medical service system: A nationwide observational study. *Resuscitation, 158*, 143–150.

Rasmussen, M. B., Tolsgaard, M. G., Dieckmann, P., Østergaard, D., White, J., Plenge, P., & Ringsted, C. V. (2020). Social ties influence teamwork when managing clinical emergencies. *BMC Medical Education, 20*(1), Article 63.

Rauch, M., & Ansari, S. (2022). Waging war from remote cubicles: How workers cope with technologies that disrupt the meaning and morality of their work. *Organization Science, 33*(1), 83–104.

Regehr, C., Goldberg, G., & Hughes, J. (2002). Exposure to human tragedy, empathy, and trauma in ambulance paramedics. *American Journal of Orthopsychiatry, 72*(4), 505–513.

Remarque, E. M. (2004). *All quiet on the western front*. London: Bloomsbury Publishing.

Resseguier, A. (2018). The moral sense of humanitarian actors: An empirical exploration. *Disasters, 42*(1), 62–80.

Ressler, E. (1978). Accountability as a program philosophy. *Disasters, 2*(2–3), 129–133.

Rice, S., & Fallon, B. (2011). Retention of volunteers in the emergency services: Exploring interpersonal and group cohesion factors. *Australian Journal of Emergency Management, 26*(1), 18–23.

Rietjens, S. J., & Bollen, M. T. (2008). *Managing civil-military cooperation: A 24/7 joint effort for stability*. Farnham: Ashgate Publishing, Ltd.

Rietjens, S. J., & Ruffa, C. (2019). Understanding coherence in UN peacekeeping: A conceptual framework. *International Peacekeeping, 26*(4), 383–407.

Rimstad, R., Njå, O., Rake, E. L., & Braut, G. S. (2014). Incident command and information flows in a large-scale emergency operation. *Journal of Contingencies and Crisis Management, 22*(1), 29–38.

Rivera, K. D. (2015). Emotional taint: Making sense of emotional dirty work at the US Border Patrol. *Management Communication Quarterly, 29*(2), 198–228.

Robert, B., & Lajtha, C. (2002). A new approach to crisis management. *Journal of Contingencies and Crisis Management, 10*(4), 181–191.

Robert, R., Kentish-Barnes, N., Boyer, A., Laurent, A., Azoulay, E., & Reignier, J. (2020). Ethical dilemmas due to the Covid-19 pandemic. *Annals of Intensive Care, 10*(1), Article 84.

Roberts, K. H., & Bea, R. (2001). Must accidents happen? Lessons from high-reliability organizations. *Academy of Management Perspectives, 15*(3), 70–78.

Rodriguez-Díaz, C. E., & Lewellen-Williams, C. (2020). Race and racism as structural determinants for emergency and recovery response in the aftermath of hurricanes Irma and Maria in Puerto Rico. *Health Equity, 4*(1), 232–238.

Rodriguez, H., Trainor, J., & Quarantelli, E. L. (2006). Rising to the challenges of a catastrophe: The emergent and prosocial behavior following Hurricane Katrina. *The Annals of the American Academy of Political and Social Science, 604*(1), 82–101.

Rosenthal, U., Hart, P. t., & Kouzmin, A. (1991). The bureau-politics of crisis management. *Public Administration, 69*(2), 211–233.

Roux-Dufort, C. (2007). Is crisis management (only) a management of exceptions? *Journal of Contingencies and Crisis Management, 15*(2), 105–114.

Rushton, C. H. (2016). Moral resilience: A capacity for navigating moral distress in critical care. *AACN Advanced Critical Care, 27*(1), 111–119.

Salvarani, V., Rampoldi, G., Ardenghi, S., Bani, M., Blasi, P., Ausili, D., … Strepparava, M. G. (2019). Protecting emergency room nurses from burnout: The role of dispositional mindfulness, emotion regulation and empathy. *Journal of Nursing Management, 27*(4), 765–774.

Sandal, G. M., Leon, G., & Palinkas, L. (2006). Human challenges in polar and space environments. *Reviews in Environmental Science and Bio/ Technology, 5*(2–3), 281–296.

Sandberg, J., & Tsoukas, H. (2015). Making sense of the sensemaking perspective: Its constituents, limitations, and opportunities for further development. *Journal of Organizational Behavior, 36*(S1), S6–S32.

Sandvik, K. B. (2016). The humanitarian cyberspace: Shrinking space or an expanding frontier? *Third World Quarterly, 37*(1), 17–32.

Sandvik, K. B., Jumbert, M. G., Karlsrud, J., & Kaufmann, M. (2014). Humanitarian technology: A critical research agenda. *International Review of the Red Cross, 96*(893), 219–242.

Sanial, G. J. (2007). *The response to Hurricane Katrina: A study of the Coast Guard's culture, organizational design & leadership in crisis.* Cambridge: Massachusetts Institute of Technology.

Sasson-Levy, O., & Amram-Katz, S. (2007). Gender integration in Israeli officer training: Degendering and regendering the military. *Signs: Journal of Women in Culture and Society, 33*(1), 105–133.

Sassoon, S. (2013). *Memoirs of an infantry officer: The memoirs of George Sherston.* London: Penguin.

Sauer, L. M., Catlett, C., Tosatto, R., & Kirsch, T. D. (2014). The utility of and risks associated with the use of spontaneous volunteers in disaster response: A survey. *Disaster Medicine and Public Health Preparedness, 8*(1), 65–69.

Scanlon, J., Helsloot, I., & Groenendaal, J. (2014). Putting it all together: Integrating ordinary people into emergency response. *International Journal of Mass Emergencies and Disasters, 32*(1), 43–63.

Schakel, J.-K., van Fenema, P. C., & Faraj, S. (2016). Shots fired! Switching between practices in police work. *Organization Science, 27*(2), 391–410.

Schakel, J.-K., & Wolbers, J. (2021). To the edge and beyond: How fast-response organizations adapt in rapidly changing crisis situations. *Human Relations, 74*(3), 405–436.

Schmidt, A. (2019). Tensions and dilemmas in crisis governance: Responding to citizen volunteers. *Administration & Society, 51*(7), 1171–1195.

Schmutz, J. B., Lei, Z., Eppich, W. J., & Manser, T. (2018). Reflection in the heat of the moment: The role of in-action team reflexivity in health care emergency teams. *Journal of Organizational Behavior, 39*(6), 749–765.

Schneider, F. E., & Wildermuth, D. (2017). *Using robots for firefighters and first responders: Scenario specification and exemplary system description.* Paper presented at the 2017 18th International Carpathian Control Conference (ICCC), Sinaia, Romania.

Schneider, R. O. (2006). Principles of ethics for emergency managers. *Journal of Emergency Management, 4*(1), 56–62.

Schneider, S. K. (1992). Governmental response to disasters: The conflict between bureaucratic procedures and emergent norms. *Public Administration Review, 52*(2), 135–145.

Scott, R., & Nowell, B. (2020). Networks and crisis management. In E. K. Stern, D. Fischbacher-Smith, S. Kuipers, A. McConnell, D. Nohrstedt, & T. Preston (Eds.), *The Oxford Encyclopedia of Crisis Analysis.* Oxford: Oxford University Press. https://doi.org/10.1093/acrefore/9780190228637.013.1582

Segal, M. W. (1986). The military and the family as greedy institutions. *Armed Forces & Society, 13*(1), 9–38.

Shanker, T., & Richtel, M. (2011). In new military, data overload can be deadly. *The New York Times*. Retrieved from www.nytimes.com/2011/01/17/technology/17brain.html

Shepherd, D. A., & Williams, T. A. (2014). Local venturing as compassion organizing in the aftermath of a natural disaster: The role of localness and community in reducing suffering. *Journal of Management Studies, 51*(6), 952–994.

Shils, E. A., & Janowitz, M. (1948). Cohesion and disintegration in the Wehrmacht in World War II. *Public Opinion Quarterly, 12*(2), 280–315.

Sidel, V. W., & Levy, B. S. (2003). Physician-soldier: A moral. In T. E. Beam, L. R. Sparacino, E. D. Pellegrino, A. E. Hartle, & E. G. Howe (Eds.), *Military medical ethics. Volume 1* (pp. 293–329). Washington: TMM Publications.

Skar, M., Sydnes, M., & Sydnes, A. K. (2016). Integrating unorganized volunteers in emergency response management: A case study. *International Journal of Emergency Services, 5*(1), 52–65.

Slim, H. (1997). Doing the right thing: Relief agencies, moral dilemmas and moral responsibility in political emergencies and war. *Disasters, 21*(3), 244–257.

Slim, H. (2021). Localization is self-determination. *Frontiers in Political Science, 3*, Article 708584.

Snook, S. A. (2002). *Friendly fire: The accidental shootdown of US Black Hawks over northern Iraq*. Princeton: Princeton University Press.

Solnit, R. (2010). *A paradise built in hell: The extraordinary communities that arise in disaster*. New York: Penguin.

Spector, B. (2019). *Constructing crisis*. Cambridge: Cambridge University Press.

Stabile, B., Simon, K., Thornton, T. E., & Grant, A. (2022). Diversity and inclusion in emergency management and first response: Accounting for race and gender in codes of ethics in the United States. *Public Integrity, 24*(1), 82–101.

Stachowski, A. A., Kaplan, S. A., & Waller, M. J. (2009). The benefits of flexible team interaction during crises. *Journal of Applied Psychology, 94*(6), 1536–1543.

Stallings, R. A., & Quarantelli, E. L. (1985). Emergent citizen groups and emergency management. *Public Administration Review, 45*(SI), 93–100.

Staw, B. M., Sandelands, L. E., & Dutton, J. E. (1981). Threat rigidity effects in organizational behavior: A multilevel analysis. *Administrative Science Quarterly, 26*(4), 501–524.

Steffen, S. L., & Fothergill, A. (2009). 9/11 volunteerism: A pathway to personal healing and community engagement. *The Social Science Journal, 46*(1), 29–46.

Steigenberger, N. (2016). Organizing for the big one: A review of case studies and a research agenda for multi-agency disaster response. *Journal of Contingencies and Crisis Management, 24*(2), 60–72.

Stein, M. (2004). The critical period of disasters: Insights from sense-making and psychoanalytic theory. *Human Relations, 57*(10), 1243–1261.

Stephenson, M. (2005). Making humanitarian relief networks more effective: Operational coordination, trust and sense making. *Disasters, 29*(4), 337–350.

Stephenson, R., & Anderson, P. S. (1997). Disasters and the information technology revolution. *Disasters, 21*(4), 305–334.

Stoddard, A., Jillani, S., Caccavale, J., Cooke, P., Guillemois, D., & Klimentov, V. (2017). Out of reach: How insecurity prevents humanitarian aid from accessing the neediest. *Stability: International Journal of Security and Development, 6*(1), Article 1.

Suarez, F. F., & Montes, J. S. (2019). An integrative perspective of organizational responses: Routines, heuristics, and improvisations in a Mount Everest expedition. *Organization Science, 30*(3), 573–599.

Sudmeier-Rieux, K. I. (2014). Resilience – An emerging paradigm of danger or of hope? *Disaster Prevention and Management, 23*(1), 67–80.

Suparamaniam, N., & Dekker, S. (2003). Paradoxes of power: The separation of knowledge and authority in international disaster relief work. *Disaster Prevention and Management, 12*(4), 312–318.

Svensson, M., & Hällgren, M. (2018). Sensemaking in sensory deprived settings: The role of non-verbal auditory cues for emergency assessment. *European Management Journal, 36*(3), 306–318.

Svensson, M., & Pesämaa, O. (2018). How does a caller's anger, fear and sadness affect operators' decisions in emergency calls? *International Review of Social Psychology, 31*(1), Article 7.

Swann, C., Crust, L., & Allen-Collinson, J. (2016). Surviving the 2015 Mount Everest disaster: A phenomenological exploration into lived experience and the role of mental toughness. *Psychology of Sport and Exercise, 27*, 157–167.

Taylor, S. E., Klein, L. C., Lewis, B. P., Gruenewald, T. L., Gurung, R. A., & Updegraff, J. A. (2000). Biobehavioral responses to stress in females: Tend-and-befriend, not fight-or-flight. *Psychological Review, 107*(3), 411–429.

Telford, J., Cosgrave, J., & Houghton, R. (2006). *Joint evaluation of the international response to the Indian Ocean tsunami: Synthesis report.* London: Tsunami Evaluation Coalition (TEC).

Tempest, S., Starkey, K., & Ennew, C. (2007). In the Death Zone: A study of limits in the 1996 Mount Everest disaster. *Human Relations, 60*(7), 1039–1064.

Ter Heide, F. J. J. (2020). Empathy is key in the development of moral injury. *European Journal of Psychotraumatology*, *11*(1), 1843261.

Terry, F. (2011). The International Committee of the Red Cross in Afghanistan: Reasserting the neutrality of humanitarian action. *International Review of the Red Cross*, *93*(881), 173–188.

Thompson, J. D., & Hawkes, R. W. (1962). Disaster, community organization and administrative process. In G. W. Baker & D. W. Chapman (Eds.), *Man and society in disaster* (pp. 268–300). New York: Basic Books.

Thornborrow, T., & Brown, A. D. (2009). 'Being regimented': Aspiration, discipline and identity work in the British parachute regiment. *Organization Studies*, *30*(4), 355–376.

Tierney, K. (2003). *Conceptualizing and measuring organizational and community resilience: Lessons from the emergency response following the September 11, 2001 attack on the World Trade Center*. Newark: Disaster Research Center, University of Delaware.

Tierney, K. (2007). From the margins to the mainstream? Disaster research at the crossroads. *Annual Review of Sociology*, *33*, 503–525.

Tierney, K. (2019). *Disasters: A sociological approach*. Cambridge: Polity Press.

Tierney, K., Bevc, C., & Kuligowski, E. (2006). Metaphors matter: Disaster myths, media frames, and their consequences in Hurricane Katrina. *The Annals of the American Academy of Political and Social Science*, *604*(1), 57–81.

Tolstoy, L. (2001). *War and peace*. Hertfordshire: Wordsworth Editions.

Trainor, J., & Barsky, L. (2011). *Reporting for duty? A Synthesis of research on role conflict, strain, and abandonment among emergency responders during disasters and catastrophes*. Newark: Disaster Research Center, University of Delaware.

Trnka, J., Lundberg, J., & Jungert, E. (2016). Design and evaluation of a role improvisation exercise for crisis and disaster response teams. *International Journal of Information Technology and Management*, *15*(3), 251–271.

Tuckey, M. R., & Hayward, R. (2011). Global and occupation-specific emotional resources as buffers against the emotional demands of firefighting. *Applied Psychology*, *60*(1), 1–23.

Turner, B. A. (1976). The organizational and interorganizational development of disasters. *Administrative Science Quarterly*, *21*(3), 378–397.

Turoff, M., Chumer, M., de Walle, B. V., & Yao, X. (2004). The design of a dynamic emergency response management information system (DERMIS). *Journal of Information Technology Theory and Application (JITTA)*, *5*(4), 1–35.

Twigg, J., & Mosel, I. (2017). Emergent groups and spontaneous volunteers in urban disaster response. *Environment and Urbanization, 29*(2), 443–458.

Tyhurst, J. (1957). Psychological and social aspects of civilian disaster. *Canadian Medical Association Journal, 76*(5), 385–393.

Uhr, C. (2017). Leadership ideals as barriers for efficient collaboration during emergencies and disasters. *Journal of Contingencies and Crisis Management, 25*(4), 301–312.

United States Congress. (2006). *A failure of initiative: Final report of the select bipartisan committee to investigate the preparation for and response to Hurricane Katrina* (0160754259). Retrieved from www.congress.gov/congressional-report/109th-congress/house-report/377/1

van Burken, C. G. (2013). The non-neutrality of technology. *Military Review, 93*(May-June), 39–47.

Van Wart, M., & Kapucu, N. (2011). Crisis management competencies: The case of emergency managers in the USA. *Public Management Review, 13*(4), 489–511.

van Wynsberghe, A., & Comes, T. (2020). Drones in humanitarian contexts, robot ethics, and the human–robot interaction. *Ethics and Information Technology, 22*(1), 43–53.

Vaughan, D. (1996). *The Challenger launch decision: Risky technology, culture, and deviance at NASA.* Chicago: University of Chicago Press.

Villar, E. B., & Miralles, F. (2021). Purpose-driven improvisation during organisational shocks: Case narrative of three critical organisations and Typhoon Haiyan. *Disasters, 45*(2), 477–497.

Vinzant, J. C., & Crothers, L. (1998). *Street-level leadership: Discretion and legitimacy in front-line public service.* Washington: Georgetown University Press.

Vivona, B. D. (2014). Humor functions within crime scene investigations: Group dynamics, stress, and the negotiation of emotions. *Police Quarterly, 17*(2), 127–149.

Vogelaar, A. L., & Kramer, E.-H. (2004). Mission command in Dutch peace support missions. *Armed Forces & Society, 30*(3), 409–431.

Von Batten, K. (2020). *The first 100 days: The effects of the Covid-19 pandemic on healthcare workers' efficacy and absenteeism in the United States and the United Kingdom.* Retrieved from https://papers.ssrn.com/sol3/papers.cfm?abstract_id=3633537

Von Clausewitz, C. (1997). *On war.* Ware: Wordsworth Editions.

Wachtendorf, T., & Kendra, J. (2006). *The waterborne evacuation of lower Manhattan on September 11: A case of distributed sensemaking.* Newark: Disaster Research Center, University of Delaware.

Wagner, S. L., Pasca, R., & Regehr, C. (2019). Firefighters and empathy: Does it hurt to care too much? *Journal of Loss and Trauma, 24*(3), 238–250.

Waldman, S., Yumagulova, L., Mackwani, Z., Benson, C., & Stone, J. T. (2018). Canadian citizens volunteering in disasters: From emergence to networked governance. *Journal of Contingencies and Crisis Management, 26*(3), 394–402.

Wallace, A. (1957). Mazeway disintegration: The individual's perception of socio-cultural disorganization. *Human Organization, 16*(2), 23–27.

Waller, M. J. (1999). The timing of adaptive group responses to nonroutine events. *Academy of Management Journal, 42*(2), 127–137.

Waller, M. J., & Uitdewilligen, S. (2008). Talking to the room: Collective sensemaking during crisis situations. In R. A. Roe, M. J. Waller, & S. Clegg (Eds.), *Time in organizational research* (pp. 208–225). London: Routledge.

Walsh, S., & Johnson, O. (2018). *Getting to zero: A doctor and a diplomat on the Ebola frontline.* London: Bloomsbury Publishing.

Wankhade, P. (2021). New development: A 'journey of personal and professional emotions' – Emergency ambulance professionals during Covid-19. *Public Money & Management,* Online first.

Waugh Jr, W. L., & Streib, G. (2006). Collaboration and leadership for effective emergency management. *Public Administration Review, 66*(S1), 131–140.

Webb, G. R. (2004). Role improvising during crisis situations. *International Journal of Emergency Management, 2*(1–2), 47–61.

Webb, G. R., & Chevreau, F.-R. (2006). Planning to improvise: The importance of creativity and flexibility in crisis response. *International Journal of Emergency Management, 3*(1), 66–72.

Weick, K. E. (1979). *The social psychology of organizing.* Reading: Addison-Wesley.

Weick, K. E. (1988). Enacted sensemaking in crisis situations. *Journal of Management Studies, 25*(4), 305–317.

Weick, K. E. (1990). The vulnerable system: An analysis of the Tenerife air disaster. *Journal of Management, 16*(3), 571–593.

Weick, K. E. (1993). The collapse of sensemaking in organizations: The Mann Gulch disaster. *Administrative Science Quarterly, 38*(4), 628–652.

Weick, K. E. (1995). *Sensemaking in organizations.* Thousand Oaks: Sage.

Weick, K. E. (1996). Drop your tools: An allegory for organizational studies. *Administrative Science Quarterly, 41*(2), 301–313.

Weick, K. E. (2004). Rethinking organizational design. In R. J. Boland & F. Collopy (Eds.), *Managing as designing* (pp. 36–53). Stanford: Stanford University Press.

Weick, K. E. (2010). Reflections on enacted sensemaking in the Bhopal disaster. *Journal of Management Studies, 47*(3), 537–550.

Weick, K. E. (2011). Organizing for transient reliability: The production of dynamic non-events. *Journal of Contingencies and Crisis Management, 19*(1), 21–27.

Weick, K. E., & Roberts, K. H. (1993). Collective mind in organizations: Heedful interrelating on flight decks. *Administrative Science Quarterly, 38*(3), 357–381.

Weick, K. E., & Sutcliffe, K. M. (2001). *Managing the unexpected.* San Francisco: Jossey-Bass.

Weick, K. E., Sutcliffe, K. M., & Obstfeld, D. (2005). Organizing and the process of sensemaking. *Organization Science, 16*(4), 409–421.

Wester, M. (2011). Fight, flight or freeze: Assumed reactions of the public during a crisis. *Journal of Contingencies and Crisis Management, 19*(4), 207–214.

Whiteman, G., & Cooper, W. H. (2011). Ecological sensemaking. *Academy of Management Journal, 54*(5), 889–911.

Whittaker, J., McLennan, B., & Handmer, J. (2015). A review of informal volunteerism in emergencies and disasters: Definition, opportunities and challenges. *International Journal of Disaster Risk Reduction, 13*, 358–368.

Wiedemann, N. J., Pina e Cunha, M., & Clegg, S. R. (2021). Rethinking resistance as an act of improvisation: Lessons from the 1914 Christmas truce. *Organization Studies, 42*(4), 615–635.

Williams, T. A., Gruber, D. A., Sutcliffe, K. M., Shepherd, D. A., & Zhao, E. Y. (2017). Organizational response to adversity: Fusing crisis management and resilience research streams. *Academy of Management Annals, 11*(2), 733–769.

Williams, T. A., & Shepherd, D. A. (2016). Building resilience or providing sustenance: Different paths of emergent ventures in the aftermath of the Haiti earthquake. *Academy of Management Journal, 59*(6), 2069–2102.

Wolbers, J., & Boersma, F. (2013). The common operational picture as collective sensemaking. *Journal of Contingencies and Crisis Management, 21*(4), 186–199.

Wolbers, J., Boersma, F., & Groenewegen, P. (2018). Introducing a fragmentation perspective on coordination in crisis management. *Organization Studies, 39*(11), 1521–1546.

Wolf, L. A., Perhats, C., Delao, A. M., Moon, M. D., Clark, P. R., & Zavotsky, K. E. (2016). "It's a burden you carry": Describing moral distress in emergency nursing. *Journal of Emergency Nursing, 42*(1), 37–46.

Wong, L., Kolditz, T., Millen, R., & Potter, T. (2003). *Why they fight: Combat motivation in the Iraq war.* Carlisle: Strategic Studies Institute, US Army War College.

Wortel, E., & Bosch, J. (2011). Strengthening moral competence: A 'train the trainer' course on military ethics. *Journal of Military Ethics*, *10*(1), 17–35.

Wu, A., Convertino, G., Ganoe, C., Carroll, J. M., & Zhang, X. L. (2013). Supporting collaborative sense-making in emergency management through geo-visualization. *International Journal of Human-Computer Studies*, *71*(1), 4–23.

Zhou, Q., Huang, W., & Zhang, Y. (2011). Identifying critical success factors in emergency management using a fuzzy DEMATEL method. *Safety Science*, *49*(2), 243–252.

Zijderveld, H. J. T., & Kalkman, J. P. (Forthcoming). Emergent organizing: Origins and evolution of temporary crisis response organizations. *Under review*.

Zook, M., Graham, M., Shelton, T., & Gorman, S. (2010). Volunteered geographic information and crowdsourcing disaster relief: A case study of the Haitian earthquake. *World Medical & Health Policy*, *2*(2), 7–33.

Index

Printed in the United States
by Baker & Taylor Publisher Services